SO-DNJ-462

THE LEGAL ASPECTS OF INDUSTRY
AND COMMERCE

THE LEGAL ASPECTS OF INDUSTRY AND COMMERCE

By

W. F. FRANK

LL.B. B.Com. M.Sc. (Econ.) Dr.jur.

HEAD OF THE DEPARTMENT OF MANAGEMENT AND BUSINESS STUDIES
LANCHESTER COLLEGE OF TECHNOLOGY, COVENTRY

AUTHOR OF
"THE GENERAL PRINCIPLES OF ENGLISH LAW"

NEW EDITION REVISED

GEORGE G. HARRAP & CO. LTD
LONDON TORONTO WELLINGTON SYDNEY

First published in Great Britain 1958
by GEORGE G. HARRAP & CO. LTD
182 High Holborn, London, W.C.1

New Edition revised 1961

Reprinted 1962

© *W. F. Frank* 1958

*Composed in Times Roman type and printed at the St Ann's Press
Park Road, Altrincham.   Made in Great Britain*

PREFACE

"Sir," said Dr Johnson, "a lawyer has no business with the justice or injustice of the cause which he undertakes . . . lawyers are a class of the community that, by study and experience, have acquired the art and power of arranging evidence, and of applying to the points at issue what the law has settled." [1]

THIS book has been written for management students preparing for the examinations of the Institute of Cost and Works Accountants, the Graduate Examination of the British Institute of Management and the examinations of other professional management bodies. It may also prove helpful to others in industry and commerce who require a brief and simple introduction to the law. Many, if not all, of the readers of this book will have never studied law before, and their impression as to what law entails is probably a confused mixture of interest in the kinds of subject discussed in some sections of the Sunday Press and of fear that law is a dry-as-dust subject. Now, the present book does not go into questions of criminal law at all, but it is the author's contention that law is not and cannot be dry if properly treated.

Law may not know all the answers to the questions posed by the poets, it may be at times, in Mr Bumble's immortal words, "an ass," but then do we know the answers to all the questions, and do we not also behave at times in an asinine way? Law is life, we live law, everything we do has legal implications and no one who is interested in himself and his fellow-men can find law uninteresting.

The purpose for which this book has been written imposes, of course, certain limitations on the treatment of the subject. A great deal more might have been written about the sources of law and its administration, and the author hopes that as many readers of this book as possible will try to read some introductory work on law so as to broaden their knowledge of the background against which the material rules of law operate. Even those, however, who do not find the time to read any other book should get a sufficient grasp of the essential principles of commercial and industrial law from reading the present work.

It is the author's firm belief that a student's grasp of law cannot be properly tested by setting questions which require a mere repetition of text-book passages learnt by heart. If the study of law has any practical value at all it should help the student to deal with situations which he may meet in his private and business life.

---

[1] James Boswell, *Journal of a Tour to the Hebrides.*

Examiners are coming round to this belief as well, and an increasing number of questions set in examinations are of the problem type. It is for this reason that the author has included in Appendix I not only a chapter-by-chapter analysis of examination questions, but also a few problems relating to the subject-matter of the various chapters, so that the student may test himself as to whether he is able to apply the principles of law to some problem which may crop up.

Some of the questions in Appendix I are the author's own work, others have been set in the examinations of the Institute of Cost and Works Accountants or in those of the British Insitute of Management. The author would like to take this opportunity of thanking these two bodies for permission to reproduce the questions.

Readers who are receiving some form of organized instruction will be guided by their tutors as to how examination questions in law should be tackled. For the benefit of those, however, who may not have the advantage of professional guidance the author wishes to remind students that examiners expect not only an answer to the question, but also reasons for it. The reasons to be given are why the law is what the writer claims it to be, and they necessitate, therefore, some 'authority.' The 'authority' may either be a section of some Act of Parliament, or it may be a past decision of a court of law. This explains the emphasis which is placed on authorities in the book, and why it is so essential that students should get thoroughly familiar with them.

The author does not claim any originality either for the views expressed in this book or for the method of presentation. He does believe, however, that this is the first book in which commercial and industrial law are treated in sufficient detail to satisfy the examination requirements mentioned. Any comments from teachers, as well as from students, about difficulties encountered in the book will be welcomed by the author.

W. F. F.

NOTE TO SECOND EDITION

IMPORTANT changes have taken place in some of the branches of law discussed in this book since the publication of the first edition. The author received many helpful letters from readers, and the writers of these will easily trace the places where the author has acted on their advice. It is hoped that the second edition will prove to be as helpful to students as the first edition has obviously been.

W. F. F.

CONTENTS

CHAPTER ONE

GENERAL INTRODUCTION

THE purpose of this book is to explain those parts of English law which deal with issues that are of direct importance to persons engaged in commerce or industry. Before approaching, however, the material parts of the law, it is necessary to discuss, even if in outline only, what English law is, and where we find the legal rules which we shall be dealing with in later chapters.

Law consists of a body of rules which regulate the behaviour of the citizens of a country. It differs from other rules that control their behaviour, such as those of good manners or of speech, in that any infringement of the legal rules may be dealt with by the machinery of the law in the shape of the courts. The breach of certain legal rules is visited by punishment of the law-breaker. We call these rules the rules of criminal law, and they are outside the scope of this book. The breach of other rules does not lead to punishment, but entitles the person who has some interest in the observance of the rule to have his rights protected by a court of law, whether by having monetary damages awarded to him, or by receiving a court order which requests the rule-breaker to rectify his breach, or by other means. These are the rules of civil law.

English law, whether civil or criminal, is basically derived from two sources—namely, statutes (Acts of Parliament) and the common law. Common law, in the broadest sense in which the term is used, means all the rules of English law which are not based on legislation. In this sense it is also referred to as unwritten law, while law based on statute is called the written law. This does not mean that common law has not been written down; the volume of any law library shows that clearly enough. What is meant is that the origin of common law is not some document where the relevant rules are expounded.

Common law in the broader sense may be divided into common law in the narrower or stricter sense and into equity. Common law in the stricter sense is that part of the non-statutory law of this country which developed from the customs of our people. It is known as common law because it applies to the country as a whole, and is so distinguished from customs which apply to parts of the country only. At first the judges were applying local customs in deciding the cases brought before them, but gradually, from the twelfth century onward, they began to mould these customs into a single unit, the common law of England. This was done by the judges quite imperceptibly when they began to introduce customary rules developed in one part of the country into other parts. Common law is, then, judge-made law in the sense that it owes its existence to the creative work of generations of judges, though they took as their raw material customs which they had found in their travels through the country.

Equity came into existence because the courts which administered the common law failed to give redress in certain cases that were brought before them. Sometimes this failure was due to the human failings of the judges, who had taken bribes from one of the parties, but more often it was due to the innate conservatism of the lawyer who is not prepared to deal with new issues on which he is asked to pronounce. The common law judges believed—wrongly, no doubt—that the law which they had collected was complete, and that if a new legal issue was brought before them which they had not heard of before they were entitled to assume that there existed no remedy in law. The dissatisfied suitors were wont to petition the King, who in the medieval political set-up was looked upon as the fountain of all justice, and ask him for his intervention. Being too busy with other matters of State, the King would hand the petitions to his chief adviser, the Chancellor, and ask him to deal with them. The Chancellor, in medieval days a clergyman, would approach the petitions from an angle different from that of the judges. He would regard them from the point of view of conscience or fairness, and, after having heard both parties, he would give a decision which in the circumstances he considered would do what was right and fair. It was for this reason that the Chancellor's jurisdiction became known as that of equity. In time the number of petitions increased to such an extent that they were addressed directly to the Chancellor instead of to the King, and the Chancellor felt compelled to set up a court of his own to deal with them. This court became known as the Court of Chancery. At first, as we have seen, the Chancellor decided each case on its merits according to his own standards of fairness. As his court became busier, and he was compelled to appoint subordinate judges to deal with the large number of petitions, it became necessary to create certain principles to be followed by those who were applying equity. The outcome was that the rules of equity were applied nearly as rigidly as the rules of common law, albeit by a different set of courts.

There existed, then, from the Middle Ages onward two main sets of courts in England, the common law courts and the courts of equity. There also existed a third set of courts which applied the law dealing with matters in which the Church had particular interest, such as matrimonial affairs and wills. The relationship between common law and equity is one of great interest. Common law had preceded equity. Equity had come into existence to deal with the defects in the common law, defects which were due partly to the unwillingness of the common law judges to deal with certain new issues and partly to their unwillingness to grant remedies of a new kind. Equity therefore supplemented common law in parts, while it also tended to override the rules of common law where their rigid application would have led to injustice. The most important remedy of the common law courts was the award of monetary damages, while the courts of Chancery granted injunctions and specific performance, both of which will be discussed in a later chapter.

The situation in which different sets of courts administered different parts of English law prevailed for a long time. It was only in 1873 that the Judicature Act radically altered the position by abolishing all the existing courts and replacing them by a single new court, the Supreme Court of Judicature. It must be clearly pointed out, however, that this step did not lead to a merger of common law and equity. These two parts of English law are still separate: it is only their administration that has been merged. The beginner may find it a little difficult to understand that our courts apply separate branches of the law. What it means is this: when a court to-day applies a remedy of equity it will expect that the same conditions should have been fulfilled which were required by the courts of Chancery in the old days, while common law remedies are granted in circumstances which would have satisfied the old common law courts. You will appreciate this point better when in connexion with the law of contract you study the situation in which the court will award damages to the plaintiff and that where it will award him specific performance of the contract.

At this point it may be helpful to discuss briefly the courts which at the present time administer the civil law.

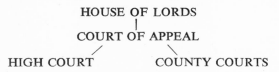

HOUSE OF LORDS
|
COURT OF APPEAL
/ \
HIGH COURT   COUNTY COURTS

Every action is initiated in a court of first instance, which will be either the High Court or one of the 450-odd county courts that are spread over England and Wales. Which type of court will be chosen depends on the nature and the value of the subject-matter. In general, where the value of the subject-matter is less than £400 the action may be started in a county court. County courts also possess jurisdiction in bankruptcy matters, in the liquidation of companies with a share capital of less than £10,000, as well as in the administration of certain social legislation—*e.g.*, the Rent Restriction Acts. All other types of action will be initiated in the High Court in London, which consists of three divisions, the Queen's Bench Division, the Chancery Division, and the Probate, Divorce, and Admiralty Division. Most common law matters are heard in the Queen's Bench Division. The Chancery Division is responsible for cases concerning company law, partnerships, the guardianship of infants, trusts, etc. The third division deals with matrimonial disputes, the proving of wills, and with legal matters concerning merchant shipping. The reason for the varied nature of the jurisdiction of this division is that it embraces all matters which before 1873 were not the responsibility of either the common law courts or of the courts of Chancery.

From the courts of first instance it is possible to appeal to the Court of Appeal in London. The judgment of this court is in general final, but in cases which raise specially difficult legal questions the Court of Appeal may, on request, permit one or both of the parties to appeal further to the House of Lords in its judicial capacity. Alternatively, the House of Lords may be asked for leave to appeal to it. The decision of the House of Lords is final, and no further appeal is possible.

As we have seen already, common law, in the broadest sense of the term, is judge-made law. It has grown over the centuries as judges have found occasion to deal with new legal issues that were brought before them. Law is never static, it must grow to keep up with the changing economic and technical environment in which it is working, and it is one of the main points in favour of our common law that it can adapt itself so easily to new demands that are made on it. It is naturally important that law should, as far as possible, be certain. If law depended entirely on the whims of the judge dealing with a case there would be little use in studying law. It is, of course, impossible to assure complete certainty in the sense that the judgment of the court should be known beforehand. If that were possible there would be no need to go to the court. What we desire is that judges should decide the cases that come before them on the basis of certain generally known principles, so that, while there might be disagreement on the facts of the case or on the question as to which legal rule should be applied, the basic principles at least should be common ground between the parties.

In order that law should be applied consistently it has been a principle of English law of some duration that judges should follow the decisions of their predecessors. This principle of *stare decisis* (keeping to past decisions) forms the cornerstone of common law. Without it common law as we know it could not have developed. It means that when a judge has decided a certain legal issue that has been submitted to him in a case his decision forms a *precedent* which should guide other judges who may have to deal with the same issue in a later case. Some judicial decisions are binding precedents, in the sense that their legal reasoning, the so-called *ratio decidendi* (the basis of the decision), *must* be applied by other judges if the same situation is brought before them. The decisions of the House of Lords are binding on all courts in England and Wales. They are binding even on the House of Lords itself in a later case, so that once a point of law has been settled in a decision of the House of Lords it will require an Act of Parliament to alter the principle. Decisions of the Court of Appeal are also binding on subordinate courts as well as on the Court of Appeal itself, but they are, of course, not binding on the House of Lords, which could overrule the statement of the law if it should be submitted to it at some time. The decisions of other courts, as well as those of courts in Scotland or in other countries which have legal systems similar to the English one, are not binding precedents at all, but they may be looked upon as persuasive precedents in that they may persuade an English court to follow them, even though it has no obligation to do so.

The only part of a court's decision which forms the precedent is the *ratio decidendi*. This is the legal proposition which the court has applied to the facts of the case in order to give its decision. Any part of the judgment which was not necessary for the purpose of finding a solution to the legal problem submitted to the court is known as an *obiter dictum* (which might be translated as an 'incidental remark'), and does not as such form part of the *ratio* and of the precedent. Thus, where a judge in giving his views on the facts of a case speculates what his decision would have been if the facts had been different his views as pronounced will be merely made *obiter*, and do not form a precedent even if the situation envisaged were really to occur at some later date.

Whenever, then, a judge has to decide a case in which some situation has to be dealt with which has occurred before, and has been decided by a superior court, the judge will follow the reasoning of the previous decision, provided always that the situation is really entirely like the earlier one. It is for the judge to decide whether the legal issue involved is the same one, and one must admit here that if the judge for one reason or another is not inclined to follow the earlier decision he has some scope for finding differences between the decided case and the case that is before him. Where, on the other hand, the situation is a new one, for which there does not exist a precedent, the judge has a fairly free hand in giving his decision. He will be guided there by decisions dealing with analogous situations, and by the general principles on which the part of the law is based that he has to apply.

From what has been said above the reader will appreciate the great importance of case law. From the student's point of view, case law together with statutes provide the authorities which he has to quote in answers when supporting some statement which he is making about the law. The citations of cases given in text-books addressed primarily to law students give the year of the decision as well as the title of the law reports and the page in them in which the case is reported. Where the year represents an essential part of the reference (because the particular series of law reports is not numbered consecutively) the year will appear in square brackets, while where the series is numbered consecutively the year appears in round brackets. As far as professional students are concerned—for whom this book is intended—it will be enough if they remember the name of each case, and they need not bother unduly about the other details, which are shown here in the table of cases only. In the citation of the case the name of the plaintiff appears first and that of the defendant second, but if the decision reported is one of the House of Lords the name of the appellant (who may well have been the original defendant) comes first, and that of the other party, the respondent, comes second. The 'v' connecting the two names stands for the Latin *versus,* meaning 'against.'

Statutes form the other main source of English law. In exactly the same way in which equity was intended to supplement the common law where it had proved to be defective, so statutes have also been used to supplement both common law and equity where they have been found wanting from the point of view of later social and economic ideas. Apart from that, statutes have been passed at times for the purpose of codifying certain parts of our law, which means bringing together in one Act of Parliament the law which hitherto may have been spread over many separate decisions or Acts of Parliament. As an example of such a codifying statute we may mention the Sale of Goods Act, 1893.

In order to give statutes their correct meaning it is necessary to interpret them. Words may mean different things to different people, and it is quite possible that the purpose which the law-makers in Parliament had in mind when they passed an Act will not in fact be attained in practice. What really matters is the meaning which the courts ascribe to an Act of Parliament, and the courts follow certain definite rules in interpreting the provisions of an Act of Parliament. Words will be construed in their ordinary meaning unless they have some generally accepted legal meaning differing from the ordinary meaning. Individual sections of an Act have to be interpreted in the light of the general meaning of the Act and not in isolation, and there are a number of other principles as well which the courts will apply. Once, however, a court has interpreted some sections or words of an Act of Parliament the principle of judicial precedent comes into operation, and these sections or words will be interpreted in the same way by any other court which is bound to follow the earlier decision.

Every Act of Parliament has three titles, a short one, a long one, and a numerical one. The short title refers to an Act by its name—*e.g.,* the National Insurance Act, 1946. The long title of the Act describes the purposes of the Act in greater detail, while the numerical title is based on the regnal year of the Sovereign which coincided with the Parliamentary session in which the Act was passed, the Act being then further identified by a number—*e.g.,* the numerical title of the above-mentioned Act is 9 & 10 Geo. 6, c. 67. The Act was passed in the Parliamentary session comprising the close of the ninth and beginning of the tenth year of the reign of George VI, and it was the 67th enactment passed in that session. The 'c' before the number stands for 'chapter,' and may be explained by the fact that in the early days 'Act of Parliament' referred to the work of the entire Parliamentary session (consisting in those days usually of a few days only), while the various items which were legislated on during the session were separated as chapter headings of the Act of Parliament. The readers need only remember the short titles of the Acts quoted here.

Finally, mention must be made of the fact that some of our law may be found in so-called statutory instruments. These are generally ministerial orders made by a Minister of the Crown under powers delegated to him by Parliament. When an Act of Parliament is passed dealing with some complicated subject-matter, such as the National Insurance Act, 1946, the Act would be unduly bulky and detailed if everything that has to be legislated on were to be contained in it. It is therefore usual to include various sections in which, after reciting some general principle, a particular Minister is empowered to fix the detailed application of the principle by regulations. These regulations have the same force as if their provisions were contained in the relevant Act of Parliament. The Minister who made the regulations is then in effect legislating, though his power to do so is restricted by the limits which Parliament has set for him when delegating the power to him. If he should exceed these limits he would be acting *ultra vires* (outside his powers) and the regulations made by him would be null and void, and would not be enforced by a court of law.

CHAPTER TWO

THE LAW OF CONTRACT

DEFINITIONS

A contract may be defined as an agreement between two parties which is intended by them to have legal consequences. This definition is to be preferred to the one often encountered which identifies a contract with a legally enforceable agreement, since there are some contracts which, for reasons to be discussed later, are not enforceable in a court of law.

A contract thus forms a subdivision of the genus 'agreement,' from which it follows that, while every contract is based on an agreement of the parties, not every agreement is necessarily a contract. In order that an agreement should qualify as a contract the parties must have shown an intention that a legal relationship between them should be set up, or, in other words, that a breach of the agreement should call for *legal* sanctions. Sometimes the parties in clear words state whether or not they wish to establish legal relations, but more often this intention will have to be deduced from the surrounding circumstances.

> *Balfour* v. *Balfour.* Husband, before departing for India, agreed with his wife to pay her a fixed monthly allowance. *Held,* that this was merely a family agreement which as such was not intended to have legal consequences.

> *Parker* v. *Clark.* The defendants, an elderly couple, asked the plaintiff and his wife, who were distant relatives, to sell their own house and come and live with the defendants. The running costs of the defendants' house were to be shared equally by the parties, but the defendant promised also to acquire a new car and to leave the house after his death to the plaintiff's wife. The plaintiff and his wife moved into the defendant's house, but after a year the arrangement broke down and they were asked to leave. *Held,* that in the circumstances it must be presumed that the parties had intended to enter into a legally binding contract.

Agreements of a commercial nature will be treated as contracts unless the parties have clearly indicated a contrary intention—*e.g.,* by declaring that the agreement was to be merely a 'gentlemen's agreement,' or was intended to be 'binding in honour only.' Many readers will be familiar with the conditions which appear on foot-ball-pool coupons providing that an entry should not give rise to a legally enforceable relationship between the parties. Thus, a person who had sent in an all-correct forecast cannot claim damages in the courts if the promoters refuse to pay out the prize to him.

In order that a valid contract between the parties should come into existence certain essential requirements must be fulfilled. They are:

1. The parties must possess legal capacity to enter into contracts.
2. One party must have made a binding offer to the other, and the offer must have been accepted by the other party.
3. The resulting agreement of the parties must have been a genuine one.
4. The contract must be supported by consideration.
5. In certain exceptional cases the contract must have been made in a particular form.
6. The object of the contract must not be one disapproved of by the law.

A contract which does not comply with the above requirements may be either void, voidable, or unenforceable. A contract is *void* if it lacks one of the fundamental requirements of a contract, so that in reality it does not exist at all. In a way, the expression 'a void contract' is a contradiction in terms, since if the contract is void there is really no contract at all.

A contract which is *voidable* is one that is valid to start with but which may be brought to an end (or *avoided*) at the option of one of the parties. If the party exercises the option the contract will cease to be valid from the time when that has happened.

A contract is *unenforceable* if it is perfectly valid in all respects except for the fact that it cannot be enforced by an action in law. This will be the case where the party wishing to enforce it lacks some particular type of evidence (such as evidence in writing) which is demanded by the law for the enforcement of this type of contract. Except for its unenforceability, such a contract is a perfectly valid one, so that if the other party were to perform it—*e.g.*, by paying a sum of money due under it—he could not reclaim it, as he could if he had paid money in pursuance of a void contract.

We shall now discuss the essential ingredients of a valid contract in detail.

THE CONTRACTUAL CAPACITY OF THE PARTIES

In general, every person, irrespective of sex or nationality, is under English law capable of entering into binding contracts. It will be therefore sufficient if we consider the exceptional cases where the contractual capacity differs from the ordinary.

B

Infants

An infant in law is a person under the age of twenty-one. An infant reaches his majority on the day preceding his twenty-first birthday. This is so because he completes his twenty-first year on that day, and law always presumes that everything which is due to happen on a particular day happens at the first minute of that day.

Contracts made by infants during their infancy were, at common law, voidable at the infant's option. The infant could thus repudiate any contract which he had made during his infancy, provided he did so either before reaching his majority or within a reasonable time afterwards. The position has been partially altered by statute. The Infants' Relief Act, 1874, provides that certain contracts made by infants are absolutely void. No action could thus be taken on these contracts, even if the infant were to ratify his contractual promise after reaching majority. The Act refers to three contracts:

1. A contract whereby an infant promises to repay money lent to him.

2. A contract whereby an infant promises to pay for goods supplied to him.

3. An account stated—*i.e.*, a promise by an infant to pay a past debt.

While no action can be taken against an infant in any of these three cases, there is nothing to stop him from discharging his obligation voluntarily. Furthermore, if the infant has already repaid the debt or paid for the goods supplied to him, he cannot reclaim what he had paid. It may be suggested, therefore, that, although the Act calls these contracts 'void,' they are in reality merely unenforceable.

In all these cases what matters is the infant's real age, and not the age which he may have given to the other party. If the infant has given a wrong age—perhaps in order to persuade a trader to supply him with goods—the infant may be prosecuted for the criminal offence of obtaining goods by false pretences, but even then payment cannot be demanded of him. If the goods supplied to the infant are still in his possession he may, however, be made to return them.

Not all contracts entered into by infants are voidable or void. There are some contracts which are valid and which may be enforced against the infant.

1. Where goods have been supplied to an infant, and these goods are 'necessaries' to him, he will be bound to pay a reasonable price for them. This means that if the price which he agreed to pay is not reasonable in the circumstances he will have to pay only what the court may consider to be reasonable. Necessaries are goods or

services intended for personal (as distinct from business) use, whether by the infant himself or by other persons for whom he is responsible. Furthermore, the infant must not be already sufficiently supplied with goods of that description, and their value must not be excessive in relation to his social standing.

Nash v. *Inman.* A tailor supplied seven fancy waistcoats to an infant undergraduate. *Held,* that while the goods were intended for personal use, and were appropriate to the infant's social standing, the infant was adequately supplied with clothing, so that they were not necessaries and he could not be made to pay for them.

2. The infant is also bound by contracts of service or of apprenticeship provided that they are, on the whole, to his benefit. The whole contract has to be considered, and if its terms are advantageous to the infant in that he is given an opportunity of earning a living or of learning a trade, the contract may be enforced against him, even those parts which, taken in isolation, would appear to be against the infant's interests.

Doyle v. *White City Stadium.* An infant professional boxer had agreed to participate in a prize fight on condition that he subscribed to the usual rules of the British Boxing Board of Control. *Held,* that he was bound by the contract even though one of its terms provided that if disqualified (as he unfortunately was) he would lose his purse.

3. As far as contracts of continuing obligation are concerned (*e.g.,* shareholding or leases of land) the old common law rule still applies, and these contracts are binding on the infant until he decides to repudiate them. This, if he wishes to do it at all, he will have to do before reaching majority or within a reasonable time afterwards. If an infant repudiates such a contract he will free himself from any future obligations under it, but he will still be bound by any debts which have accrued already (*e.g.,* rent for the time for which he has occupied premises) and he will not be able to recover any monies paid already.

Steinberg v. *Scala (Leeds), Ltd.* An infant applied for and was allotted shares in a company. Subsequently, she asked for her name to be removed from the list of shareholders. *Held,* that she was entitled to this, but that she could not reclaim the money paid for the shares.

Persons who are insane or drunk

Contracts made by persons of unsound mind are valid, except where the person contracting was unable, because of his insanity, to understand the nature of the contract *and* the other party was aware of the fact. In that case the contract could be avoided by the person of unsound mind as and when he regained his sanity.

The position of a person who was drunk when entering into a contract is the same; he also will be able to avoid the contract only if he can prove that because of drunkenness he did not know what he was doing *and* that the other contracting party was aware of it.

Persons who were drunk, as well as those of unsound mind, are still liable to pay a reasonable price for necessaries supplied to them.

Corporations

The parties to a contract must be legal persons, but a legal person need not necessarily be a physical person; it can also be a corporation. A corporation is a group of physical persons associated for some common lawful purpose, where the group is treated by law as a person in its own right, separate from the legal personalities of the individuals constituting it. Corporations, the members of which are in existence at the same time, are known as corporations aggregate. They may come into existence in three ways:

1. By the grant of a Royal Charter. This method is restricted to-day to corporations established for educational, charitable, and similar purposes (*e.g.*, universities) and to local government corporations—*i.e.*, boroughs.

2. By Act of Parliament. The various nationalization statutes have set up corporations to run the industries brought under public ownership (*e.g.*, the National Coal Board and the British Transport Commission).

3. The most frequently used method of creating a new corporation is by following the procedure laid down in the Companies Act, 1948 (discussed in Chapter 7), or in one of a small number of other Acts with similar provisions. These Acts make it possible for persons who wish to be formed into a corporation to register their intention with a public official, and if they satisfy this official that they have complied with the legal requirements he will grant to them a certificate of incorporation.

The most important feature of a corporation is that in law it has a separate existence from that of its members. It is therefore possible for members of a corporation to make contracts with it and to take legal action against it. This is so even if the member concerned has a large proprietary interest in the corporation, and controls the running of its affairs.

Salamon v. *Salamon and Company, Ltd.* S. held all the shares in the company, except for six which were held by other members of his family. He had also advanced some money to the company for which he had received loan certificates (debentures) entitling him to repayment before other creditors. The company went into liquidation, and the court *held* that although S. was, commercially speaking, the owner of the business, legally he and the company were separate persons and there was no reason why the company could not be indebted to him. This meant that he had a prior claim to the available assets of the company and nothing was left for the other creditors.

The extent of a corporation's contractual capacity depends on the method of its creation. No corporation can enter into contracts which only a human being can make. With that exception, however, chartered corporations have unlimited contractual capacity, and may enter into any kind of contract. Statutory and registered corporations, on the other hand, can enter only into contracts which fall within their objects. The objects of a statutory corporation are found in the Act of Parliament which created it, while those of a registered corporation are found in its memorandum of association (see page 109). If a contract made by a corporation falls outside its objects it is *ultra vires* (outside its powers), and therefore void.

> *Ashbury Railway Carriage and Iron Company, Ltd.* v. *Riche.* The objects of the company referred only to the manufacture and sale of railway carriages. The company purported to buy a concession to build a railway in Belgium. For this purpose a meeting of the shareholders was convened and those present approved the scheme. *Held*, that as long as the company's memorandum had not been altered to cover also such transactions, the company had no legal capacity to enter into this contract, whatever the shareholders might say.

At common law all contracts of corporations had to be made under seal. Corporations formed under the Companies Act were exempt from this requirement and were allowed to make contracts in exactly the same form as is demanded for physical persons. The Corporate Bodies' Contracts Act, 1960, has now extended this rule to all other corporations as well.

OFFER AND ACCEPTANCE

The first step towards the formation of a contract is taken by the party who makes an offer to the other party. The offer must express a definite intention on the part of the person making it (called the 'offeror') to enter into a contract with the person to whom it is addressed (known as the 'offeree'). An offer may be addressed to one particular person, who would then be the only one who could accept it, or it may be addressed to a group of people, any of whose members could accept it, or to the world at large, when anyone could accept it.

An offer, as an expression of a definite intention to enter into a contract with the offeree, must be clearly distinguished from a mere statement that the person making it is willing to negotiate a contract. Such a statement is referred to as an *invitation to make an offer*. The person making it invites some particular person, or perhaps any member of the general public, to make an offer to him which he will consider on its merits and accept if he should think fit to do so. Goods exhibited in a shop-window with or without a price ticket attached to them do not represent an offer by the shopkeeper, but merely constitute an invitation by him to any member of the general public to make him an offer. A customer who enters the shop and asks for one of the exhibited articles is making an offer to the shop-keeper, and the latter may accept or reject the offer as he pleases; he has the final word in the matter.

> *Pharmaceutical Society of Great Britain* v. *Boots.* This case concerned a self-service store operated by the well-known firm of cash chemists. By law, certain drugs may be sold only under the supervision of a qualified pharmaceutical chemist. The Society claimed that Boots had broken this rule by allowing customers to select their preparations from the shelves. *Held,* that no infringement had taken place, as a contract between the chemists and their customer came into existence only when the customer brought his selection of goods to the pay desk, where they were examined by a qualified chemist. The customer offered to buy the goods; it rested with the chemist whether the offer was accepted.

The position is the same even where a price ticket is attached to the goods. The purpose of the ticket is to indicate to the customer the price which he should offer. The same applies also to goods which are advertised in the Press. The offer comes from the reader who writes to the advertiser and not from the advertiser.

An offer must be communicated to the offeree. If a person does something which might constitute the acceptance of an offer when, however, he had no knowledge of the offer when he did the act in question, no contract will have come into existence. Thus, a person who returned some lost property to the owner, not knowing that a reward has been offered for the return, could not legally claim the reward.

The offeror may attach any conditions he likes to the offer, and these conditions will be binding on the offeree if he accepts the offer with knowledge of the conditions. The conditions must, however, have been properly communicated to the offeree. If that is so he will be bound by them even if he has not understood or appreciated them. He will have neglected to study them at his own risk and expense.

Where, as part of the making of a contract, a printed document containing conditions is handed by the offeror to the offeree the conditions will be treated as having been properly communicated to the offeree if there is some reference to them on some part of the document where a reasonably careful person would notice them. The application of this rule is particularly important where the contractual document happens to be a ticket, such as a railway or bus ticket. In that case it is obviously impossible for the conditions to be printed in full on the limited space available on the ticket, but it has been held to be sufficient if there is a reference to the existence of conditions on the face of the ticket, and the detailed conditions are available on request from the person or organization who has issued the ticket.

> *Thompson* v. *L.M. and S. Railway.* The plaintiff had bought an excursion ticket from the defendants. On the front of the ticket the words were printed: "For conditions see back," and on the back of the ticket it was intimated that the conditions could be found in the company's time-table. The passenger made no attempt to obtain a copy of the time-table. One of the conditions provided that the company would not be responsible for injuries suffered by the holders of excursion tickets. The plaintiff was injured. *Held,* that the conditions had been properly communicated to the plaintiff, whose action failed.

The document containing the conditions or the reference to them must be a 'contractual document' in the sense that its handing to the offeree represents an essential part of the performance of the contract. It may be presumed that the offeree will study such a document with care, while he could not be similarly expected to study a non-contractual document—*e.g.*, a receipt—with the same attention. Conditions referred to on such non-contractual documents would not be considered as properly communicated, unless some other means of communication had been used as well.

> *Chapelton* v. *Barry U.D.C.* The plaintiff hired a deck-chair from an attendant employed by the defendants. He received a receipt for the hire which he paid. The receipt stated that the authority accepted no responsibility for the structural soundness of the chairs. The chair collapsed under Chapelton, and he was injured. *Held,* that the defendants were unable to rely on the exempting clause as the condition had not been properly communicated to the plaintiff, the receipt not being a contractual document.

An offer may be revoked by the offeror at any time as long as it has not been accepted by the offeree. The offeror may revoke the offer even if he has given the offeree some time for acceptance. The sole purpose of giving the offeree time for acceptance is to indicate to him that the offer will lapse automatically if he has failed to accept within the time-limit set. Where no time-limit for acceptance has been set the offer will also lapse when a reasonable time has expired. What is a reasonable time is a question of fact, depending mainly on the value and importance of the subject-matter of the offer. The more important the subject-matter, the longer will be the time which the offeree has for considering his answer, assuming always that no specific time has been laid down by the offeror.

If the offeree wants to ensure that the offer should not be revoked before a certain time has expired he may do so by obtaining an *option* from the offeror. An option is in effect a separate contract, made between the offeror and the offeree, whereby in return for some consideration the offeror agrees to keep the offer open for a fixed time. Should the offeror then revoke the offer before that time, the offeree could sue him in damages for breach of the option contract.

If the offeree wishes to accept the offer he must do so unconditionally. Where the offeror has laid down how the offer is to be accepted the acceptance must comply with the offeror's requirements, otherwise it will not be effective. A conditional acceptance by the offeree amounts in law to a rejection of the offer, coupled with the making of a counter-offer. Where an offer has been rejected, whether expressly or impliedly by the making of a counter-offer, the original offer ceases to be operative, and the offeree cannot later fall back on it and accept it. Thus, if I offer my house to B for £2000 and he replies saying that he is prepared to give £1900 for it no contract has come into existence. My original offer has lapsed, and I may now decide whether or not to accept B's counter-offer. If I decide not to accept it he cannot accept my original offer to sell for £2000, as that offer no longer stands. He may offer to buy my house for that sum, but it is then up to me whether I wish to accept his offer.

The offeree must accept the offer within the time laid down for it by the offeror. If no time has been fixed by the offeror the offer must be accepted within a reasonable time. The acceptance is not operative until it has been communicated to the offeror. If it never reaches the offeror there is no contract. There are, however, two exceptions to this rule. In the following two cases an acceptance will lead to the formation of a contract although it has not reached the offeror:

1. Where the offer is one which is intended to be accepted by being acted upon there is no need to communicate acceptance to the offeror.

Carlill v. *Carbolic Smoke Ball Company*. The defendants were the manufacturers of a patent preparation which was supposed to prevent the common influenza. They advertised that they would pay £100 to anyone who after using the preparation in accordance with the instructions nevertheless contracted the 'flu within a certain time. The plaintiff bought and used a smoke ball, and contracted 'flu. She claimed £100. *Held*, that there existed a contract between the plaintiff and the defendants, since the defendants had indicated that use of the preparation should take the place of a formal acceptance of their offer.

2. Where the offeror has postulated, expressly or impliedly, that the acceptance should be made by post the acceptance is operative from the moment when the letter of acceptance has been entrusted to the post-office, irrespective of whether the letter reaches the offeror. The agreement of the parties that the acceptance of the offer should be effected by post need not be an express one; it may be implied from their conduct, such as where the offer has been sent by post, or even in those cases where it is customary in the ordinary course of business that the parties should contact each other by post.

It is important to note here that, while an acceptance by post is operative from the moment of posting, the offer, or the revocation of an offer, is not operative until it actually reaches the offeree.

Henthorn v. *Fraser*. A sent an offer to B by post. The offer reached B with the first morning post. He replied by post at 3.30 P.M. accepting the offer. A had written at 12 noon revoking his offer. A's revocation reached B at 6 P.M. the same day. B's acceptance was delivered to A the next morning. *Held*, that a contract had come into existence at 3.30 P.M.

As the rule about acceptance by post forms an exception to the general principle according to which an acceptance is not operative until it actually reaches the offeror, it must be applied restrictively. Its application may not be extended to similar cases, such as acceptances by telephone or by teleprinter, though it probably applies to acceptances by telegram, where this method of acceptance is contractually permitted.

Entores, Ltd. v. *Miles Far East Corporation*. The plaintiffs in London made an offer by Telex to the defendants in Holland. The defendants accepted the offer by the same method. A breach of contract took place and the plaintiffs wished to sue the defendants in the London courts. This was possible only if the contract had been *made* in England. A contract is made when a valid offer is accepted. *Held*, that the contract had been made in London, since the defendants' acceptance of the plaintiff's offer was not complete until actually received by the plaintiffs.

The offeree is always free to ignore an offer completely. If the offeror attaches a time-limit to his offer this merely means that the offer will have lapsed if not accepted within the time. It does not allow the offeror to claim that it has been accepted if he does not receive a reply rejecting it within the time stated. Any notice by the offeror purporting to claim that the offer will be treated as accepted if not rejected within a given time may thus be safely disregarded.

A mere mental acceptance of an offer is also insufficient to complete a contract. The acceptance must have been communicated in fact to the offeror. If this has been overlooked there is no acceptance even if the offeree intended to accept.

> *Felthouse* v. *Bindley.* A wrote to B offering to buy B's horse for £30. He added that if he had not heard from B to the contrary within a day he would assume that the horse was his. At the time the horse was in the hands of C, an auctioneer, for sale. B wanted to accept A's offer and informed C, who nevertheless sold the horse by auction. A sued C for conversion. *Held,* the action failed. A had not become the owner of the horse, since B had not communicated to him his acceptance of A's offer.

The agreement between the parties, established by offer and acceptance, must be a complete one, which means that nothing must have been left for future negotiation between the parties. If the parties have agreed on the major items of the proposed contract, but there is still something of importance which has not been settled between them, a complete agreement has not been reached, and therefore there is no contract. Examples of this may be found frequently in contracts involving the sale of land or houses, where the agreement between the parties for the sale of the property is stated to be 'subject to contract.' This means in effect that neither party is prepared to be legally bound by the agreement reached so far until such time as a formal contract has been drawn up by them (or, more likely, their solicitors) and has been signed by them. There is no certainty, however, that the parties will in effect sign the contract when it is prepared, and therefore no binding contract has as yet been established.

Similar considerations apply also in other cases where the agreement between the parties contains terms which are not sufficiently clear or capable of being made clear.

> *Scammell* v. *Ouston.* In a contract for the sale of a motor-van it was provided that part of the purchase price was to be paid by the buyer on "the usual hire-purchase terms" over a period of two years. No "usual hire-purchase terms" were in existence in that trade at the time. *Held,* that an essential part of the agreement not being clear, no binding contract had come into existence.

The legal principle involved is sometimes stated as that "there can be no contract to make a contract." You cannot agree, with legal binding force, that you will make a contract at a future date. This sweeping statement has to be interpreted with a grain of salt. It is, in fact, possible to make a contract for the purpose of contracting in the future, *provided* that all the details of the contract to be made in the future are either certain or ascertainable. After all, an engagement to marry is a contract to make a contract. As an example of a binding contract to make a contract we may quote:

Foley v. *Classique Coaches, Ltd.* F. had sold some land to the defendants on condition that they should buy all the petrol required for their business from him at a price to be agreed upon between them from time to time. It was further provided that, if the parties should be unable to agree on the price, the question of price should be submitted to arbitration. The defendants contended that as the question of price had been left open there was no binding contract. *Held,* that a binding contract had come into existence, as the price of future petrol supplies was ascertainable in view of the arbitration provision included in the contract.

GENUINENESS OF THE AGREEMENT

The parties to a contract must not only have agreed, but they must have agreed freely, and the agreement must not have been secured either by some form of external compulsion, or by misleading statements made before the contract or on an entirely wrong assessment of the situation. Contracts made under any of the above circumstances would not be valid, though the exact effect of the situations described would vary. We may discuss these situations under three headings: (1) mistake, (2) misrepresentation, and (3) duress and undue influence.

(1) *Mistake*

One cannot truly say that the parties to a contract have agreed if one or both of them were mistaken about some essential condition of the subject-matter which they were contracting about. Even so, not every mistake that either or both parties may make in the formation of a contract will invalidate the contract. Mistakes of law—*i.e.*, mistakes as to what the law provides—are never reasons for invalidating a contract. This is so because of the fiction that every one is supposed to know the law. This does not really mean that every person is expected to understand the law in all its ramifications, but law imposes on every person the duty of finding out the legal implications of anything which he proposes to do. He neglects this duty at his own risk.

If a mistake is to invalidate a contract it must be, then, a mistake of fact, and even then not every mistake of fact will have this effect. The mistake of fact must be an operative mistake—*i.e.*, a mistake which really undermines the agreement of the parties, and not one merely concerned with some incidental issue of their agreement. Operative mistakes of fact are in general discussed under three headings:

1. *A mistake as to the existence or the identity of the subject-matter.* These mistakes must be either common or mutual mistakes, in the sense that either both parties must have been mistaken about the same thing or about each other's intentions; a mistake of one party only would not be sufficient to invalidate the contract. A mistake as to the existence of the subject-matter arises where both parties believed the subject-matter to be in existence (a common mistake), while, in fact, the subject-matter had ceased to exist, or had perhaps never existed. No contract has come into existence in these circumstances, because the agreement of the parties rested on the implied understanding that the subject-matter which they were contracting about was actually in existence. The subject-matter need not necessarily be a tangible thing; it might be a state of affairs which both parties impliedly took for the basis of their contract.

> *Galloway* v. *Galloway.* A separation agreement between husband and wife whereby the husband promised to pay his wife a weekly allowance *held* to be void when it transpired that the marriage between the parties was not valid.

A mistake as to the identity of the subject-matter is one where the parties enter into a contract, each believing that the contract referred to a different thing—*i.e.,* a mutual mistake.

> *Raffles* v. *Wichelhaus.* A cargo of cotton was sold off the s.s. *Peerless,* described as being in the port of Bombay. Unknown to the parties, there were two ships of the same name in the port. The seller was thinking of one and the buyer of the other. *Held,* that no contract had come into existence.

The mistake in the identity of the subject-matter must be distinguished from a mere mistake in quality. If seller and buyer have agreed on the subject-matter of the contract, but one or both of them believe it to be something different (*e.g.,* in value) from what it really is, the contract will still be valid.

> *Fred. E. Rose, Ltd.* v. *W. H. Pim and Company, Ltd.* The parties wanted to enter into a contract for the supply of *féveroles.* Both of them believed that *féveroles* was merely another name for Moroccan horse-beans, and the contract was formulated in terms of the latter. It was later discovered that *féveroles* were not Moroccan horse-beans, but another variety of beans. *Held,* that the contract for Moroccan horse-beans was valid as the mistake of the parties was one of quality of the subject-matter and not one as to its identity. When they made

the contract the parties wanted to deal in Moroccan horse-beans, even though they believed them to possess a quality which they did not possess.

2. *A mistake in the identity of the other party.* Not every mistake in the identity of the person with whom a contract is made will suffice to make the contract void. The identity of the other party must in some way be material to the contract. It stands to reason that this type of mistake is an unilateral one, which can affect one of the parties only. In exactly the same way in which we had earlier to distinguish between a mistake in the identity and in the quality of the subject-matter, so we have also to distinguish between a mistake in the identity and in the quality of the other party. If I know with whom I am making a contract, but I mistakenly believe him to be a person of substance, while in fact he is a crook, the contract will stand, and it makes no difference that the other party has represented himself as a person of substance. It will be shown later that this situation could be covered by the law relating to misrepresentation. Three cases may help us in showing where mistake will and where it will not affect the validity of a contract.

Cundy v. *Lindsay.* X was induced by a man named Blenkarn to supply goods to him. Blenkarn had intentionally signed his letter to X in such a way as to make him believe that it came from the well-known firm of Blenkiron and Co. It was *held* that as X had never intended to contract with Blenkarn, there was no contract between them, and X was entitled to recover the goods from an innocent purchaser to whom Blenkarn had resold them.

King's Norton Metal Company v. *Edridge.* X had notepaper printed showing some large, albeit non-existing, factory premises and a whole string of foreign agencies. With the help of this notepaper he obtained on credit from the plaintiffs a quantity of goods which he resold to the defendants, who acted quite innocently. X then disappeared with the proceeds of the sale. The plaintiffs claimed the goods from the defendants, alleging that the plaintiffs' contract with X was void on the ground of mistake. If that was so X could not have passed a good title to the goods to the defendants. *Held,* that the plaintiffs' action failed. Their contract with X was not void, as they had known that they were selling to X, though they had been mistaken about his business standing.

Ingram v. *Little.* The plaintiffs advertised a car for sale. A rogue, giving the name of Hutchinson, replied and offered a cheque in payment for the car. The plaintiffs, who had no knowledge of the buyer, refused at first to accept the cheque, but then, having looked up the address given by H. in a directory and finding that a person of this name lived at that address, accepted the cheque. Within a few days, H. sold the car to the defendant in part-exchange for another car. The cheque was dishonoured as the real Hutchinson was in no way connected with the buyer. The plaintiffs now claimed the return of the car from the defendant. *Held*, that the contract between the plaintiffs and H. was void on the ground of mistake and that they were entitled to the return of the car or its value. A majority of the Court of Appeal held that the offer to sell the car had been made to the real Hutchinson and that it could therefore not have been validly accepted by the rogue using that name.

3. *Mistake as to the nature of the contract.* If A enters into a written contract with B believing it to be a contract of an entirely different kind the contract will be void. The mistake must be one as to the nature of the contract, and not merely one concerning its contents. If you know that you are entering into a contract for the purchase of goods, but you have failed to study the terms of the document embodying the contract before signing it, you will still be bound by the contract.

L'Estrange v. *Graucob.* The plaintiff bought an automatic machine from the defendants and signed a purchase agreement containing certain conditions in small print. These exempted the defendants from liability if the machine should not work. *Held*, that as the plaintiff had signed the agreement she was bound by its terms.

Where the meaning of the terms of a contract signed by a party has been misrepresented by the other party the terms will not be binding on the party misled.

Curtis v. *Chemical Cleaning and Dyeing Company, Ltd.* The plaintiff, when handing in a wedding dress for cleaning, was asked to sign a receipt containing certain conditions. She was told by the assistant that the conditions meant that the company would not accept liability for damage to sequins. When the dress was returned it was badly stained. The clause in fact exempted the company from all liability for damage to cleaned goods. *Held*, that the company could not rely on the exempting clause.

Where there is a mistake as to the *nature* of the contract entered into the contract will be void even if it was negligent on the person's part to enter into the contract. If, however, the contract entered into took the form of a negotiable instrument, liability may be avoided only if the person who signed it can prove that he was not negligent in making the mistake.

Foster v. *Mackinnon.* An old man suffering from bad eyesight signed a bill of exchange believing it to be a guarantee. *Held*, that he was not liable on the bill as in the circumstances he had not been negligent in not discovering the mistake.

(2) *Misrepresentation*

Misrepresentation is an untrue statement of fact, made by one party to a contract to the other, either at or before the time of entering into the contract, with the intention that the person to whom the statement is made should act upon it, and where he has in fact acted upon it.

Misrepresentation must always be a statement of fact and not one of law, since, as has been shown already, every one is supposed to know the law. The statement must have been made by a party to the contract or by some one acting on his behalf, and not by a stranger to the contract. The statement must have been made at some time before the completion of the contract, since a statement made after the contract had already been made could not induce a person to enter into it. Lastly, the person to whom the statement was made must have believed in it and must have acted upon it. If he ignores the statement and enters into the contract for a different reason, the validity of the contract will not be affected. If the statement is embodied in the contract it becomes a term of it, and if it is proved to be untrue the innocent party will have the ordinary remedies for breach of contract, and not those for misrepresentation. Here we are concerned with those cases only where the statement is not embodied in the contract.

A misrepresentation may be innocent or fraudulent. It is fraudulent where the person making the statement knows that it is untrue or makes it recklessly not caring whether it is true or not, or where he makes the statement not himself believing it to be true. Any other case of misrepresentation comes under the heading of innocent misrepresentation.

The difference between innocent and fraudulent misrepresentation is important, because of the remedies which are open to the party who had been misled into making the contract. Where the misrepresentation was an innocent one the innocent party may either refuse to perform the contract or he may ask the court to rescind the contract—*i.e.*, set it aside. Rescission of contracts is a remedy of equity which used to be unknown at common law. At common law there existed, in effect, no remedy for innocent misrepresentation. As the purpose of rescission is that the parties should revert to their position before the contract was made, it is obvious that there can be no rescission if this aim cannot be attained —because, for instance, the subject-matter of the contract has been altered in shape, or has been consumed. Furthermore, as with all other remedies of equity, an action for the rescission of a contract must be started promptly. If it is delayed unreasonably the court will be unable to grant rescission.

Leaf v. *International Galleries.* L. bought a drawing of Salisbury cathedral from the defendants, who claimed that it was the work of

Constable. This was not true, but the defendants did not know that themselves. Five years later, when the buyer wanted to sell the drawing, he discovered that it was not an authentic Constable. *Held,* that too long a time had elapsed to justify a rescission of the contract.

A person who has been fraudulently misled into making a contract has the same remedies, but in addition he may also claim damages for fraud from the other party.

The party who has been misled by an untrue statement has the remedies described above even if he could have easily found out for himself that the statement was untrue. You may always rely on a statement made to you by the other party. A person is, however, not bound to volunteer any information to a party who has not asked for it. Keeping silent will not be construed as a statement. When entering into a contract you need not volunteer to the other party all the defects from which the subject-matter of the contract may be suffering. You may leave it to the other party to find out the defects for himself. There are only two cases where a duty is imposed on a person to volunteer information in connexion with the formation of a contract and where the withholding of this information would be treated as misrepresentation.

1. Where a person has made a representation, and then before the other party has entered into the contract with him the representation which at first was true has become untrue, he will be bound to let the other party know of the changed position.

With v. *O'Flanagan.* A doctor who was negotiating for the sale of his practice informed the prospective buyer that the practice yielded about £2000 a year. The negotiations took some time, and during this period, because of the selling doctor's illness, the income of the practice declined to an average of £5 a week. When the buyer who had bought the practice discovered this it was *held* that the contract could be set aside at his request on the ground of misrepresentation.

2. In entering into a contract of utmost good faith (a contract *uberrimæ fidei*) a person has to make a full disclosure of all relevant facts to the other party. Contracts of utmost good faith are those in which because of their very nature certain facts can only be known to one of the parties. The only true contract of this kind is one of insurance. In such a contract the insured has to volunteer to the insurer all facts which may have an influence on the latter's decision whether and on what terms to insure. In a continuing contract of partnership each partner has to disclose to the other information that pertains to the partnership affairs, and in a sale of land the seller must disclose to the buyer all legal defects in his title, though not the physical defects of the property.

Conditions and Warranties. Representations must be distinguished from contractual terms. Where a person makes a statement
in connexion with the formation of a contract we have a representation. It becomes a term of the contract if it has been embodied in
the contract. Where the person making the statement intends to
accept legal responsibility for it, and the statement is proved to be
untrue, a claim for damages will succeed.

Oscar Chess, Ltd. v. *Williams.* The defendant, when buying a car
from the plaintiffs, gave his own old car in part-exchange. He described the car as a "1948 Morris 10 saloon." This description was
based on the car's registration book, and he was credited with the
value of a car of that year's make. Some months later the plaintiffs
discovered that a previous owner of the car had altered the entry on
the registration book, and the car was really a 1939 model, the value
of which was smaller. *Held,* that the plaintiffs could not recover the
difference in value, as it could not be assumed that the defendant's
statement about the age of the car was intended to be a warranty.

It has been shown already that the only remedy for an innocent
misrepresentation is a rescission of the contract, which has to be
applied for promptly. Where, however, the statement has become a
term of the contract and it is untrue the other party has the usual
remedies for breach of contract, which he may exercise within the
normal period of limitation (in general, six years).

Contractual terms in the broad sense as described above may
be sub-divided into conditions and warranties in the narrow and
technical sense. The difference between these will be discussed in
Chapter 4, dealing with the law relating to the sale of goods.

(3) *Duress and Undue Influence*

Where one of the parties to a contract was not a free agent when
he entered into it the contract will be set aside at his request. This
situation may arise where the party has been subjected either to
duress or to undue influence. A contract is entered into under
duress where a party has been coerced into making it, either by
violence or by threats of violence or by having some of his property
seized or by threats of criminal proceedings. The person threatened
in all the above circumstances may be either the contractual party
himself or some one else who is so close to him that a threat to
that person could be treated as a threat to the contractual party
himself. If a person enters into a contract under the threat. express
or implied, of criminal proceedings the contract will be voidable
by him irrespectively of whether there existed some foundation for
the taking of criminal proceedings, the reason being that it is an

c

abuse of criminal proceedings to use the threat of them as a lever with which to extort some contractual concessions.

A contract is voidable on the ground of undue influence where there existed between the parties a relationship of such a kind that one of them was guided or influenced by the views of the other party. It is always possible to prove the existence of such a relationship, but in certain cases law presumes its existence. This applies to the relationships between parent and child, solicitor and client, doctor and patient, guardian and ward, trustee and beneficiary, and a minister of religion and a member of his congregation. Where a contract has been entered into between any one of these persons and the other party in the pair the contract will be voidable at the option of the weaker party. The presumption of undue influence may be, however, rebutted if it can be shown that the weaker party had independent legal advice before entering into the contract. It should be noted that there is no presumption of undue influence in contracts between husband and wife.

While duress was recognized at common law, undue influence was a ground for having a contract set aside in equity only. From this follows that he who wishes to have a contract set aside on the ground of undue influence will have to go to court as soon as possible after the influence has ceased to operate.

CONSIDERATION

It is a principle of English law that a contract, except where made by deed, must be supported by consideration if it is to be legally valid. A contract is basically a form of exchange; one party receives in return for his act or promise something from the other party, and this something is referred to as consideration. We distinguish between good consideration and valuable consideration. Good consideration consists of such things as gratitude, thanks, or love which a person may return for a promise that has been made to him. Needless to say, good consideration is insufficient for legal purposes. What law requires is valuable consideration, and that has been defined in *Currie* v. *Misa* as "some right, interest, profit or benefit accruing to one party or some forbearance, detriment, loss, or responsibility given, suffered or undertaken by the other." What this means is that if A makes a promise to B, B's consideration for the promise may take the form either of some kind of benefit extended to A or of some forbearance or detriment suffered by B, even though it may not have directly benefited A. It stands to reason that the consideration, whatever it may be, must have been agreed upon by the parties, and cannot be unilaterally selected by B.

The parties to a contract are the persons who have provided consideration. The relationship that exists between them is known as one of *privity of contract*. A person who has not provided any part of the consideration, but who was to benefit from the contract, may not bring an action for breach of contract if the contract has not been performed, as privity of contract did not exist between him and the party who failed to carry out his contractual promises.

Tweddle v. *Atkinson*. A was about to marry B. Before the wedding A's father agreed with B's father that each of them would pay £100 to the bridegroom on the day of the wedding. The bride's father failed to pay, and the bridegroom sued the estate of his father-in-law (who had died in the meantime). *Held,* that the action failed, since privity of contract did not exist between the groom and the promisor.

There exists now one exception to the principle that absence of privity of contract makes an action impossible, and that is in respect of resale price-maintenance agreements. If manufacturer A sells some goods to B, a wholesaler, who resells them to C, a retailer, there is no contract between A and C. A may have laid down certain terms as to the conditions, mainly the price, on which the goods may be resold. Until fairly recently A could not have enforced these conditions against C, but he may do so now, thanks to the provisions of Section 25 of the Restrictive Trade Practices Act, 1956. This Act provides that where a person acquires goods with knowledge of the existence of certain conditions about resale prices, he will be bound to observe these conditions.

As has been stated above, consideration is required for the validity of any contract not made by deed, even though the contract may be in writing, and is otherwise in accordance with the law. The following points should be noted, however, about valuable consideration:

1. *Consideration need not be adequate.* There is no need for the value of the counter-promise to be anywhere near that of the promise which is supported by it, as long as the consideration has some value and is not just 'good' consideration. Gross inadequacy of consideration may be, however, possible evidence of fraud, though this would have to be proved also by other facts. Behind this principle lies the reasoning that persons of full age are free to enter into any contract they like, and that it is for them to decide whether the terms offered to them are satisfactory ones.

2. *Consideration must be real.* This means that the party making the sacrifice loses something which, at least at the time when he made the sacrifice, appeared to him to be something of value. Thus, if a person merely promises to do something which he is bound to

do already he does not make a real sacrifice, and there is no real consideration. The best illustration of that is where a debtor promises to discharge his debt to the creditor by the payment of a smaller sum. Even if the creditor accepts this payment "in full settlement" he will still be able to claim the balance, as he has received no real consideration for his promise not to claim the balance.

Foakes v. *Beer.* Mrs B. agreed not to claim interest from her debtor, Dr F., if he repaid his debt by stated instalments. F. did so, but after he had paid off the principal sum Mrs B. claimed the interest. *Held*, that she was entitled to succeed, as she had received no real consideration from Dr F. for her promise not to claim; he merely did what he was legally bound to do in any case.

The principle that the acceptance of a smaller sum in settlement of a larger debt will not discharge the debt in full applies, of course, only where the creditor has not, in addition to the sum of money, received some other consideration for his promise not to claim more. Thus, the debt is discharged by the payment of a smaller sum if the payment has been offered and accepted earlier than it was due, or at a different place from where it was due, or in a form other than that in which the creditor was entitled to claim payment. The earlier payment or the payment at a different place or in a different form would be looked upon as real consideration for the creditor's promise to accept less than he was entitled to. It should be noted that payment by cheque or bill of exchange is something to which the creditor is not entitled, since he can only demand legal tender, and if a cheque or bill of exchange is given and accepted in full settlement the debt will be discharged.

Where a debtor tenders a cheque for a smaller sum of money in full settlement of a larger debt, and the cheque is accepted by the creditor, the debt will be discharged only if it can be shown that the creditor intended to take it in full settlement.

Neuchâtel Asphalte Company, Ltd. v. *Barnett.* The N. Co. had agreed to do some work for B. at a cost of £259. B. paid £125 on account, but subsequently he claimed that the work had been done badly, and that he was entitled to a reduction because of this. He sent eventually a cheque for £75 in respect of the work, and typed on the back of the cheque the words: "In full and final settlement of account. Signed . . . Dated . . ." The account was not enclosed with the cheque. The secretary of the company, who did not know about the customer's claim for a reduction, signed the receipt on the cheque. *Held*, that in the circumstances it could not be supposed that the company had any intention of receiving the cheque in full settlement of the account.

The importance of the principle in *Foakes* v. *Beer* has been further reduced as a result of more recent developments in our law.

Central London Property Trust v. *High Trees House.* The plaintiffs, before the War, had let a block of flats to the defendants. In the first year of the War many flats were unoccupied, and the defendants were contemplating terminating the lease when the plaintiffs offered to reduce the rent. Because of this promise, the defendants kept on the lease. After the War the plaintiffs again demanded the full rent. Denning, J. *held* (a) that the plaintiffs could at any time demand the full rent again, as they had received no consideration for their promise to reduce the rent, (b) they could not claim any of the arrears of rent, because by their conduct in allowing a reduction they had induced the defendants to do something (*i.e.*, to retain the lease) which they otherwise would not have done.

In more general terms, the principle in the *High Trees case* may be stated as follows. If A, without consideration, makes a promise to B which is accepted and acted upon by B, and the parties intended this promise to be a legally binding one, then B will be able to set up this promise by way of defence if he is sued by A. Note the words 'by way of defence.' The principle may be employed only as a weapon of defence; it is not possible to base an action on it.

Combe v. *Combe.* A husband separated from his wife. He agreed to make an annual allowance to her, and the wife, because of this, failed to apply for a court order for maintenance against him. The husband never made any payments, and the wife by her delay had made it impossible to claim through the court. In an action by the wife against her husband it was *held* that she could not rely on his promise as she had not given any consideration and the High Trees rule did not apply, as it could be used by way of defence only.

If A is already under a contract to B to do something a subsequent promise made to C to do the same thing will be valuable consideration for a counter-promise by C, since in the event of A's failure to carry out the promise he would be subjected to two actions for breach of contract, one by B and one by C.

Shadwell v. *Shadwell.* A young barrister was engaged to be married. His uncle promised him that he would make him an annual allowance if he got married. *Held,* that a contract had come into existence between uncle and nephew, although the nephew had promised to do something (*i.e.*, marry) which he was already obliged to do because of his engagement to his fiancée.

3. *Consideration must be legal.* This point will be discussed in a later paragraph in connexion with legality of contracts in general.

4. *Consideration must not be past.* If A makes a promise to B, B's consideration must come after A's promise. Thus, if A promises something to B in return for a service which B has rendered to him

already B's consideration would be past, and would thus be insufficient to support the contract.

It is sometimes argued that past consideration may be acceptable where B's service has been rendered in circumstances raising the presumption that it would be paid for, the subsequent promise of A to pay being merely the means by which the price payable is fixed. For instance, I may call in a jobbing gardener to do a job for me, and when he has finished promise to pay him for his services. In fact, however, this type of situation does not create an exception to the principle that past consideration will not be valuable consideration, since we must presume that when the jobbing gardener rendered his service to me there existed already an implied agreement between us that a reasonable amount would be paid for his service. The consideration for the promise to pay was thus created simultaneously with the promise.

There exists one real exception to the rule that consideration may not be past. A bill of exchange is stated by the Bills of Exchange Act, 1882, to have been given for valuable consideration, even though the consideration was a past one.

THE FORM OF CONTRACTS

The general rule is that a contract validly entered into between parties capable of entering into contracts is enforceable irrespective of the form in which it has been made. Contracts may be divided, according to the form in which they have been made, into specialty contracts and simple contracts. Specialty contracts are contracts made by deed, while simple contracts are those made in any other form, whether in writing, or orally (parol contracts), or even by the conduct of the parties.

A deed is a written instrument which has been signed, sealed, and delivered. To-day, when few persons other than corporations have their own seals, any kind of seal will suffice, and even a paper wafer in the shape of a seal will do. The deed is not complete, however, until it has been delivered by the party executing it. A deed which has not been delivered yet is known as an *escrow*. Delivery can be actual, where the party executing the deed hands it to the other party in person, but in practice it is generally constructive, where the executing party places a finger on the seal on the deed in the presence of a witness and states: "I deliver this as my act and deed." The witness then signs the deed to show that it has been delivered in his presence.

The main differences between specialty contracts and simple contracts are the following:

1. A specialty contract does not require to be supported by consideration.

2. A right of action under a simple contract is barred after six years, while the corresponding period for specialty contracts is twelve years. (Limitation Act, 1939, see page 48.)

3. Where the parties have entered into a simple contract concerning a certain subject-matter, and subsequently make out a deed to cover the same subject-matter, the simple contract is said to have been merged into the deed, and thereby becomes extinct.

Deeds are used in practice on those occasions only where formality is essential in order to impress upon the parties the importance of the transaction. Not all the examples given below relate to contracts: some of them relate to transfers of property (conveyances) which follow the making of a contract and are intended to pass property rights. Deeds will then have to be employed in the following cases:

(1) contracts which are not supported by valuable consideration;
(2) leases of land for more than three years;
(3) the transfer of shares in a British ship;
(4) the transfer of the title to land.

Where a transaction is required to be made by deed, non-compliance with this requirement would invalidate the transaction.

The following transactions (contracts and transfers) have to be made in writing, though not necessarily by deed. Where the transaction in any of these cases is not made in writing it would again fail to be legally operative.

(1) a contract of marine insurance (though not other contracts of insurance);
(2) bills of exchange, cheques, and promissory notes;
(3) an acknowledgment of a statute-barred debt (page 49);
(4) contracts under the Moneylenders Act, 1927;
(5) hire-purchase contracts, if subject to the Hire Purchase Acts, 1938–54;
(6) the transfer of shares in a limited company;
(7) the assignment of a copyright.

Apart from the cases where contracts have to be *made* in writing if they are to be valid at all, there are also other contracts which, while they may be made in any form, cannot be enforced by court action unless it is possible to prove their existence and their terms by some written evidence. In the absence of this evidence any of the contracts mentioned below will be valid, but unenforceable.

1. A contract of guarantee (Section 4 of the Statute of Frauds, 1677). This is a contract whereby one person (the guarantor) promises another that he will be responsible for the debt or wrong-doing of a third party. The guarantor's liability is conditional upon the creditor being unable to obtain satisfaction from the main debtor. In this way it differs from a contract of indemnity where a person promises to be responsible for the payment of a sum of money independently of another's indebtedness. If I say to X, who is about to sell something to Y, "You may safely grant credit to him, because if he should not pay I will" that is a guarantee. If, however, in similar circumstances I say to X: "I shall be responsible for payment" that is a contract of indemnity. Such a contract may be enforced even if there is no written evidence to prove it, though, of course, there would have to be some other evidence.

2. Any contract for the sale or other disposition of land (Section 40 of the Law of Property Act, 1925). The other dispositions referred to cover such transactions as leases or mortgages.

A contract of guarantee or a contract for the sale or other disposition of land may not be enforced unless it can be evidenced in writing. The best evidence in writing would be a written contract, but even if the contract is not in writing other written evidence would be sufficient, provided it satisfies the requirements of what the law calls a 'note or memorandum in writing.'

1. The memorandum must contain the names of the parties. Normally, these will be expected to appear on the same document, except that in the case of a letter the envelope in which the letter was sent may be produced as additional evidence to satisfy the requirement.

2. The document must describe the subject-matter of the contract in detail. This includes all the important terms of the contract.

> *Hawkins* v. *Price*. A sold a house to B for £1000. It was agreed that vacant possession should be given on completion of the contract. The only written evidence of the contract was a receipt signed by the vendor, for the deposit of £100 which the buyer had paid. The receipt contained no reference to the date when possession of the house would be granted. *Held,* that the receipt was not a sufficient memorandum in writing to allow the buyer to enforce the contract against the vendor.

3. The memorandum must state the consideration which has been agreed, except for a guarantee, where this is not necessary.

4. The memorandum must have been signed by or on behalf of the person against whom it is to be used in evidence. The signature need not necessarily appear at the end of the document as long as it

is clear that the person against whom the document will be used accepted responsibility for its contents.

5. Any written document satisfying the above requirements may be introduced in evidence, irrespective of the purpose for which it has been prepared, provided that it was in existence at the time of the commencement of the action. It could be a private letter, a receipt, or anything else of that sort.

6. The 'memorandum in writing' may consist of two documents provided that the document signed by the party to be charged contains, expressly or by necessary implication, a reference to the other document. When this is so parol evidence may be given to identify the other document—*e.g.*, a letter not containing the name of the addressee may be supplemented by producing the envelope in which it was sent.

Timmins v. *Moreland Street Property Company, Ltd.* The plaintiff, by an oral agreement, sold some property to the defendants. The defendants made out a cheque, payable to the plaintiff's solicitor, for the deposit, and the plaintiff himself wrote out a receipt which identified the property, the parties, and the purchase price. The defendants subsequently repudiated the agreement. *Held*, that the cheque signed by the defendants could not be used as a memorandum together with the plaintiff's receipt, since it was impossible to spell a reference to the plaintiff's letter out of the defendants' cheque, which was made payable, not to the plaintiff himself, but to his solicitors.

A contract which had to be evidenced in writing could not be enforced at common law in the absence of written evidence. Equity took a more lenient view by applying the *doctrine of part performance*. This doctrine is applied where a contract for the sale or lease of land has been validly entered into, but there does not exist any written evidence of that fact. The conditions to be fulfilled for the application of this doctrine are the following:

1. The party wishing to enforce the contract must himself have partly performed the contract. The act of part performance must be one that is exclusively referable to the contract to be enforced. This means that what the plaintiff has done is something that can be explained only on the assumption that he had made a contract with some one. The payment of a sum of money would not be a sufficient act of part performance, as there are many possible reasons why a person may have paid a sum of money to another.

2. The situation is one where it would be fraudulent on the defendant's part to take advantage of the absence of written evidence.

3. The remedy which the court will grant to the plaintiff will be

that of ordering the defendant to perform his part of the contract. Damages would not be granted.

4. The plaintiff must be able to prove the terms of the contract by sufficient evidence in some other form.

> *Rawlinson* v. *Ames*. A. had verbally agreed to take a twenty-one years' lease of the plaintiff's flat. In order to meet A.'s special requirements the plaintiff had to make certain structural alterations to the flat. The defendant followed the progress of the work, and frequently made suggestions about improvements. When the work was completed the defendant refused to take the flat. *Held*, that as the plaintiff had performed his part of the contract it would be wrong to allow the defendant to take advantage of the absence of writing, and she must complete the contract by signing a proper lease.

ILLEGALITY

A contract which is illegal is absolutely void. It may be illegal either because it is forbidden by the law, or because a court will not enforce it on the grounds of 'public policy,' or because the contract has been entered into for an illegal or immoral purpose.

Contracts declared illegal by statute

A gaming or wagering contract is illegal (Gaming Act, 1845). A contract of gaming or wagering is one under which a person agrees to pay a sum of money to another on the happening of some uncertain event in return for an immediate payment or for a payment which is to take place if the event does not materialize. The parties must have no interest in the subject-matter of the wager other than the stake. This is the difference between this contract and one of insurance, which otherwise closely resembles a wager. The difference between wagering and gaming contracts is that in the latter case the bet is one on the result of some game or pastime, while in the former case it is one on any other event or fact—*e.g.*, on the results of an election.

An essential feature of a gaming or wagering contract is that both parties stand to win or lose. Where, as with a football pool competition or the totalizator at a race meeting, one side cannot lose, the contract is not one of gaming in the legal sense of the word. It could therefore be enforced by court action unless the parties have indicated that they do not wish it to have legal consequences.

Contracts opposed to public policy

The term 'public policy' is a technical legal term, and should not be identified with the policy of the Government in office. The list of contracts which are deemed to be 'opposed to public policy' is by now complete, and it is most unlikely that the courts will add further contracts to the list. The following contracts may be mentioned as examples of contracts which are opposed to public policy:

1. A contract in *absolute* restraint of marriage—*i.e.,* a contract whereby a person promises not to marry at all. A contract whereby a person promises not to marry a particular other person or a person belonging to a certain class of people, (*e.g.,* a Roman Catholic) would be valid, provided that the restriction was one which could be clearly interpreted by the courts.

2. A contract tending to impede the administration of justice. The main example is a contract whereby a person agrees for a consideration not to prosecute some one who has committed a criminal offence—*e.g.,* not to prosecute a burglar provided he returns some of the property which he has taken. We call this an agreement to stifle a prosecution. Where the victim of the offence has the choice either of prosecuting the offender for the crime or of suing him for a civil wrong (a tort) he may agree not to take any criminal proceedings against the offender—*e.g.,* in a case of assault.

3. A contract tending to injure the public service. This includes the sale of a public office, or the receipt of bribes to procure some favour from a Government department or to obtain some award.

Parkinson v. *Royal College of Ambulance.* An agreement to obtain the award of a knighthood in return for a large donation to a charity was *held* to be illegal.

4. A contract involving trading with the enemy in war-time is illegal unless made with the licence of the Crown. An 'enemy' for the purposes of this contract is any person resident in enemy or enemy-occupied territory, irrespective of his nationality.

5. A contract of champerty or maintenance is illegal. Maintenance means assisting a person in bringing or defending a legal action where the person giving the assistance has himself no legal interest in the subject-matter of the dispute. Champerty is the same as maintenance, except that the person giving the assistance has been promised a share in the proceeds of the action.

6. A contract having as its purpose the breaking of the laws of a friendly country is opposed to public policy.

Regazzoni v. *L. C. Sethia* (1944), *Ltd.* The parties entered into a contract for the export of jute from India. To the knowledge of both parties, the jute was intended for re-export to the Union of South Africa. Under Indian law, the export of goods to South Africa was forbidden. *Held,* that the contract would not be enforced by an English court.

7. A contract interfering with the performance of parental or

marital duties is illegal, such as where a person agrees to an
adoption of his child otherwise than by means of a legal adoption.

8. A contract in unreasonable restraint of trade is opposed to
public policy, and therefore illegal. These contracts will be further
discussed on page 136.

Contracts entered into for an illegal or immoral purpose

Where a contract, legal in itself, is entered into for an illegal or
immoral purpose the court will refuse to enforce it.

> *Alexander* v. *Rayson*. The landlord of a block of flats entered into
> an agreement with the prospective tenant of a luxury flat, whereby
> the rent should be paid partially as compensation for certain services
> which in fact were not provided. The reason for this agreement was
> that the landlord did not want the rating authority to find out the
> true rental value of the premises. It was *held* that the contract had
> been entered into for an illegal purpose—namely, depriving the local
> authority of some of their rateable revenue—and that for that reason
> it was illegal and would not be enforced by the court.

The effects of illegality

An illegal contract is not necessarily a criminal one. Illegality
with reference to contracts merely means that they will not be enforced by a court of law. As soon as the court discovers that a
contract is illegal it will refuse to help the plaintiff any further.
There is a legal maxim which states *in pari delicto potior est con-
ditio defendentis* (where the guilt of the parties is equal the position
of the defendant is the stronger one). This means that, if both
parties are equally responsible for the illegality, the defendant is in
a stronger position, because the court will not help the plaintiff to
recover anything from him. Thus, if a contractor has done work
for you for which a Government licence is required, and no licence
has been obtained, the court will not order you to pay him the
agreed price for the work which he has done. An illegal contract
will never be enforced by the court, but in some exceptional cases
the court may allow a party to recover money which he has paid
to the other party under an illegal contract. This will happen in the
following cases:

1. Where the guilt of the parties is not equal, and the plaintiff
is less to blame for the illegality than the defendant. A mere mistake
of law on the part of the plaintiff will be no help to him, as he is
presumed to know the law; but a mistake of fact induced by the
defendant would help. Thus, where in the above example the householder was told by the contractor that he had obtained the licence,
and the householder, who had no reason to disbelieve the contractor,

paid to him a sum of money by way of advance on the contract price, he would be able to recover it even though the contract was illegal.

2. Where the illegal purpose of the contract is not carried out because one of the parties repents in time, and prevents the illegality being carried out, the repenting party will be able to recover anything which he may have paid to the other party. Repentance is, however, possible only if it takes place when it would still have been feasible to perform the contract. If the illegal purpose could not be attained, for some reason outside the plaintiff's control, he will be unable to recover his payment from the other party.

> *Bigos* v. *Bousted.* A agreed with B that B should supply some Italian currency to A's wife, who was about to visit Italy. This contract was illegal, as it offended against the exchange control regulations. A deposited some securities with B as guarantee that he would settle the debt in England. B then refused to supply A's wife with currency when she asked him for it in Italy. A sued B for the return of the securities. *Held,* that A's action had to fail, as it could not be said that he had repented. In the court's words, "there can be no true repentance when it has become impossible to sin."

The position concerning illegal contracts may, then, be summed up as follows: it is never possible to enforce a contract which is illegal, and, with the exception of the two cases mentioned above, it is also impossible to recover money that has been paid on an illegal contract.

Where the contract between the parties is legal, but the performance of the contract by one of the parties happened to involve the commission of a criminal offence (though it need not have done), the other party will be unable to withhold payment.

> *St John Shipping Corporation* v. *Joseph Rank, Ltd.* A ship had been chartered for the carriage of a cargo of wheat. The shipowner allowed the ship to be overloaded, which involves the commission of a criminal offence, for which the master of the ship was duly fined. The charterers withheld from the shipowners a sum of money equal to the extra profit which the owners had made by allowing the ship to be overloaded. *Held,* that they were not entitled to do so, since a contract which is legal and made for a legal purpose does not become illegal by being performed in an illegal manner.

DISCHARGE OF CONTRACTS

A contract is discharged when it ceases to be operative, so that all rights and obligations which had existed under it become extinguished. A contract may be discharged in the following ways:

1. *Discharge of the contract by agreement.* A contract, having

come into existence by agreement between the parties, may be discharged in the same way in which it has been made. This means that in order for the discharge to be fully operative valuable consideration will have to be given to the other party. Where neither party has as yet performed their respective promises under the contract (in legal terminology, the contract is still in its 'executory' stage) a mutual release will be fully operative, as the consideration for the release of one party by the other is the similar undertaking of the party to be released.

Where, however, one of the parties has already performed his undertaking under the contract, and now wishes to release the other party, that party will have to provide some fresh consideration. We call this a discharge of the contract by accord and satisfaction, as, in addition to the accord (agreement) of the parties, the party to be released from his original obligation is providing some satisfaction (consideration) for the other party.

Another way of discharging a contract by agreement is by replacing the old contract by a new one, either made between the same parties but embodying some new terms, or made by one of the parties with a third person. We call this a discharge of the contract by *novation*. Let us illustrate how novation works by means of an example. Assume that A has sold a book to B for £2. A and B then may make a new contract whereby the parties agree that A should receive as consideration for the book a turkey instead of the agreed £2. Alternatively, C may agree with A that he (C) will buy the book for £2, provided that A releases B from his obligation to pay this sum, and provided, of course, also that B is willing to be released.

It is always possible to dissolve or amend a contract. No particular form is required for this purpose, except that where the contract is one which by law has to be in writing it may be dissolved by an oral agreement of the parties, but it can be amended only by a written agreement. A parol agreement to amend the terms of a written contract of this type would therefore be disregarded by the court. Where the terms of a written contract are ambiguous the court will be prepared, however, to accept parol evidence to interpret the terms of the contract.

A contract is also discharged by agreement where the contract contains a term providing that it should be discharged on the happening or non-happening of some future event or on the fulfilment or non-fulfilment of some condition, or by either party giving notice. During the last war many contracts were entered into which were stated to be 'for the duration of the War,' and that meant that they were treated as discharged once the War had officially ended.

2. *Discharge of the contract by performance.* A contract is dis-

charged if both parties have performed their respective undertakings under the contract. If one party tenders performance, and this is without good cause rejected by the other party, the effect of the tender will vary according to whether goods or money had been tendered. Where goods have been tendered in performance of a contract, and they are not accepted, the party tendering will be discharged from his obligation. A tender of money, not accepted by the creditor, does not discharge the tenderer, but he may pay the sum into court if sued by the creditor. This means that he deposits the amount which he acknowledges to owe with the office of the appropriate court in favour of the creditor, giving notice to the creditor that he has done so. The most likely occasion on which this may happen is where the creditor claims a larger sum than that which the debtor acknowledges. If the money has been paid into court by the debtor, and the creditor in his action does not recover more than this amount, the creditor will have to pay the costs of the legal proceedings.

When money is tendered in settlement of a debt the money must be offered in the form of legal tender. Bank of England notes are legal tender up to any amount, silver is legal tender up to two pounds, threepenny (cupro-nickel) pieces are legal tender up to two shillings, and coppers up to one shilling. Cheques and other similar credit instruments are not legal tender at all. If a creditor accepts a cheque in settlement of a debt the debt is discharged by accord and satisfaction rather than by performance, because the creditor has accepted payment in a different form from that to which he was entitled. The debtor must always tender the correct sum, as the creditor is not bound to provide change. Tender of payment must take place at a reasonable time, which, if the creditor is in business, must be during ordinary business hours. It is the debtor's duty to ensure that the payment reaches the creditor, unless the creditor has specifically prescribed some method of conveying the money to him. If the debtor sends the money by post it is at his risk during transit, and if it were lost he would not have discharged his debt. If the creditor has asked for the money to be sent by post, and the debtor has exercised all the usual precautions of a reasonably careful businessman (e.g., registering a letter containing notes, crossing cheques, etc.) then the loss, if it should materialize, would fall on the creditor. It should also be noted that where payment is made by cheque or some other credit instrument, then, unless the parties have agreed otherwise, it will be presumed that the discharge of the debt is conditional upon the credit instrument being honoured.

Where a debtor owes several debts to the same creditor, and then makes a payment which is insufficient to discharge all of them, it may be of some importance to decide which of the outstanding debts have been discharged. The reason is that some of the debts, if not discharged, may presently become unenforceable on the ground of being statute-barred (see Section 3 below). When the debtor makes the payment he has the right of deciding at the time of payment which debt he wishes to discharge. If the debtor does not choose the creditor may appropriate the payment to any of the outstanding debts, even to those which have already become statute-barred. Where the debtor has a current account with the creditor (*i.e.*, an account the balance of which is carried forward, payments made being deducted from the balance and further debts added to it), the presumption is that a payment made will discharge the oldest debt.

3. *Discharge of a contract by lapse of time.* A contract is discharged by lapse of time only where the contract has been made for a specific period of time—*e.g.*, a contract of employment made for one year. In all other contracts, where time is not a material ingredient of the contract, the mere passing of time will not discharge the contract.

While, then, a contract will not be discharged by the lapse of time except in special circumstances, a contract may become unenforceable (statute-barred) if it is not enforced within a certain period of time. The reason for this rule is that there must be an end to all litigation, and parties should not be put to the expense and trouble of having to defend actions based on stale causes. The periods of limitation are now governed by the Limitation Act, 1939.

Actions based on simple contracts will be statute-barred after six years, while actions based on specialty contracts, and those brought in order to recover land, will be barred after twelve years. The periods mentioned are reckoned from the time "when the cause of action first arose," which is when the plaintiff could have brought his action for the first time. This is generally not the time when the contract was made, but the time when the contract was first broken, though it is possible, of course, that the contract was broken immediately it was made.

If the plaintiff was an infant or lunatic at the time when the cause of action first arose the period of limitation will not begin to run until his disability has ended, but once the period of limitation has begun to run it will not be stopped by any subsequent incapacity of the plaintiff.

Where the plaintiff has failed to discover the existence of a cause of action because of the defendant's fraud, or where he is bringing an action based on the defendant's fraud, or one asking for a contract to be set aside on the ground of mistake, the period of limitation will begin to run, not from the time when the cause of action first arose, but from the time when the plaintiff first discovered its existence, or from the time when, with the exercise of reasonable care, he should have discovered it.

The passing of the period of limitation does not discharge a contract; its sole effect is that the plaintiff's right of action will be barred. Thus, if the debtor of a statute-barred debt pays the debt at a time when he could not have been sued for it he will be unable to recover the money which he had paid, as he paid a valid, though unenforceable, debt. A right of action which has become statute-barred may be revived in one of two ways:

(a) where the debtor pays a sum of money on account of principal or interest;

(b) where the debtor acknowledges the existence of the debt in writing.

In either of these cases a new period of limitation will commence to run from the time of the payment or from the acknowledgment of the debt.

4. *Discharge of a contract by breach.* Strictly speaking, a contract is not discharged by a breach, but a breach gives the innocent party a right to treat the contract as discharged if he wishes to. A contract may be broken in various ways. A party may fail to fulfil his obligatons under the contract, or he may repudiate his liability under the contract at some time before he was due to perform his obligations, or he may do something which will make it impossible for himself to perform the contract.

Every breach of contract entitles the innocent party to claim damages from the party guilty of the breach. Not every breach, however, entitles the innocent party to treat the contract as discharged. He may treat the contract as discharged only where the breach is a total one, and not merely a partial one. A breach is a total breach if it affects some vital part of the contract or if it clearly shows that the contract-breaker has no intention of performing the contract.

Where a party repudiates his obligations under a contract the innocent party may treat the contract at once as discharged or he may decide to wait in the hope that the other party will change his mind and will perform the contract after all. The second possibility is fraught with danger, in that, if the contract in the meantime becomes discharged for some other reason—*e.g.*, impossibility—the innocent party will have lost his opportunity of treating the contract as discharged by breach and cannot claim damages for that breach. If A has engaged B to work for him as from January 1, and A informs B on November 1 that he will not be requiring his services, B can treat the contract at once as discharged and sue A for damages.

D

If he decides, however, to wait for January 1, hoping that A will change his mind, and A is killed in an accident on Christmas Eve, the contract will have become discharged by impossibility, and B will be unable to sue A's estate. If he had treated the contract as discharged in November, and had immediately sued A, the action would continue against A's estate.

Where a person makes it impossible for himself to perform a contract this will be treated in the same way as a repudiation of the contract. If X promised to marry Y next Easter, and some months before that he marries Z, Y will be able at once to sue him for breach of promise of marriage.

Where a breach has taken place in a contract which is to be performed by instalments it is always a question of fact whether the innocent party may consider the breach a total one, and thus treat the entire contract as discharged, or whether the breach is a partial one affecting the particular instalment only. In *Maple Flock* v. *Universal Furniture Products, Ltd*, it was held that the main considerations are "first, the ratio quantitatively which the breach bears to the contract as a whole and, secondly, the degree of probability or improbability that such a breach will be repeated."

5. *Discharge of a contract by subsequent impossibility*. If a person contracts to do something which according to our present scientific knowledge is impossible the contract will be void because of the absence of real consideration for the other party's promise. If he contracts to do something which can be done, but he cannot do it, the contract will be valid, and he will have to accept the legal consequences of his inability to perform.

Difficulties may arise where a contract was possible of performance when made but becomes subsequently impossible. The general rule which will guide us is that parties are bound by the contracts which they have freely entered into. Thus, where I have promised to do something and it has now become quite impossible for me to perform it the contract will not be discharged. I should have anticipated the possibility of circumstances intervening which would interfere with performance, and I should have safeguarded myself by including a term in the contract providing for this contingency. In some circumstances, however, a contract will be discharged by subsequent impossibility:

(*a*) A contract will be discharged where it becomes legally impossible (*i.e.*, forbidden) to perform it.

Baily v. *De Crespigny*. A had leased some land to B, and had promised that no buildings would be erected on the adjoining land. A railway company, possessed with statutory powers of compulsory acquisition of land, bought the land from A and erected a station on it. *Held,* that A's contractual obligation to B had become discharged.

(b) A contract of personal service (but not other contracts) is discharged by the death of either party, and also by the illness of the employee, where that illness makes the performance of the contract impossible.

Robinson v. *Davison.* A pianist who had agreed to give a concert on a certain day was unable to appear because of illness. *Held,* that the contract was discharged.

More will be said in Chapter 9 about the effect of illness on contracts of service.

(c) A contract is discharged where it expressly or impliedly rests on the continued existence of a subject-matter, and this subject-matter has been destroyed.

Taylor v. *Caldwell.* A hired the Surrey Music Hall from B. As a result of an accidental fire the theatre was burnt to the ground. *Held,* that the contract was discharged, and that neither party could claim anything from the other.

This rule applies only where the contract rests on the continued existence of the subject-matter. If I engage a driver for my car, and the car is accidentally destroyed, the contract with the driver will not be discharged unless he has been engaged specifically for the car which I originally owned.

(d) Where a contract has been entered into in contemplation of a future event or state of affairs, and the event or state of affairs does not materialize, the contract will be discharged. Naturally, both parties must have contemplated the event in question.

Krell v. *Henry.* The coronation procession of King Edward VII had to be cancelled at short notice. The defendant had hired a room overlooking one of the streets through which the procession had been expected to pass. *Held,* that the contract had become discharged when the procession was called off.

(e) A contract will also be discharged where its commercial purpose has been frustrated. It should be stated at once that the courts will not readily find that a contract has been discharged for this reason. As has been mentioned already, it is assumed that, where the parties could have foreseen a future situation arising which would alter the commercial effect of the contract, they should have done so. The situation in which a court will be prepared to treat a contract as discharged on the ground of frustration has been described by

Lord Radcliffe, in *Davis Contractors* v. *Fareham U.D.C.* (see below) as follows: "Frustration occurs whenever the law recognizes that, without the default of either party, a contractual obligation has become incapable of being performed because the circumstances in which performance is called for would render it a thing radically different from that which was undertaken by the contract."

Joseph Constantine Steamship Line, Ltd. v. *Imperial Smelting Corporation, Ltd.* A ship had been chartered to proceed to an Australian port with a view to loading a cargo there. Before her arrival at the port an explosion took place on board which substantially delayed her arrival. The lateness of her arrival frustrated the commercial purpose of the contract, as the charterers had to make other arrangements for the shipping of their goods. The charterers sued the shipowners for damages for breach of contract. *Held,* that the action failed as the contract had become discharged by frustration.

It should be noted, however, that the explosion in the above case had taken place without the fault of the shipowners. If they had been negligent they could not have relied on the frustration of the commercial purpose, and the contract would not have been treated as discharged.

Davis Contractors, Ltd. v. *Fareham U.D.C.* Plaintiffs had contracted with the defendants to erect for them 78 houses within eight months for a fixed sum. Because of shortage of labour and material and bad weather, the contract took much longer to complete, and in view of rising costs the plaintiffs found themselves out of pocket. They claimed that the contract had been discharged by frustration, and that, in the absence of the contract, they were entitled to be paid the actual cost of the work done. *Held,* that even if because of an unexpected turn of events the contract had proved to be more onerous for the plaintiffs than they had expected, they could not treat this as a ground for being relieved from their contractual obligation, since the nature of their performance had not changed in any fundamental way.

Gaon v. *Société Interprofessionelle des Oléagineux Fluides Alimentaires.* A consignment of Sudanese groundnuts had been sold to the defendants "c.i.f. Nice." This meant that the price included the cost of transport from Port Sudan to Nice. Before the contract had been performed the Suez Canal was closed to traffic because of the hostilities in that area. There existed an alternative route round the Cape, but this was four times as long and five times as expensive. *Held,* that the contract had not been discharged since it could not be said that the performance of the contract had become something radically different from what the parties had envisaged when making it.

Where a contract has been discharged by subsequent impossibility in any of the above ways the financial settlement between the parties is governed by the Law Reform (Frustrated Contracts) Act, 1943. This Act provides that:

(*a*) Anything paid by a party in pursuance of a contract subsequently discharged by impossibility may be recovered by the party, and any sums still due will cease to be payable.

(*b*) If one party has incurred any expenses in connexion with a contract subsequently discharged he may recover at the discretion of the court part or all of the expenses (including a proportion of his overheads) from the other party, or retain for this purpose money already paid to him.

(*c*) The Act does not apply to the following contracts, among others:

    (i) contracts of insurance;
    (ii) contracts of carriage of goods by sea;
    (iii) contracts containing specific terms dealing with the effects of frustration;
    (iv) contracts for the sale of specific goods which perish before the property has passed to the buyer.

Assignments of Contractual Rights

A person's rights under a contract may be assigned to a third party, provided that the conditions laid down in the Law of Property Act, 1925, have been fulfilled. Three rules have to be observed:

1. The assignment must be in writing.

2. Written notice of the assignment must be given to the debtor.

3. The assignment must be absolute, and not by way of charge only. This means that it is impossible to assign (*a*) part only of the assignor's contractual right, or (*b*) the whole of it but subject to some condition, or (*c*) the whole or part of it by way of charge so that the assignee would become entitled to be paid out of a certain fund without the fund itself being assigned to him.

All contractual rights to the payment of a sum of money are assignable, and so also are other rights arising under a contract. The only contractual rights which are not assignable are rights to personal services or other rights which are so tied up with personal considerations that the other party would be placed at a disadvantage if his contractual partner were to be allowed to assign his contractual rights.

Kemp v. *Baerselman.* A farmer had contracted to supply a baker with all the eggs and butter which he might require in his business. The baker sold his business to another baker, and purported also to assign the benefit of his contract with the farmer to the purchaser of the business. *Held,* that the contractual benefit was not assignable, as the extent of the farmer's obligation depended on the scale at which the bakery business was operated, and this might well be altered when the business passed into new hands.

If the farmer in the above case had agreed to supply x dozen eggs and y pounds of butter weekly, there would have been no reason why the baker could not have assigned his right to receive the goods.

An assignment of contractual rights is always said to be 'subject to equities.' That means that any defences or counter-claims which the debtor had against the assignor will survive against the assignee. If A owes £5 to B, and B owes £2 to A, B could sue A only for the balance of £3. If now B were to assign to a third party the debt of £5 owing to him by A, the assignee would also be able to claim £3 only from A.

Contractual obligations are not assignable. The only way in which a debtor under a contract may rid himself of his obligation is by means of a novation (see page 46), where by agreement between him and his creditor the latter is prepared to accept another person as a substitute for the debtor.

Some monetary debts are embodied in written instruments which have been endowed by law with special privileges. These instruments are known as negotiable instruments, and will be discussed further in Chapter 5.

REMEDIES FOR BREACH OF CONTRACT

Every breach of contract, whether total or partial, entitles the innocent party to claim damages from the party responsible for the breach. The damages to which the plaintiff will be entitled may be either liquidated or unliquidated damages. They are liquidated when their amount has been agreed upon by the parties themselves in the contract. They are unliquidated if they have to be assessed by the court.

Where a contract contains a clause providing for the payment of agreed damages if a breach of the contract should take place the innocent party will be able to claim the sum agreed upon irrespective of the extent of the loss which he has actually suffered. It is important to distinguish, therefore, between liquidated damages in their true legal sense and a penalty, because a penalty clause will not be enforced by the court. Thus, where the court holds agreed damages to constitute a penalty the plaintiff will have to be satisfied with unliquidated damages. In order that the agreed damages should be liquidated damages in the true legal sense, they must represent a true and fair estimate (at the time of agreement) of the loss likely to be suffered by the plaintiff in case of breach of contract. If the agreed damages do not represent a true and fair estimate of the likely loss they are a penalty, and will not be enforced by the court.

As with other technical legal terms, it does not matter what the parties call the agreed damages; all that matters is the fairness of the estimate. Agreed damages do not become a penalty merely because the plaintiff's loss turns out to be much smaller than had been expected, provided that the forecast of the loss embodied in the agreed damages was a reasonable one.

The court will always hold agreed damages to represent a penalty where the obvious purpose of the agreement was, by the size of the damages, to terrorize the other party into performing the contract rather than the making of a fair estimate of the likely loss.

Lamdon Trust, Ltd. v. *Hurrell.* The defendant bought a motor-car from the plaintiffs on hire-purchase terms. The purchase price of the car was £558. After the defendant had paid altogether £302, he defaulted on further instalments. The plaintiffs recovered possession of the car and sold it for £270. The agreement between the parties had provided that if the hire was terminated the hirer should pay the difference, if any, between what he had paid already on the car and £425. The plaintiffs claimed from him now £123. *Held,* that the figure of £425, which was approximately three-quarters of the purchase price, could not be regarded as a genuine pre-estimate of damage, and was therefore a penalty and not recoverable in law.

Where the contract provides for the payment of a single sum of money in the event of any of a possible number of breaches, some of which are more serious than others, it will also be a penalty. It is so also where the contract provides that a larger sum of money is to be paid on the non-payment of a smaller sum. If A has agreed to pay B £100 on January 1, and has further agreed to pay £120 if he should fail to discharge his debt on the due date, the agreed damages —£20—would constitute a penalty, because this amount is payable by way of damages whether payment is delayed by one day or by one month, while the real loss of the creditor cannot be the same in these two eventualities.

Where the parties have not agreed on the size of the damages, the court will have to assess the plaintiff's loss. The basic principle is that the plaintiff should be compensated, but no more than compensated, for the *financial* loss which he has suffered as a result of the defendant's breach of contract. This rule is, however, subject to the further reservation that the defendant cannot be made responsible for all the consequences that have followed from his breach. Some of the loss suffered by the plaintiff may have been too remote in relation to the defendant's breach of contract. It is therefore essential to determine the exact limits of the defendant's responsibility. The present rule as to the measure of damages recoverable by a plaintiff for breach of contract is based on the nineteenth-century case of

Hadley v. *Baxendale.* A miller sent a broken crankshaft by means of carrier to a firm of engineers for repair. He informed the carrier that it was a matter of urgency, and the carrier agreed to deliver the crankshaft without any delay. The miller failed to inform the carrier, however, that without the crankshaft the mill would be standing idle, and the carrier had no reason to believe that the crankshaft was such an essential part of the machinery of the mill. The carrier delayed delivery of the crankshaft to the engineers, and the mill was idle for longer than it need have been. In an action for damages the court *held* that the defendant was not liable for the loss of profits during the enforced idleness of the mill. In giving their decision the court laid down two general principles, namely:

1. The damages to be awarded to a plaintiff for breach of contract should cover such of his losses as may be fairly considered to arise naturally (*i.e.,* in the usual course of events) from the breach of contract.
2. Where the plaintiff suffered some unusual loss he will be able to recover damages for this loss only if it has been in the reasonable contemplation of the parties—*i.e.,* if the parties entered into the contract foreseeing the possibility of this loss if the contract should be broken.

In a way the second principle in *Hadley* v. *Baxendale* covers also the first one, since, if no special circumstances have been brought to the notice of the defendant, he can foresee such loss only as would arise normally from the breach of contract in the circumstances known to him. 'Reasonable foreseeability' is thus the essential principle on which the assessment of damages by the court will be based.

The principle of foreseeability does not mean that all possible risks must be brought specifically to the notice of the other party; certain risks must always be presumed to be in the reasonable con· templation of the parties, who are assumed to be endowed with reasonable intelligence.

Victoria Laundry (Windsor), Ltd. v. *Newman Industries, Ltd.* The plaintiffs had ordered a reconditioned boiler from the defendants, and the defendants had promised to deliver it in June. Delivery was in fact delayed until November of that year. As a result of the delayed delivery the plaintiffs lost the profit on additional laundry work which they could have accepted if the boiler had been installed, and they were also unable to take up a remunerative dyeing contract offered to them by the Ministry of Supply. *Held,* that the plaintiffs could claim under the first heading, as the defendants must have realized that a laundry would be unable to do its normal work if deprived of some expected piece of equipment, but they could not claim under the second heading, as this loss was not foreseeable when the contract was entered into.

The rule that the plaintiff is to be compensated for his loss but no more than compensated is well illustrated by *British Transport Commission* v. *Gourley,* where the House of Lords held that if the plaintiff's loss consisted of taxable income the damages (not taxable) payable to him should be based on the net income (*i.e.*, after tax deduction) which he lost and not on the gross income which he had been deprived of.

The plaintiff who has suffered a loss as a result of a breach of contract must do everything in his power to minimize the loss. Thus, a seller who finds that the buyer of goods refuses to accept them will have to dispose of them elsewhere at the best price obtainable. If the plaintiff has failed to minimize his loss he will be unable to recover more than the amount which he would have lost if he had done so.

> *Brace* v. *Calder*. The plaintiff was employed by a partnership. A change in the membership of the partnership took place, and by law this operates as a notice of dismissal to all employees. The remaining partners offered the plaintiff re-engagement on his previous terms of employment, but he refused to accept it. The court *held* that, while the plaintiff's 'dismissal' operated as a breach of contract, he had failed to minimize his loss, and could therefore claim nominal damages only.

In cases such as *Brace* v. *Calder,* where there has been a breach of contract but the plaintiff is found to have suffered no loss, he will be awarded nominal damages only—*i.e.*, the court will award him a few shillings for the formal breach of the contract, but no more.

In exceptional circumstances the court may award the plaintiff penal damages. Such damages exceed the actual loss which he has suffered, and are intended to compensate him not only for his financial loss but also for the loss of reputation caused by the breach of contract. There are two instances only when penal damages will be awarded for breach of contract—namely, in an action by a woman for breach of promise of marriage and in an action by a businessman for the wrongful dishonour by his bank of one of his cheques.

Damages are the usual remedy for breach of contract, but they are not the only one. In exceptional cases the court may award specific performance of the contract or an injunction. Both these remedies are remedies of equity, and as such are awarded at the absolute discretion of the court. It is up to the party wanting one of these remedies to satisfy the court that the conditions for it are present. Even then the judge may award damages instead if he feels that this would meet the needs of the plaintiff quite adequately.

When the court awards a decree of specific performance it orders the defendant to carry out a contractual promise which he has undertaken. If he should fail to do so he would be guilty of contempt of court, for which he might be fined or imprisoned. Specific performance is never granted to enforce a contract for personal service, as the court would not feel competent to supervise the execution of the order in such a case. Specific performance is mainly granted in connexion with contracts for the sale of land, but it has been also granted to enforce contracts for the sale of goods, where, because of the uniqueness of the goods in question, the purchaser would not get a fair deal by being awarded merely damages, which would not help him to buy the goods elsewhere.

An injunction is a court order requiring a person to desist from doing something which he has contractually or otherwise bound himself not to do. Where he has already completed the action which he had agreed to refrain from doing the injunction may compel him to undo it again, such as by pulling down some structure which he had erected in breach of a contractual undertaking. An injunction will be granted also in connexion with contracts for personal service where specific performance would not be ordered, but, as with a decree for specific performance, it will not be available where the court could not enforce obedience to its orders.

PAYMENT OF INTEREST

Where a person owes a sum of money he will have to pay the principal sum; but interest on the debt will be payable in the following circumstances only:

1. where the parties have expressly or impliedly agreed that interest should be paid;

2. where a bill of exchange has not been paid on the date on which it has fallen due for payment;

3. where a person has wrongfully obtained or retained money belonging to another person;

4. the court may also allow interest in an action for the recovery of a sum of money if in the opinion of the court it is just and fair that interest should be paid (Law Reform (Miscellaneous Provisions) Act, 1934).

Compound interest will be payable only if specifically agreed upon by the parties.

CHAPTER THREE

THE LAW OF AGENCY

Definition

An agent is a person who possesses authority to act on behalf of another person (known as the principal), with a view to establishing contractual relationships between the principal and a third party. The legal definition of an agent is therefore a narrower one than that which is used in everyday speech. Not every person who acts for another is in law his agent; the essence of agency rests in the agent's power to enter into contracts which will be legally binding on his principal.

The contract which the agent makes on the principal's behalf is the principal's contract, and the principal must therefore possess capacity to enter into contracts. The agent need not possess such capacity, since he is not contracting on his own behalf, and an infant, for instance, could as agent enter into contracts for his principal which the infant could not make on his own behalf.

The agent may acquire his power to act on the principal's behalf in one of two ways—namely, expressly by grant by the principal or impliedly. Where the principal expressly authorizes another person to represent him the authority need not be given in any special form, except where the agent is to execute a deed on his principal's behalf. In this case the agent's authority (referred to in this case as a *power of attorney*) would have to be given by deed as well. Where the agent has agreed with the principal that he will enter into a contract for him there may or may not exist a contractual relationship between the two persons. Everything depends on whether the agent receives some consideration for his promise to represent the principal in the making of the contract. Thus, if I ask a friend to buy 20 cigarettes for me he has my authority to make a contract on my behalf, but there exists no contract between me and my agent. We shall later see what influence this has on the duties which we owe to each other. If, on the other hand, I were to ask a friend to attend an auction sale on my behalf and bid there for certain articles, and if I were to promise to pay him £1 for his trouble, he would be under a contractual obligation to me to act as my agent.

An Agent's Implied Authority

The various instances of implied authority which are discussed below have got one thing in common, and that is that law holds one person (the principal) responsible for the contracts made by another (his agent by implication) although he has given no actual authority to the person to act on his behalf. You will appreciate from the examples why law adopts this attitude.

1. *Authority may be implied from certain relationships.* Where one partner enters into a contract in connexion with the affairs of the partnership he is presumed to be acting as agent of all the partners, irrespective of whether he has really obtained their authority for the transaction in question. A more important example still is the relationship of husband to wife. A wife is presumed in law to be her husband's agent for the purpose of making contracts for the purchase of necessaries for the household. The meaning of necessaries is the same as that given for the same term in connexion with the contracts of infants (page 18). The wife's agency exists, however, only if she is actually living with her husband, and the husband may rebut the presumption that she is authorized to charge his credit for necessaries by proving that he has provided her with sufficient cash to pay for all the necessaries for the household.

2. *Authority may be implied by necessity.* This means that if A, who is B's agent for certain purposes, has to act on B's behalf in an emergency he may enter into contracts on B's behalf which he has not been expressly authorized to make. Note, however, that A must already be B's agent; if he were a stranger he would not, even in an emergency, be authorized to make contracts on B's behalf. The following conditions must be fulfilled before this emergency authority arises:

(a) The emergency must be a real one, in which it is essential to act at once in the principal's interest.

(b) The agent is unable to contact the principal. If he is able to contact him he should get his instructions.

(c) The agent acts to the best of his ability in representing the principal's interests.

The following examples may help to illustrate the situations in which such an authority is likely to arise:

(a) Where a wife has been deserted by her husband she is authorized to charge his credit (incur debts on his behalf) for necessaries, provided, however, that she has no means of her own. If she has means she has to use them, and obtain a court order for maintenance against her husband.

(b) The master of a ship requiring some repairs may have these repairs undertaken without the owner's authority if it is essential that the work should be done at once, and the owner cannot be contacted.

(c) A person who has been left in charge of some one's property has a similar authority if it is absolutely essential that something should be done to the property to safeguard it.

3. *Authority by ratification.* This is really a case of authority bestowed in arrears. It applies to a situation where a person has made a contract on behalf of another without his authority, and the principal, when discovering what has happened, decides to ratify the act of the unauthorized agent. Where an unauthorized act is properly ratified the ratification dates back to the time when the act was done, so that the position is the same as if the agent had his principal's authority from the very outset. The ratification is valid only if the following conditions have been satisfied:

(*a*) The principal, before ratifying the agent's act, has received full information from him about what he has done.

(*b*) The principal must have been in existence and capable of entering into contracts at the time when the agent acted on his behalf, and he must still be capable of making the contract when he ratifies the agent's act. Thus, where the promoter of a company has made a contract on behalf of the company about to be formed, the contract cannot be ratified when the company has been set up, because the company did not exist, and thus had no contractual capacity, at the time when the agent (the promoter) acted on its behalf. (See *Kelner* v. *Baxter*, page 63.)

(*c*) The act of the agent which the principal purported to ratify must have been a legal one. An illegal act has in law no existence, and thus cannot be ratified.

> *Brook* v. *Hook.* A young man forged his uncle's signature on a promissory note. The note came eventually into the possession of A., who discovered the forgery and intended to institute proceedings against the forger. The young man's uncle then purported to ratify his nephew's act in signing the note, but later he refused to honour it. *Held,* that since a forgery is an illegal act it is legally a nullity, and as such it cannot be ratified.

Where, however, the principal by pretending to ratify an illegal act prevents the other party from taking legal proceedings he will be held to his ratification.

> *Greenwood* v. *Martins Bank.* G. discovered that his wife was forging his signature on cheques. He took no steps to inform the bank. G.'s wife eventually died, and he then claimed that the bank had no right to debit his account with the cheques forged by his wife. *Held,* that though a forgery cannot be ratified, G. could not claim a refund of the monies paid out, since by his conduct he had prevented the bank from taking steps against his wife during her lifetime.

(*d*) The agent must have acted for an identifiable principal. This means that where the agent purported to act on his own behalf, or at least failed to inform the other party that he was acting for a principal, his act cannot be subsequently ratified by another person.

4. *Authority arising from estoppel.* 'Estoppel' is a rule of evidence according to which a person who, by words or conduct, has led others to believe that a certain state of affairs existed will not be allowed subsequently to deny the existence of that state of affairs. Thus, if A by words or conduct lets C believe that B is his (A's) agent, he will be bound by B's acts as if he were in fact his agent. Whether or not A's words or conduct raise such a presumption is a question of fact. The authority which B appears to possess because of what A has said or done is known as his apparent, or ostensible, authority. Provided, then, that B has acted within the limits of this ostensible authority with which he has been endowed by A's behaviour, A will be legally liable on the contracts which B has made. Where, for instance, a businessman instals some one as manager of his shop, and instructs him as to the type of contract which he may make, the manager's actual authority is limited by these instructions, but his ostensible authority is that which a shop manager normally possesses. A third party who has no knowledge of the arrangements between the owner of the shop and his manager may rely on the manager's ostensible authority, and any contract falling within this authority will be legally binding on the principal —*i.e.*, the shop proprietor.

> *Watteau* v. *Fenwick.* The owner of a public house installed a manager and instructed him to place all orders for supplies through the owner, and not to buy anything himself. The manager, even so, bought some cigars and other goods from a traveller. *Held,* that the owner had to pay for them, as the purchase fell within the ostensible authority of his agent.

Another example of ostensible authority may again be found in the relationship of husband and wife. A married woman has as such no implied authority to buy goods which are not necessaries on her husband's behalf. If she does buy a luxury which is not a necessary the person who supplied her will only be able to claim from her, and not from her husband. Assume, however that the husband pays for the goods without indicating to the seller that he is doing so on this occasion only. In that case the husband, by his conduct, has led the seller to believe that the wife has authority to charge his credit, and if she buys something from the seller again the husband will have to pay. Once a person has by his conduct led others to believe that an agency exists, this agency will continue until direct notice that the agent's authority has been cancelled has been given to all persons entitled to assume that the agent has authority to act on the principal's behalf. The husband in my earlier example will have to write to the shopkeepers whose bills he has been in the habit of paying, informing them that he will do so no longer in the future, except where the debts have been incurred by him in person. To insert an advertisement to this effect in the local paper is not enough, as the interested parties need not necessarily read it, but it may perform a useful purpose in warning persons who have not dealt with the wife before (and who therefore have as yet no claim against the husband) that in dealing with the wife they will have to look to her only for payment.

The Agent's Liability on Contracts made for the Principal

Where the agent makes a contract on the principal's behalf he does not in general incur any personal liability on the contract, as the contract is one between the principal and the third party only, and does not directly affect the agent, who merely acted as intermediary between the parties. There are, however, certain exceptional situations in which the agent will be personally responsible to the third party for the performance of the contract by his principal.

1. Where the agent acted without authority, either because he never possessed it or because the authority had expired, the third party if unable to claim against the principal may claim against the agent. This is based on the principle of the law of agency according to which a person who purports to act as agent warrants or guarantees to the party with whom he is making a contract on the principal's behalf that he possesses the authority which he claims to possess. If it is proved that he did not possess authority the third party may sue him for breach of warranty of authority.

Kelner v. *Baxter*. A agreed to sell a hotel to B, who purported to act on behalf of a company which was about to be formed. *Held*, that as an agent cannot act for a non-existing principal, B was personally responsible for the performance of the contract.

In passing, it may be mentioned that the principle in *Kelner* v. *Baxter* does not apply in reverse—*i.e.*, so as to allow a person who contracted as an officer of a non-existing company to enforce the contract in his own name.

Newborne v. *Sensolid* (*Great Britain*), *Ltd.* The defendants bought a quantity of tinned food from Leopold Newborne (London), Ltd, a company which at that time had not yet been registered. The contract was signed on behalf of the company by Leopold Newborne, who described himself as one of its directors. The defendants subsequently refused to take delivery of the goods. *Held*, that Leopold Newborne could not enforce the contract in his own name. A company, as a legal person, cannot sign a contract itself; the contract has to be signed by one of its officers. The signature of that officer is not that of an agent acting on behalf of the company but is part of the company's signature, and, since the company did not exist at the time of the contract, no contract had in fact been made.

Starkey v. *Bank of England.* A trustee forged the signature of his fellow-trustee on a letter to their stockbroker instructing him to sell certain Government bonds for which the trustees were jointly responsible. The transfer was registered with the Bank of England. When the forgery was discovered, the Bank had to compensate the owner whose stock had been wrongfully transferred, and they claimed damages from the broker for breach of warranty of authority. *Held*, that as the broker's authority was partially forged, he had no right to order the transfer of the bonds, and he had to compensate the Bank for the loss which they had suffered.

2. Where the agent has acted on behalf of an undisclosed principal the third party, after discovering the existence of the principal, may choose whether to claim performance of the contract from the agent or from the principal. This choice may be made as long as he has not obtained judgment against one of the parties. Thus, if X buys goods from Y and Y discovers that X has been buying really on Z's behalf, Y will be able to claim payment either from X or from Z.

3. Where the agent entered into a contract on a principal's behalf without clearly indicating the fact that he was doing so solely as agent he may be personally responsible on the contract. This is so especially where the contract has been made in writing and signed by the agent without clearly showing that he is signing as agent and not as principal.

4. Where the agent signs a bill of exchange for his principal without clearly indicating that he is signing as agent only.

THE AGENT'S DUTIES TOWARDS HIS PRINCIPAL

The duties which will be discussed below apply, of course, to those cases only where the agent has acted under an express authority. An agent whose authority is implied only has no duties towards the principal. The duties of an agent acting on an express authority are the following:

1. The agent must perform the agency transaction in person. The Latin maxim which is applied here is that of *delegatus non potest delegare* (an agent may not sub-delegate his authority), and sub-delegation will be permitted only where the principal has agreed to it, or where it is customary in the trade that agents should sub-delegate part or all of their authority, or where it is a case of absolute necessity such as one caused by the sudden illness of the agent

which makes it impossible for him to act. Where an agent has validly sub-delegated his authority to a sub-agent the sub-agent owes the same duties to the main principal as the agent does.

2. The agent must perform his duties with due care. The standard of care that may be expected from the agent depends on whether or not he has received consideration for his services. A paid agent must exercise such skill as he claims to possess, while an unpaid agent need only exercise such skill as he actually possesses.

3. The agent must not allow his personal interest to come into conflict with his duties to the principal. Thus, an agent who has been authorized by the principal to sell something may not buy it himself unless the principal agrees.

4. The agent must not make a secret profit out of the agency transaction, nor may he take bribes. He would make a secret profit if he failed to pass to the principal any gain that had resulted from the agency transaction. If the principal tells the agent to sell something for £10, and he sells it for £11, he would be making a secret profit if he kept the extra pound. Where an agent has made a secret profit, or taken a bribe, the principal has the following remedies:

(a) He may recover from the agent the profit or bribe.

(b) He may refuse to pay to the agent any remuneration which would have been due to him.

(c) He may repudiate the contract with the third party if the third party has bribed the agent.

(d) Criminal proceedings may be started against agent and third party under the Prevention of Corruption Act, 1906, where the agent has taken a bribe.

5. The agent must not disclose confidential information which he has acquired during the agency.

6. The agent must submit proper accounts to the principal.

The Principal's Duties towards the Agent

1. The main duty of the principal towards the agent is that of paying the agent the agreed commission. Both the amount of the commission as well as the circumstances in which it becomes payable depend on the terms of the contract between principal and agent. Where the agent is a professional agent, such as an estate agent, who has asked his principal-client to sign a standard agreement prepared by the agent, the court will interpret the terms of the agreement strictly and the agent must have complied exactly with the terms of the agreement before the commission will become payable to him. Where, for instance, the contract provides that the agent should become entitled to the commission if he presents a client who is "able and willing to buy" on the principal's terms, he

E

will not be entitled to the commission unless the buyer whom he introduces is one who is prepared to enter into a legally binding contract. Thus, if the buyer signs an agreement that he will buy 'subject to contract' he has not entered into a legally binding contract (see page 26), and the agent will not be entitled to his commission.

> *Peter Long and Partners* v. *Burns.* The defendant employed the plaintiffs, a firm of estate agents, in connexion with the sale of his business. He agreed to pay their commission on their "introducing a person ready, willing and able to enter into a binding contract." A buyer was introduced who contracted to buy the business. Subsequently the buyer discovered that the estate agents, acting on information provided by the defendant, had wrongly informed him about the effects on the business of a town and country planning scheme. Because of this misrepresentation the contract was voidable at the buyer's option, and he was released from the contract. In an action by the plaintiffs for their commission it was *held* that since the contract entered into with the buyer was voidable at his option it was not a binding contract and the plaintiffs had thus not become entitled to their commission.

The principal's duty to pay commission normally ends when the agency has terminated. It is only where there is a special provision in the agreement between principal and agent to that effect that the agent will become entitled to commission on business done by his former principal with customers introduced by him.

2. The principal is bound to indemnify the agent against any liabilities which he may have incurred in connexion with the performance of the transaction for the principal.

SPECIAL AGENCIES

1. A *del credere agent* is an agent who has undertaken to guarantee to the principal that the third party with whom he has made a contract on the principal's behalf is solvent. If the principal should be unable to obtain payment from the third party because of his insolvency, he could claim from the agent. The agent will usually be rewarded for the extra risk which he is taking by receiving a slightly higher rate of commission. It must be noted, however, that the agent is responsible only for the solvency of the third party, and not for his possibly rejecting goods which are delivered to him in a contract for the sale of goods. A *del credere* agency agreement is really a contract of guarantee tagged on to a contract of agency, but since the guarantee is merely subsidiary to the main contract it is not subject to the requirement of Section 4 of the Statute of Frauds, 1677, according to which contracts of guarantee must be evidenced in writing in order to be enforceable.

2. A *factor* (or *mercantile agent*) is an agent who in the customary course of his business as agent has authority to sell or buy goods or to raise money on the security of goods on behalf of others. The legal position of factors is governed by the Factors Act, 1889. In order to qualify as a factor an agent must be in business—*i.e.*, he must habitually act as agent for others, and not merely occasionally.

A principal may be bound by the acts of a mercantile agent employed by him in circumstances where he would not be bound by the acts of another agent. If the mercantile agent has obtained possession of goods with the consent of their true owner, then any sale, pledge, or other disposition of the goods made by the agent in the ordinary course of his business will be as binding on the owner as if he had actually authorized it. This means that if a person acquires from a mercantile agent, acting in the ordinary course of his business, goods which the agent had no right to sell he will obtain a good title to them provided that he was not aware of the agent's want of authority.

The essential point is that the owner must have voluntarily entrusted the agent with the goods. If the agent has obtained the goods by theft, or otherwise without the consent of the true owner, the third-party buyer will not have a good title to them. It does not matter, however, that the agent has induced the owner to part with the goods by fraudulent means.

Du Jardin v. *Beadman.* A dealer in cars obtained possession of a second-hand car from a garage proprietor by pretending that he would be able to sell it. He left behind as security a cheque (which was subsequently dishonoured) and his own car, which he later secretly removed. He then sold the car to a third party, who bought it in good faith and not knowing about the seller's want of title. *Held,* that as the owners had consented to the dealer's possession of the car, the bona-fide buyer was entitled to retain it.

Where the goods that have been entrusted to the factor take the form of a motor vehicle the dealer must also have been entrusted with the registration book, since a buyer who buys a car without the appropriate registration book will not be deemed to have acted in good faith.

3. An *auctioneer* is an agent who has received goods from his principal for the purpose of selling them by public auction. He has authority to receive the purchase price of the goods from the buyer and to give a receipt for it. He has also ostensible authority to sell the goods at any price, so that where the owner has fixed a reserve price below which the goods are not to be sold, and the auctioneer sells them nevertheless at a lower price, the bona-fide buyer will be entitled to the goods. Where the auctioneer has made known, how-

ever, that the sale is subject to a reserve price, and he by mistake knocks down the goods to a bidder at a lower price, the owner of the goods will not be bound by the sale, as the bidder had knowledge of the existence of a limitation on the auctioneer's power to sell.

TERMINATION OF THE AGENT'S AUTHORITY

The authority of an agent bestowed on him by the principal terminates in the following ways:

1. It terminates automatically on the death of either party, on the bankruptcy of either party, and also where the principal becomes insane, or where because of outbreak of war between this country and his own country he becomes an enemy alien.

2. The principal may at any time withdraw the agent's authority. This revocation of the agent's authority must be distinguished from a termination of the contract of agency. The contract of agency, under which the agent may be entitled to some form of payment, may be terminated only in the same way as any other contract, but the agent's authority to represent the principal may be taken away from him by the principal at any time. If the agent has some contractual rights against the principal these would naturally survive.

Where the principal withdraws the agent's authority he must remember, however, to inform third parties who were aware of the agent's authority that it had been terminated, since otherwise he would remain responsible for the agent's contracts on the basis of the doctrine of estoppel.

The principal is unable to withdraw the agent's authority where the authority is one 'coupled with an interest.' This means that an authority given by way of consideration for an act or promise of the other party would be irrevocable, such as where a debtor has authorized his creditor by way of settlement of the debt to collect on the debtor's behalf sums of money owing to him from third parties.

CHAPTER FOUR

THE SALE OF GOODS

DEFINITION

A contract for the sale of goods is a contract whereby the seller transfers or agrees to transfer the property in goods to the buyer for a money consideration, called the price. The law concerning the sale of goods is found in the Sale of Goods Act, 1893. All references to sections in the present chapter relate to the sections of this Act.

The term 'goods' includes all personal chattels with the exception of money. In other words, all movable objects come under the heading of goods, but immovable things, such as land, houses, and other things which are permanently attached to land are excluded.

The definition of a contract for the sale of goods implies that there are two types of this contract—namely, a sale, this being a contract providing for the immediate transfer of the property in goods to a buyer, and an agreement to sell, under which the property is to pass at some future date. More will be said about these two contracts later.

The consideration for the goods must be one of money. Where goods are exchanged for goods—*i.e.,* a barter contract—we do not have a contract for the sale of goods, but it is permissible for money consideration and some other goods to be given in exchange for the goods which are being sold.

A contract for the sale of goods must also be distinguished from a contract for work and materials, since the latter type of contract is not governed by the Sale of Goods Act. We have a contract for work and materials where the main purpose of the contract is that some special work should be done, the worker providing also the materials which will eventually become the property of the person for whom the work is being done. Thus, if I buy a picture in an exhibition I am entering into a contract for the sale of goods, but if I contract with a portrait-painter that he should paint a portrait of my wife I am making a contract for work and materials, although the canvas, paint, etc., provided by the painter will become my property. This does not mean that every contract where a job is ordered to be done is outside the scope of the Sale of Goods Act. A contract to have a suit made to measure would be a contract for the sale of goods. What matters is whether the essence of the contract lies in the work (*e.g.,* the skill of the painter) or in the material that is being supplied (*e.g.,* the cloth in the suit).

The price for the goods may either have been agreed upon directly by the parties or they may have agreed that it should be fixed by a third party. Where it is understood that a price will be payable, but nothing has been said about its amount, the price payable will have to be a reasonable one.

No particular form is now required for the making of a contract for the sale of goods; in particular, it need not be made in writing in order to be legally valid (Law Reform (Enforcement of Contracts) Act, 1954).

STIPULATIONS IN THE CONTRACT

A contract for the sale of goods—as, indeed, any other contract—consists of an exchange of promises between the parties. These promises or terms of the contract are known as stipulations (Latin for 'promises'). Contractual stipulations may be either conditions or warranties. It does not matter what the parties themselves have called them, what matters is whether the parties intended the stipulation to 'go to the root of the contract'—*i.e.,* to represent an essential term of the contract—or whether they wanted the stipulation to be one which would not be basic to the existence of the contract. In the former case the stipulation is a condition, while in the latter it will be a warranty. Only rarely will the parties to the contract in so many words state whether they deem the stipulation to be an essential one. It will then be necessary for the court to examine the contract as a whole, and on that basis to decide what the view of the parties would have been if they had thought about this matter when they made the contract.

Whether a stipulation is a condition or a warranty is of great importance in connexion with the remedies which are open to the innocent party where the terms of the stipulation have not been complied with. A breach of condition entitles the innocent party to treat the contract as discharged—*i.e.,* it operates as a total breach of contract—while a breach of warranty is looked upon merely as a partial breach of contract for which damages could be claimed, but which will not enable the innocent party to treat the contract as at an end. The innocent party has, however, always the option of treating a breach of condition as a breach of warranty, which means not avoiding the contract, but merely claiming damages (Section 11 (1) (*a*)). Once the buyer has accepted goods he is compelled to treat any breach of condition on the part of the seller as a breach of warranty (Section 11 (1) (*c*)).

Conditions as well as warranties may be either expressly agreed by the parties or they may be implied by the Act. The Act contains a list of conditions and warranties which have to be implied in every contract for the sale of goods.

The following is the list of implied conditions:

1. The seller stipulates that he has a right to sell the goods (Section 12 (1)). Having a right to sell the goods means not only that the seller is either the owner of the goods, or has the owner's authority to sell, but also that there are no other reasons (such as a possible infringement of another person's patent or trade-mark) why he should not sell the goods.

2. Where the goods are sold by description the seller stipulates that the goods will correspond with the description (Section 13). Whenever the seller has made any kind of descriptive statement about the goods, such as identifying them by name, colour, etc., there is a sale by description. If the buyer has not seen the goods before he bought them there must have been a sale by description.

3. Where the goods are sold by sample the seller stipulates:

   (a) that the bulk of the goods shall correspond with the sample;
   (b) that the buyer shall have a reasonable opportunity of comparing the bulk with the sample;
   (c) that the goods are free from any defect rendering them unmerchantable which would not be apparent on a reasonable examination of the sample (Section 15).

Godley v. *Perry.* A boy of six was injured when firing a stone from a toy plastic catapult bought from a shop. The catapult fractured, and a piece of it hit the child in the eye. In the action which the boy brought against the retailer claiming that the catapult was not of merchantable quality, the retailer brought in the wholesaler as a third party. The fragility of the catapult could have been easily discovered by squeezing together the two prongs of the catapult. The retailer had in fact examined the toy, but had merely pulled back the elastic. *Held,* that the Act referred to "reasonable" and not to "practicable" examination. Thus, the wholesalers had to indemnify the retailer for the damages paid out to the infant.

Where the sale of the goods is one by sample as well as by description the goods as supplied must correspond both with the sample and the description (Section 13).

A sale of goods is one by sample where there is a provision in the contract, expressed or implied, to that effect. There would be an implied clause where the seller has shown a sample prior to the making of the contract and the buyer has then placed an order with him for the goods. When talking about the 'bulk' we mean the goods which are actually supplied by the seller.

4. Where the buyer expressly or by implication makes known to the seller the particular purpose for which the goods are required, so as to show that he relies on the seller's skill and judgment, and the goods are of a description which it is in the course of the seller's business to supply, the seller stipulates that the goods are reasonably fit for such purpose (Section 14 (1)).

The general rule of our law is that of *caveat emptor* (let the buyer beware), and it is up to the buyer to ensure that he gets what he wants. The present implied condition as to fitness for a particular purpose is one of the few exceptions to the rule. The reader should, however, note the following points:

(*a*) The seller must be in business selling goods of the kind in question.

(*b*) The purpose for which the goods are required must have been communicated to him. Where goods are generally used for one purpose only the purpose has been communicated to him by implication.

Frost v. *Aylesbury Dairy Company, Ltd.* The defendants supplied the plaintiff with milk. For some unexplained reason the milk contained typhoid germs, and the plaintiff's wife died after drinking some of it. *Held*, that the dairy had committed a breach of condition in supplying milk not reasonably fit for the purpose for which they must have presumed that it would be used.

(*c*) The buyer must have shown that he relied on the seller's skill and judgment in advising him. From this follows, as is also specified in the Act, that where a buyer asks for goods by their trade or patent name the seller is in no way responsible for their quality, since the buyer cannot have relied on the seller's skill in advising him (Section 14 (1)).

(*d*) The goods must be reasonably fit for the purpose for which they are intended. They need not be of the best quality as long as they could be used if reasonably handled.

Heil v. *Hedges*. A lady bought a pork chop from her butcher. The chop was prepared by her maid, who did not cook it enough, so that it was partly raw when eaten. The pork contained worms, and the lady who had eaten the chop became ill with trichinosis. *Held*, that there had been no breach of condition by the butcher, as the chop would have been fit for human consumption if it had been properly cooked.

5. Where goods are bought by description from a seller who deals in goods of that description there exists an implied condition that the goods are of merchantable quality (Section 14 (2)).

This is another exception to the principle of *caveat emptor*. Goods are not of merchantable quality if they are in a state which makes them unsuitable for their ordinary use—*e.g.*, vegetables which are rotting, hot-water bottles with holes in them. If the buyer has examined the goods there is no implied condition as regards any defects which his examination should have revealed.

There are also two implied warranties referred to in the Act:

(1) that the buyer shall have and enjoy quiet possession of the goods (Section 12 (2)). Quiet possession means possession undisturbed by third parties who may have some prior rights to the goods.

(2) that the goods are free from any charge or incumbrance in favour of a third party, not declared or known to the buyer before or at the time when the contract is made (Section 12 (3)).

It is possible for the parties to exclude by agreement both express and implied conditions. Naturally, such an agreement is very much to the disadvantage of the buyer, since all the implied conditions and warranties contain promises by the seller. The courts interpret such agreements strictly, and they will require clear evidence that the parties really intended to enter into a contract for the sale of goods without any conditions or warranties attached. Even then it has been held that some conditions cannot be excluded by agreement of the parties. This is said to be true of those conditions embodying an 'essential term' of the contract, though it is sometimes difficult to distinguish between conditions which do and those which do not embody such an essential term.

Karsales (Harrow), Ltd. v. *Wallis.* A bought a car from B. When A had inspected the car it was in perfect condition and good running order, but when the car was delivered it had to be towed, as all essential parts had been removed and good parts had been replaced by poor ones. A refused to accept the car. B relied on a term in the contract by which all conditions and warranties, express as well as implied, had been ruled out. *Held,* that A was entitled to repudiate the contract, since it was an essential term of any contract for the sale of goods that the article supplied was basically the same as that regarding which the contract had been made.

Apart from the conditions and warranties which are implied by the Sale of Goods Act, there is also a principle of common law to be noted according to which the seller of dangerous goods is bound to warn the buyer of their dangerous features.

Clarke v. *Army and Navy Co-operative Society, Ltd.* The plaintiff bought a tin of disinfectant powder. She had not been warned that the powder could be dangerous if it got into a person's eyes. While prising open the tin some of the powder got into her eyes. *Held,* that the defendants were liable in damages for not having informed the plaintiff of the dangerous character of the goods sold.

The liability of the seller of goods to provide goods which are reasonably fit for the purpose for which they are intended exists only in relation to the buyer with whom the contract was made. Where, then, a manufacturer places goods on the market through middlemen there will be no privity of contract between the manufacturer and the ultimate buyer of the goods. If the goods turn out to be unfit for the use for which they are intended the buyer may claim from the immediate seller, provided the conditions of Section 14 (1) have been satisfied, but he cannot claim for breach of contract from the manufacturer. He is, however, not entirely without remedies against the manufacturer. He may have an action for negligence where the manufacturer has allowed goods to go out in a state in which they may be dangerous to the ultimate user, and has by the packing chosen or in other ways made it impossible for intermediate dealers to interfere with the goods. In these circumstances law assumes that the manufacturer owes directly a duty of care to the ultimate consumer, and he will be liable in damages to him if the consumer should suffer injury through the defective quality of the goods.

Donoghue v. *Stevenson.* Two ladies visited a restaurant. One ordered a drink for herself and an ice-cream with ginger-ale poured on for her friend. The ginger-ale was supplied in a sealed opaque bottle. When the bottle had been emptied it was found that it contained the decomposed remains of a snail. The lady who had been drinking the ginger-ale was ill for some time. She had no remedy against the proprietor of the restaurant, as she had not bought the ale from him; her friend who had bought it could not claim, as she had not suffered any loss. *Held,* that an action lay against the manufacturers of the ginger-ale for permitting it to go out in a state in which it was dangerous to consumers.

THE TRANSFER OF PROPERTY IN GOODS

It is important to ascertain the time when the property in goods sold passes from the seller to the buyer, because as a rule the risk of loss or damage to the goods falls on the owner (Section 20), and it is essential to know who the owner has been at some point of time.

The Act states that the property passes at such time as the parties by their agreement wish it to pass (Section 17). If the parties have not shown any definite intention property will pass according to certain rules enumerated in the Act (Section 18). In order to understand these rules it is necessary to distinguish between specific and unascertained goods. Goods are unascertained if they are described in the contract only by reference to their kind or type—*e.g.,* ten pounds of sugar. Where the goods have been described in such a way that they are distinct from other goods of a similar kind they are specific goods, such as when I have picked a sugar bag from the grocer's shelves and put it aside for myself.

. The rules concerning the passing of property are:

1. Where there is an unconditional contract for the sale of specific goods in a deliverable state the property passes when the contract is made even if delivery and payment are to follow later.

2. Where there is a contract for the sale of specific goods which are not in a deliverable state, in that the seller has to do something to them—such as alter them—the property will pass when this has been done and the buyer has been informed.

3. Where in a sale of specific goods in a deliverable state the goods have to be weighed, tested, or measured in order to ascertain the amount payable by the buyer the property will pass only when this has been done and the buyer has been informed.

4. Where the seller has supplied goods on approval to the buyer the property will pass when the buyer has accepted them, whether expressly or by doing something to them signifying acceptance, or where he has retained the goods without rejecting them for a time longer than that laid down by the seller, or, where no time has been laid down by the seller, for longer than a reasonable time.

5. In a sale of unascertained goods the property passes to the buyer only when the goods have been specified, which means that goods of the appropriate description have been appropriated to the contract by the seller with the consent of the buyer or by the buyer with the consent of the seller. In general the buyer in advance assents to the appropriation to be done by the seller. Where the parties have agreed that the goods should be sent to the buyer through the post or through some other carrier, delivery of the goods by the seller to the carrier is a sufficient appropriation of them to the contract, so that the property passes at once to the buyer. If the goods are then lost in transit the loss will fall on the buyer.

SALE BY SOME ONE WHO IS NOT THE OWNER OF THE GOODS

The general principle of our law is that *nemo dat quod non habet,* which means that a person who has no title to the goods cannot make the buyer the owner of the goods. In general, then, if you buy goods from a person who has no right to sell them you will be bound to return the goods to their true owner, irrespective of your own innocence in the matter, and without being able to claim from the owner the refund of the money which you had paid to the seller. You are, of course, entitled to claim this money from the seller, as he has been in breach of the implied condition according to which a seller stipulates that he is entitled to sell. There are, however, a number of exceptional circumstances in which a person who bought goods from some one not entitled to sell will nevertheless acquire a good title to the goods. They are:

(1) buying goods from a mercantile agent acting in the ordinary course of his business. (Section 21 (2) (a)). This has been discussed already (page 67);

(2) sale in an 'open market' (*market overt*). (Section 22). Where a person acting in good faith buys goods in an open market from a seller dealing in goods of that description he will obtain a good title even if the seller had no title to the goods.

Not every market ranks as an 'open market' for the above purpose. The market in question must have acquired the privilege either by custom or by charter or by Act of Parliament. Further, it must be open to the general public, and not just to a limited membership. By custom, all shops in the City of London are treated as one single 'open market.' The sale must have taken place, however, in a part of the shop which is open to the general public, and not in a private part of the shop

A sale in an 'open market' means always a sale by the dealer to the customer, and not by the customer to the dealer.

Where goods which at some previous time have been stolen are sold in an open market the original owner will be able to recover them from the buyer in market overt only if he first has prosecuted the thief, and a conviction has been recorded against him (Section 24 (1)).

(3) Sale by a person in possession. Where a person, having sold goods, remains in possession of the goods or of the documents of title to them, any further sale of the goods to a buyer who takes the goods in good faith and in ignorance of the previous sale will pass a good title to the buyer (Section 25 (1)). Thus, if A sells goods to B but, for some reason, retains possession and then sells the same goods to C, who takes possession of them, C's title to the goods will be better than that of B.

(4) Where the owner of goods by his behaviour allows an innocent party to pay money for the goods to a person

THE SALE OF GOODS

having no right to sell the owner will be estopped from denying that the seller had a right to sell. This principle is based on a dictum of Ashhurst, J., in *Lickbarrow* v. *Mason,* where the learned judge said: "Wherever one of two innocent parties must suffer by the acts of a third, he who has enabled such third person to occasion the loss must sustain it." This does not mean, however, that the mere fact that the owner of goods has entrusted another one with possession for some limited purpose will prevent the owner from claiming the goods from a third party to whom they have been wrongfully transferred.

Jerome v. *Bentley and Company.* The plaintiff entrusted a ring to X for the purpose of sale. If he had not sold the ring within seven days he was to return it to the plaintiff. After the seven days had expired X sold the ring to the defendants, who bought it in good faith, and appropriated the purchase price. *Held,* that the plaintiff was entitled to claim the ring from the defendants; since he had done nothing which would mislead the defendants.

THE PERFORMANCE OF THE CONTRACT

The contract is performed by the seller delivering the goods to the buyer and the buyer paying for them (Section 27). If nothing has been agreed to the contrary payment and delivery have to take place concurrently, so that the seller need not part with the goods unless he is paid, nor need the buyer pay unless he receives the goods (Section 28).

The actual conditions of delivery will depend on the contract of the parties, but where the contract is silent the following rules would apply (Section 29). The goods have to be delivered at the seller's place of business. If the parties have agreed that the goods are to be sent to the buyer the seller has to send them within a reasonable time. If the goods are not in a deliverable state when the contract is made the cost of putting them into a deliverable state will have to be borne by the seller.

The buyer performs his part of the contract by accepting the goods and paying for them. Once the buyer has accepted the goods he is bound to pay for them, and he can no longer reject them. Section 35 states that acceptance takes place when:

1. The buyer intimates to the seller that he has accepted the goods;

2. The buyer does something to the goods (*e.g.,* writing his name into a book) which is inconsistent with the seller's rights of ownership;

3. The buyer retains the goods for more than a reasonable time without informing the seller that he has rejected them.

Section 30 contains rules which apply where the delivery of goods is a faulty one. Where the seller delivers a quantity which is either larger or smaller than that ordered by the buyer the buyer may do one of three things: he may reject the delivery, or he may accept and pay for those goods only which are in accordance with the order, and reject the rest, or he may accept the whole delivery and pay for it at the contract rate. Where the seller delivers goods of the kind ordered mixed with goods of another description the buyer may either reject the lot or accept the part which is in accordance with the contract and reject the rest.

RIGHTS OF THE UNPAID SELLER

The seller is an 'unpaid seller' when payment has fallen due and he has not been paid yet (Section 38). In these circumstances he has certain remedies against the buyer as well as against the goods.

1. *Remedies against the buyer.* Where the property in the goods has passed to the buyer the seller may sue him for the price of the goods (Section 49). This action is also available to the seller even though the property may not yet have passed to the buyer where the price was due on a certain date which has passed already.

When the property in the goods has not yet passed to the buyer, and he is unwilling to accept the goods, the seller has an action for damages for non-acceptance. The measure of the damages will be the estimated loss which directly and naturally results in the ordinary course of events from the buyer's refusal to accept (Section 50 (1)). Where there is an available market for the goods the measure of damages will *prima facie* be ascertained by the difference between the contract price and the market price at the time when the goods should have been accepted by the buyer (Section 50 (2)).

There can be an 'available market' only if the seller should find it easy to sell the goods to another person, but it has also been pointed out that the existence of a market presupposes a fluctuating price, based on bargaining between buyers and sellers, so that where the price is a fixed one there can be no 'market.'

Charter v. *Sullivan.* The defendant bought a Hillman Minx car from the plaintiff at its official list price, but later refused to accept it. The car was sold to another buyer within a week. The seller claimed damages amounting to his lost profit on the sale; the buyer countered by pointing to the fact that there was an available market and that the difference between contract price and market price was nil. *Held,* that as the price was fixed there existed no 'market.' The plaintiff's loss directly resulting from the breach of contract was merely a nominal one. He did not lose his profit, because he had only a limited allocation of these cars and he could not have sold more cars than he did.

2. *Remedies against the goods.* In addition to his personal remedies against the buyer, the seller also has certain remedies against the goods. These remedies are important, because the practical value of proceeding against the buyer may occasionally be small where the buyer has no funds to satisfy a judgment that might be given against him. The seller's rights against the goods depend on whether he has still possession of the goods.

(*a*) Where the seller is still in possession of the goods sold, he may exercise a *right of lien* (Section 41). This is the right of retaining the goods until the price has been paid. The right of lien does not by itself imply that the seller may resell the goods. He may only use pressure on the buyer by keeping the goods from him. He will have a right of resale only where the goods are perishable, or where he has given notice to the buyer that he intends to resell and the buyer has not within a reasonable time paid for the goods, or where the seller has in the contract expressly reserved for himself the right of resale in such a situation (Section 47 (3-4)).

(*b*) Where the seller is no longer in possession of the goods, but the goods are in the hands of a carrier taking them to the buyer, the seller may *stop the goods in transit* if he is unpaid *and* if the buyer has become insolvent (Section 44). Stoppage in transit is effected by informing the carrier that the goods are not to be delivered but are instead to be returned to the seller, who will have to pay the return freight.

The seller's right of stoppage in transit is defeated once the goods have come into the possession of the buyer or of some one acting as the buyer's agent. Where the buyer has resold the goods while they are still in transit the seller will nevertheless be able to stop them. If, however, a bill of lading has been issued in respect of the goods and the buyer has endorsed the bill of lading to a bona-fide purchaser for value, the seller's right of stoppage in transit will have been defeated (Section 47).

REMEDIES OF THE BUYER

1. Where the seller has failed to deliver the goods altogether the buyer has a right of action for damages for non-delivery (Section 51). The measure of damages will be assessed on similar lines to those of an unpaid seller suing for non-acceptance. This means that

the buyer may claim the estimated loss naturally resulting from the breach of contract, but where there is an available market the measure of damages will be *prima facie* the difference between the contract price and the market price at the time when the goods should have been delivered. According to the general principles relating to damages for breach of contract (see page 56), the buyer will be able to claim damages for loss of profit on resale only where the resale of the goods by the buyer was in the contemplation of the parties when the contract was made. The same also applies where the buyer suffers any other exceptional loss because of the seller's non-delivery.

2. The buyer can claim specific performance of the seller's promise to deliver only where in the opinion of the court monetary damages would not be a sufficient remedy in the circumstances, such as where the article bought is something of an unique kind—*e.g.*, a rare first edition of a book (Section 52).

3. Where the seller has committed a breach of condition or of warranty the remedies of the buyer will be those which have been discussed already earlier in this chapter.

SALE OF GOODS BY AUCTION

Section 58 deals with the sale of goods by auction. It contains the following main provisions:

1. Where goods are sold by auction in lots each lot will be deemed to be the subject of a separate contract for the sale of goods.

2. The offer in an auction sale is made by the bidder, and it is accepted by the auctioneer by the fall of his hammer. Until the auctioneer has accepted the offer in this way, the bidder may withdraw his offer.

3. The owner of the goods sold may not himself bid in the auction unless he has expressly reserved this right. If he were to bid, directly or through an agent, in contravention of this rule the sale could be treated as fraudulent by any buyer. The purpose of the rule is to prevent the owner of the goods from driving up the price by bids placed by himself.

4. The sale by auction may be notified to be subject to a reserve price. If this has been done, and the highest bid did not reach the reserve price, the auctioneer would be entitled to refuse to 'knock down' the goods to the highest bidder.

HIRE-PURCHASE CONTRACTS

A hire-purchase contract is a contract whereby one party, the owner, delivers goods to another party, the hirer, on the understanding that the hirer will make periodical payments to the owner, and that, after having paid a certain number of hire payments, he will have the option of becoming the owner of the goods. It must be emphasized that the goods, while in the possession of the hirer, remain the owner's property until the final hire payment has been made. In this way a contract of hire-purchase differs from a contract for the sale of goods by instalments, where the buyer becomes the owner at once but agrees to pay the price by stated instalments.

Hire-purchase contracts and credit-sale agreements are not governed by the Sale of Goods Act, 1893, but by the Hire Purchase Acts, 1938-54. These Acts apply to those hire-purchase and credit-sale transactions only where the total price does not exceed £300, or £1000 where livestock is concerned. The purpose of the Acts is to protect the hirer against unscrupulous dealers who might take advantage of the credulity of the poorer sections of the community, who are the main people interested in hire-purchase.

The owner must, before the contract is entered into, state in writing the cash price of the goods to be sold, except where the hirer has inspected them and the cash price is indicated on a price ticket. Furthermore, the contract will not be legally enforceable unless a memorandum has been made out and signed by the hirer, who must be given a copy, containing the following terms:

(1) a statement of the hire-purchase price and the cash price;
(2) details about the dates and amounts of the instalments;
(3) a list of the goods;
(4) a notice in a prescribed form as to the hirer's legal rights under the Acts.

The most important of these rights of the hirer is that of terminating the hire-purchase agreement at any time. If he does so he will be bound to pay to the owner any instalments which were due at the time when notice was given together with the sum, if any, needed to bring the total of instalments paid and due up to half the hire-purchase price. Naturally, the hirer would have to return the goods, and make good any damage to them, other than such as has been caused by normal wear and tear.

Another important protection for the hirer is that the owner may not recover possession of the goods otherwise than by court action, once the hirer has paid one-third of the hire-purchase price.

The implied conditions and warranties laid down by the Sale of Goods Act do not apply to hire-purchase contracts, but the Hire Purchase Acts provide that instead the following conditions are to be implied in such contracts:

1. That the goods are of merchantable quality (except where the goods have been sold as second-hand goods), but the hirer cannot

F

complain about any defects of which the owner could not have reasonably been expected to know, or which the hirer who inspected the goods should have discovered.

2. That the owner has a right to sell the goods.

3. Where the hirer has made known to the owner the purpose for which the goods are intended, that they shall be reasonably fit for that purpose.

Many traders selling goods on hire-purchase terms do not have the necessary finance for this. The procedure followed in these cases is that when the details have been settled between the owner and the hirer the owner sells the goods to a finance company, who then enter into the hire-purchase contract with the hirer. The important effect of this is that there is no contract between the trader and the hirer, so that in general representations made by the original owner will not affect the hire-purchase contract made between the finance company and the hirer.

Where, however, the dealer expressly warrants that the goods are of a certain quality or fit for a particular purpose, and the customer because of this statement enters into the contract with the finance company, the customer will have a right of action against the dealer if the goods sold should fail to come up to the representation.

Andrews v. *Hopkinson.* The plaintiff was shown a 1934 saloon car by the defendant, a dealer in cars. The defendant claimed that it was in excellent condition; and that he would stake his life on it. The plaintiff arranged to buy the car on hire-purchase terms through a finance company. A week after the contract was made the plaintiff was seriously injured in a collision caused by the defective steering of the car, the defect being one which any competent mechanic examining the car would have noticed. *Held,* that the plaintiff was entitled to claim damages from the defendant because he relied on the defendant's warranty in entering into the hire-purchase agreement with the finance company.

In order to prevent members of the public from being misled by untruthful advertisements issued by dealers selling goods on hire-purchase terms the Advertisements (Hire Purchase) Act, 1957, was passed. This Act provides that if a dealer advertises goods as being available on hire-purchase or credit-sale terms, and there is a statement that a deposit is or is not payable or an indication of the amount of any of the instalments, then the advertisement must state the exact amount of the deposit or the proportion of the total price which is represented by it, the amount of each instalment, the total number of instalments payable, the length of the period in respect of which each instalment is payable, the number of instalments payable before delivery of the goods, and the sum which represents the cash price of the goods. This means that if the advertiser (whether in the Press or in a window display) gives *any* information about the hire-purchase or credit-sale terms which he is offering he must provide the *complete* information and not merely a selected part of it. Non-compliance with the provisions of the Act will make the offending dealer liable to a fine.

CHAPTER FIVE

THE LAW OF NEGOTIABLE INSTRUMENTS

DEFINITION

IN Chapter 2 we have discussed the position concerning the assignability of rights existing under a contract. We have seen that the assignment of a contractual right—mainly the right to receive a sum of money—is possible subject to the requirements of the Law of Property Act, 1925, having been complied with. There are, however, certain contractual rights to receive sums of money which, because they are embodied in instruments endowed by law with special privileges, and referred to as negotiable instruments, may be transferred from one person to another without the above requirements having to be satisfied.

Most instruments which possess the quality of negotiability do so because of commercial custom, though some of them have been given the status of a negotiable instrument by Act of Parliament. It is rather unlikely that new negotiable instruments would be created at the present time. The most important negotiable instruments in existence to-day are bills of exchange, cheques, and promissory notes (all three of which are governed by the Bills of Exchange Act, 1882), dividend warrants (warrants drawn by a company on its bank in favour of a shareholder to whom a dividend is payable), share warrants (documents evidencing the shareholding of a shareholder), debentures payable to bearer, and Treasury Bills. Postal and money orders are not negotiable instruments.

A negotiable instrument differs from any other document evidencing a contractual debt in the following ways:

1. A negotiable instrument may be transferred by mere delivery without the necessity for a formal assignment. The only exception to this rule is represented by bills of exchange payable to order which, in addition to delivery, require also an endorsement.

2. Where a negotiable instrument is properly transferred or negotiated the transferee, provided that he has given valuable consideration for it, acquires a good title irrespective of the quality of the title of the transferor. This means that while the assignment of a contractual right is "subject to equities" (the assignee will not have a better position than the assignor), a negotiable instrument is transferred "free from equities," in that the title of the holder for value does not depend on the title of his predecessor.

The remainder of this chapter will be devoted to a discussion of bills of exchange and cheques, the two main types of negotiable instruments. References to sections are to be interpreted as relating to the Bills of Exchange Act, 1882.

BILLS OF EXCHANGE

A bill of exchange is an unconditional order in writing, addressed by one person to another, signed by the person giving it, requiring the person to whom it is addressed to pay on demand or at a fixed or determinable future time a sum certain in money to or to the order of a specified person, or to bearer (Section 3 (1)). It will help in our discussion of bills of exchange if a draft of a typical bill is produced.

£100   *Rochester, 1st January, 1961*
Three months after date pay to Samuel Johnson or Order the sum of one hundred pounds for value received.
                                        CHARLES DICKENS
To Robert Browning,
 The Old House,
  Newtown.

There are three parties to every bill of exchange. The person who gives the order (Dickens, in our example) is known as the drawer, the person to whom the order is given (Browning) is the drawee, and the person to whom payment is to be made (Johnson) is the payee. It is possible for the drawer to be named also as the payee, but where the drawer has drawn the bill on himself the bill could be treated as a promissory note (Section 5).

The following points in the definition of a bill of exchange deserve special attention:

1. The drawer's order must be an unconditional one. If the order to pay addressed to the drawee is subject to certain conditions, such as that he should pay only if something or other has been done or has happened first, the order would be conditional, and the document would not be a bill of exchange. This is important in connexion with the practice of bank customers who pay their debts by cheque having printed on the back of the cheque a receipt form which the recipient of payment is asked to sign. If the instruction were to be worded so as to indicate to the bank that they were not to pay the cheque unless the receipt form had been signed the document would not be a proper cheque (cheques being, as we shall see, a type of bill of exchange).

2. The bill of exchange must be for a definite sum of money. It is, however, quite permissible to provide for this sum to be paid by

stated instalments or with interest at a rate fixed by the bill. There is no objection in principle to bills of exchange being made out in terms of a foreign currency, perhaps with an embodied rate of conversion of that currency into sterling (Section 9).

3. The bill of exchange must be payable either to a specified person or to bearer. From this point of view, bills are divided into two classes—namely, order bills and bearer bills. A bill is payable to order (this means to the person named in the bill or to anyone else to whom he might order payment to be made instead) if

(a) the bill itself states so, or

(b) the bill is made payable to a specified person without containing further words prohibiting transfer (Section 8 (4)). Thus, a bill payable to John Jones will be an order bill even if the words 'or order' are not added after his name, but if the bill were to be payable to John Jones *only*, then it would not be an order bill. Indeed, while such a document would certainly be a valid authority to the drawee to pay the sum mentioned to the payee, it is doubtful whether it would be a bill of exchange in the legal sense, because transferability is an essential element of a bill of exchange.

A bill of exchange will be treated as a bearer bill where:

(a) the bill states so, or

(b) the last or only endorsement on the bill is an endorsement in blank (Section 8 (3)), or

(c) the bill is made payable to a fictitious or non-existing person (Section 7 (3)). A non-existing person is one who has never existed, or at least does not exist at the present time, while a fictitious person is one who does exist, but who has never been intended by the drawer to receive payment on the bill.

Bank of England v. *Vagliano*. A employed a clerk, X. X fraudulently drew a bill in the name of B, a person well known to A, on A for the benefit of C, another well-known business man. X put the bill before A, who accepted it. X then forged C's signature on an endorsement and put the bill into circulation. *Held*, that since C had not been intended by B to receive any payment, he was a fictitious payee, the bill was a bearer bill, and the holder of it could claim irrespective of the forged endorsement.

A bill may be made payable to two persons jointly (*e.g.*, Mr and Mrs A. Brown), or to two payees in the alternative (Mr or Mrs A. Brown), or to the holder of a particular office (*e.g.*, the Borough Treasurer of X) (Section 7 (2)).

4. The bill must be payable either on a date specified on the bill or one which may be ascertained by consulting the calendar (*e.g.*, the first Tuesday after Easter 1961) or it may be payable on demand (at sight). Where a bill is stated to be payable on a fixed or ascertainable date the payment is not actually due on that day, since by law three days (the so-called days of grace) have to be added. It does not matter if the bill is stated to be payable on a Sunday, but if the third day of grace falls on a Sunday or public holiday the bill will be due for payment on the preceding business day. If the third day of grace falls on the second of two successive public holidays, then the bill will be payable on the next following business day (Section 14).

PRESENTING A BILL FOR ACCEPTANCE

The fact that some person has been named on a bill of exchange as drawee does not mean that he has a legal liability to pay the bill. The payee has therefore no certainty that he will be paid by the drawee until the drawee has agreed to pay in accordance with the drawer's order. This he does by 'accepting' the bill. The acceptance is effected by the drawee signing his name across the face of the bill, usually adding also the date (Section 17). It is in general a matter for the holder of the bill to decide whether or not to present a bill for acceptance. Bills which are payable 'at sight' cannot be presented for acceptance (*cf.* cheques), since when the holder presents the bill in such a case he presents it already for payment. There are only three cases where a bill of exchange must be presented for acceptance (Section 39).

1. Where the bill itself demands so.

2. Where the bill is payable so many days 'after sight' or 'after demand.' The reason is that presentment for acceptance will specify the day from which the period will be counted.

3. Where the bill is payable at some place other than the drawee's residence or place of business. Such a bill is said to be 'domiciled,' and the place where it is likely to be payable will be a bank. The reason for insisting on its being presented for acceptance is to inform the drawee so that he may make arrangements for having funds ready at the chosen place to meet the bill.

The presenting of a bill for acceptance must be done at a reasonable hour of the day. Where there is more than one drawee the bill will have to be presented to all of them. If the drawee has died the bill will have to be presented to his personal representative.

Where the bill has been presented to the drawee and the drawee has refused to accept it, or where it has been impossible to find the drawee, the bill is said to be dishonoured by non-acceptance (Section

47). The effect of this will be discussed later. The holder must be satisfied with nothing less than an unqualified acceptance. Where the drawee is prepared to accept the bill, but for a smaller sum of money only, or on some condition, or payable at a different time or place, the holder should consider the bill to be dishonoured by non-acceptance, since if he were to be satisfied with such an acceptance he would lose his rights of recourse against the other parties to the bill (Section 44).

The Transfer of Bills

An order bill is transferred by delivery coupled with an endorsement. An endorsement is represented by the signature of the transferor placed on the back of the bill. Endorsements may be of various kinds (Sections 34-35):

1. Special endorsements, where the endorser apart from signing his name also indicates the name of the person to whom payment is to be made.

2. Endorsements in blank, consisting of the endorser's signature only. A blank endorsement may always be extended by a subsequent holder of the bill into a special endorsement by writing his own name in front of the endorser's signature. It has been shown already that where the last or only endorsement on the bill is an endorsement in blank the bill may be treated by the holder as a bearer bill.

3. An endorsement *sans recours,* where the endorser adds these words after his signature to show that he is not prepared to accept any liability for the eventual payment of the bill.

4. A restrictive endorsement, where the endorser indicates that he is transferring the bill to the endorsee for a named purpose only —e.g., to allow the endorsee to collect the amount of the bill from the drawee or acceptor, but without having authority to negotiate the bill to another party.

A bill may be endorsed before or after it has been presented for acceptance.

A bearer bill is transferred by the delivery of the bill to another party (Section 31 (2)).

Presentment of the Bill for Payment

A bill of exchange must be presented for payment immediately when it is due (Section 45). In the case of a bill stated to be payable on a certain date this means that it must be presented on the third day of grace. A bill payable on demand falls due at once, and that means that if it is not presented for payment within a reasonable time from being drawn the bill will be treated as overdue. If a bill is not presented for payment when due the bill will not cease to be valid, nor will the acceptor, if there is one, be discharged from his liability, which continues for the length of the period of limitation. There exists, however, the general principle that when a bill has been dishonoured, whether by non-acceptance or by non-payment, every person who has placed his name on the bill (as drawer or endorser) will be liable to pay the bill. If the bill is not presented for payment on the date when it is due this right of recourse will be lost.

The holder need not present the bill for payment, and he may treat it as dishonoured for the purpose of utilizing his right of recourse, where the drawee or acceptor cannot be found after reasonable care has been taken, where the drawee is dead or bankrupt, or is a person who does not possess contractual capacity (Section 46).

In the case of dishonour, the holder must give notice at once to all the persons against whom he wishes to use his right of recourse. Anyone not informed of the dishonour will not be liable to pay the bill. No special form of notice is required, but it will generally be given in writing. Delay in giving notice would be excused if it has been impossible to give notice for reasons outside the holder's control. In practice, the holder would normally claim from his immediate predecessor on the bill, who, after having paid the holder, would claim from his predecessor, and so on until eventually the bill would be returned to the drawer, who would have no one against whom to have recourse. The amount that the holder may claim is the amount of the bill together with 5 per cent. interest from the date when the bill was due, as well as his expenses.

Section 50 (2) provides that notice of dishonour is dispensed with:

1. when, after the exercise of reasonable diligence, notice cannot be given or does not reach the addressee;

2. when the addressee has in advance waived the need to give notice, or when he does so after the holder's failure to give notice to him;

3. as regards the drawer, where (a) he is the same person as the drawee, (b) where the drawee is a fictitious person, or has no capacity to contract, (c) where the drawee is under no obligation between himself and the drawer to accept or pay the bill, (d) where the drawer has countermanded payment;

4. as regards an endorser, where the drawee is a fictitious person or is incapable to contract, and the endorser knew this when he endorsed the bill, also where the bill has been made out for his accommodation.

When it is likely that a bill will be dishonoured the holder may feel in want of some official proof of this fact. This is particularly important where recourse proceedings may have to be taken abroad.

This proof of dishonour is obtained by means of a document, known as a *protest* (Section 51). In order to have the bill protested it is handed to a notary public, who will present it to the drawee for payment. If the drawee is unwilling to pay the notary will record on a document the exact words used by the drawee, together with a recital of the wording of the bill. The protest must contain:

(1) the name of the person who asked for it;
(2) the date and place where the bill was presented; and
(3) the demand made to the drawee and his words of reply.

A protest may tend to be expensive, as it has to be stamped, and it is therefore possible by way of precaution to have the bill *noted*. This means that the same procedure is followed as has been described, but the protest is not prepared until it is actually required. In the meantime the notary merely notes on the bill the essential details of the presentation.

Where a notary public is not available a protest may be prepared by a householder acting with the help of two witnesses.

The Rights of the Holder of a Bill

The holder of a bearer bill has the right to demand payment from the acceptor. He does not possess the right of recourse of the holder of an order bill, but if the bill should be dishonoured he may be able to claim damages from his immediate predecessor. This is so because the transferor of a bearer bill warrants to the transferee that the bill is what it purports to be, that he has a right to transfer it, and that he is not aware of any fact rendering it worthless (Section 58 (3)).

For the holder of an order bill it is important to prove that he is a *holder in due course*. A holder in due course is defined by Section 29 as a holder who has taken a bill which at the time of negotiation to him was

(1) complete and regular on the face of it;
(2) before it was overdue;
(3) without notice that it had been dishonoured, if such was the fact;
(4) in good faith;
(5) for value; and
(6) without notice of any defect in the title of the person who negotiated it.

The reason why it is important for a holder of an order bill to show that he is a holder in due course is because only such a holder is able to enjoy the full benefits of the instrument being a negotiable one. Only a holder in due course has thus a good title to the bill irrespective of the title of his predecessor. Every holder is, however, deemed to be a holder in due course until the opposite has been proved.

With reference to the above definition, it must be added that a holder acts in good faith where he acts honestly, whether or not negligently (Section 90). As far as the valuable consideration is concerned that must have been given for the bill, bills of exchange form an exception to the rule that past consideration is not valuable. Furthermore, the consideration need not have been given by the holder himself; if one of his predecessors has given valuable consideration for the bill the present holder will be treated as a holder for value.

FORGERIES ON A BILL

A forged signature on a bill is wholly inoperative, and no person can acquire any rights under it, even if he has acted in good faith (Section 24). Certain exceptions exist to this rule in favour of banks handling cheques, but these will be discussed specifically under the heading of cheques.

Where a bill is materially altered without the consent of all the parties who are liable on the bill the bill will be avoided, except as against the party who made, authorized, or assented to the alteration, as well as against subsequent endorsers of the bill. Section 64, which deals with such alterations, mentions the following as being material: alteration of the date, the sum payable, the time of payment, the place of payment. If the bill has been materially altered, but the alteration is not apparent, and the bill is in the hands of a holder in due course, he may enforce the bill according to its original wording as if it had not been altered.

CHEQUES

A cheque is defined as a bill of exchange drawn on a banker payable on demand (Section 73). As a cheque is a type of bill of exchange, the general law relating to bills of exchange applies also to cheques, except that a cheque cannot be presented for acceptance or accepted because it is payable on demand. The Act contains, however, a number of provisions which are specific to cheques, but before discussing these it will be useful to examine briefly the legal relationship between a banker and his customer.

The relationship of banker and customer

The relationship of banker and customer is primarily that of debtor and creditor with the customer, provided he has a credit balance on his account, being in the position of the creditor. In addition, however, the banker may also be acting as agent for his customer where he is making payments on his behalf or is collecting money for him. Furthermore, the banker frequently acts as bailee, where the customer has deposited valuables with him for safe custody.

In his capacity as debtor, the banker is bound to honour the customer's cheques, provided that they are within the customer's credit balance or within an agreed overdraft that the banker has granted to the customer. The banker is not bound to honour a customer's cheque where the cheque is made out for an amount in excess of the customer's balance, even if the excess is a small one. The banker's authority to honour the customer's cheques is terminated in the following circumstances:

1. Where the authority has been expressly countermanded by the customer. The banker must make sure, however, that it is the customer himself who has countermanded payment of a cheque since if he were to dishonour a cheque without justification he would be liable to the customer for breach of contract.

2. Where the customer has died and the banker has received notice of his death.

3. Where a receiving order in bankruptcy proceedings has been made against the customer.

4. Where a court of law has ordered the banker to stop further payments out of a particular account. Such an order is likely to be made in *garnishee proceedings,* where a creditor of the customer has obtained judgment against him and by way of execution of the judgment has applied for a garnishee order. The effect of the order is that the debtors (and that includes the banker) of the judgment debtor are ordered not to make any repayments to him until the order is discharged.

A banker is supposed to know his customer's signature, and if he were to pay a cheque purporting to be drawn by the customer, but in fact a forgery, the loss would fall on the banker. On the other hand, however, the customer is expected to use reasonable care in drawing cheques so as to prevent unauthorized persons from raising the amount of the cheque.

London Joint Stock Bank, Ltd. v. *Macmillan and Arthur.* M. and A. entrusted to one of their clerks the duty of filling in details of cheques to be signed by the partners. The clerk presented a bearer cheque to one of the partners for signature. The amount of the cheque (£2) was written in figures in the appropriate space, but the sum was not given in words. After the cheque had been signed by one of the partners the clerk altered the figure to £120, and wrote in this amount also in words. He then collected this amount and kept it. *Held,* that the bank was entitled to debit the customers' account for the full amount because of their negligence in signing the cheque.

Crossed cheques

A cheque is a crossed cheque if two parallel transverse lines are drawn across the face of the cheque (Section 76). Words may, but need not, be written between the lines.

Where there are no words written between the lines, or only the words '& Co.,' the cheque is crossed generally. Where the name of a banker, and possibly also that of a branch of that bank, is written between the lines, the crossing is a special one. The writing of the words 'not negotiable' between the lines means that the cheque ceases to be a negotiable instrument. This does not mean that such a cheque may not be transferred; it merely means that the title which a transferee acquires cannot be better than that of the transferor. Lastly, there is a crossing 'account payee only.' This crossing, though accepted by commercial custom, is not actually referred to in the Act. Its effect will be discussed below in connexion with the banker's duties. Any crossing is deemed to be a material part of the cheque, and its removal would count as an unauthorized alteration of the cheque. It is possible, however, for any holder to cross an uncrossed cheque, or to add anything to a crossing, such as by converting a general crossing into a special one.

Since bankers handle daily an enormous number of cheques, it would be a serious hindrance to this essential branch of commerce if the liability of a banker were to be the same as that of any other person handling a bill of exchange. The Bills of Exchange Act, 1882, and the Cheques Act, 1957, contain, therefore, provisions which grant special protection to bankers. For this purpose it is necessary to distinguish between the paying banker and the collecting banker. The paying banker is the banker on whom the cheque is drawn, while the collecting banker is the banker who is collecting a cheque for a customer. It is, of course, quite feasible that the same bank may be acting as paying as well as the collecting banker.

Bills of Exchange Act, 1882. Section 60

"When a bill payable to order on demand is drawn on a banker, and the banker on whom it is drawn pays the bill in good faith, and in the ordinary course of business, it is not incumbent on the banker to show that the endorsement of the payee or any subsequent endorsement was made by or under the authority of the person whose endorsement it purports to be, and the banker is deemed to have paid the bill in due course, although such endorsement has been forged or made without authority."

In order to appreciate the importance of this section we have to consider what the banker's position would be if that section had not been included in the Act. Assume that A has drawn a bill on his banker in favour of C. C endorses the bill to D. D's signature is forged on an endorsement in favour of E. E presents the bill to the banker for payment, and receives payment. A forgery is a nullity, and legally, therefore, D was still the owner. D could therefore claim that the bank had paid the wrong person, and they would have to pay the bill again, this time to D. The following points about Section 60 should be noted:

1. It protects the paying banker.

2. It refers to order bills drawn on a banker payable on demand. Though this would include cheques, the position of a banker paying cheques drawn upon him is now specifically governed by the Cheques Act, 1957.

3. The banker must have paid the bill in good faith and in the ordinary course of business. The 'ordinary course of business' is the recognized course of business of the banking community as a whole, so that if the business methods of a particular bank were to differ from those followed in normal banking practice, the banker would not have acted 'in the ordinary course of business.'

4. The bill must contain a full chain of endorsements, the endorser in each case being the endorsee in the preceding endorsement. The bank is not protected where they paid a bill in which an endorsement was missing, only where it was forged.

Cheques Act, 1957. Section 1

"Where a banker in good faith and in the ordinary course of business pays a cheque drawn upon him which is not endorsed or is irregularly endorsed, he does not, in doing so, incur any liability by reason only of the absence of, or irregularity in, endorsement and he is deemed to have paid in due course."

The effect of this section is that the protection which a paying banker enjoys in respect of order bills payable on demand is now extended if these bills happen to be cheques. In that event, the banker may dispense altogether with the need for endorsement, but he will still enjoy his statutory protection only if he has acted in good faith and in the ordinary course of business. It should be noted that the section does not say that endorsements are not required; it merely grants protection to the banker even if there is no endorsement or where the endorsement is irregular. The banker may, if he wishes, still insist on an endorsement.

Section 1 of the Cheques Act, 1957, applies not only to cheques but also to bankers' drafts, drawn by one branch of a bank on another branch as well as to other documents drawn by a bank customer on his bank which are intended to enable some person to receive from the bank payment of a sum of money mentioned in the document.

Bills of Exchange Act, 1882. Section 80

"Where the banker on whom a crossed cheque is drawn, in good faith and without negligence pays it, if crossed generally, to a banker, and if crossed specially, to the banker to whom it is crossed, or his agent for collection being a banker, the banker paying the cheque ... shall ... be entitled to the same rights and be placed in the same position as if payment of the cheque had been made to the true owner thereof."

If Section 80 were not in the Act the paying banker would be responsible for seeing that the payment should actually go to the person entitled to receive it, even though the cheque was collected through the medium of another banker.

1. This section again concerns the paying banker, but it is limited to crossed cheques. Where a cheque is crossed the paying banker must pay the cheque to another banker, or to the banker named in the crossing, where the cheque is crossed specially. He must not pay the cheque directly to the payee over the counter. If he were to do so he would be liable to the true owner of the cheque, assuming him to be a person other than the one to whom payment had been made, for any loss which he had suffered (Section 79 (2)).

2. If, however, the paying banker pays the cheque in accordance with its crossing, and does so in good faith and without negligence, he will be in the same position as if he had paid the cheque to the true owner. The responsibility for ensuring that the payment goes to the true owner falls, then, on the collecting banker, who is in direct contact with the person presenting the cheque and can make sure that it is being collected for the rightful owner.

Cheques Act, 1957. Section 4

This section has repealed and largely re-enacted Section 82 of the 1882 Act. It applies, however, not only to cheques, but also to bankers' drafts, documents not in the form of a cheque drawn on a bank by a customer ordering the payment of money to some named party, and documents drawn on the Paymaster-General ordering the payment of money out of Government funds. The provisions of the 1882 Act applying to crossed cheques have also been extended to the above-mentioned documents.

Section 4 provides that "where a banker, in good faith and without negligence, (a) receives payment for a customer of an instrument to which this section applies; or (b) having credited a customer's account with the amount of such an instrument, receives payment thereof for himself; and the customer has no title or a defective title to the instrument, the banker does not incur any liability to the true owner of the instrument by reason only of having received payment thereof. . . . A banker is not to be treated for the purposes of this section as having been negligent by reason only of his failure to concern himself with absence of, or irregularity in, endorsement of an instrument."

1. This section provides a measure of protection for the collecting banker. If the section did not exist, and indeed also where the section does not apply because the collecting banker had not satisfied the conditions to be examined below, he would be liable to the true owner of a cheque which he had collected for another person on the ground of being guilty of the wrong (tort) of conversion. He would then have to compensate the true owner for the loss which he had suffered.

2. The banker is entitled to the protection of Section 4 only where he collected the cheque for a 'customer.' A customer is a person who has an account with the banker, as distinct from a casual caller at the bank. It does not matter that the collection of the cheque was the first transaction passing through the account. The reason why the Act insists that the cheque must have been collected for a customer is because a banker may not open an account without making careful inquiries about the new customer.

3. The Bills of Exchange (Crossed Cheques) Act, 1906, had already provided that a banker "receives payment of a crossed cheque for a customer," notwithstanding the fact that he has credited the customer's account with the amount of the cheque before having actually collected it. This, of course, is common banking practice. The 1906 Act has now been repealed and this provision has been embodied in the Cheques Act, 1957.

4. The collecting banker must have acted 'in good faith and without negligence.' The meaning of this phrase depends largely on the facts of each case, and special reference must be made to the observance of the normal precautions taken by reasonable bankers. The following list of instances where negligence would be presumed is not necessarily exhaustive:

(a) It is negligent for a banker to open an account without making careful inquiries about the identity and the business of the customer.

Hampstead Guardians v. *Barclays Bank, Ltd.* A man, giving his name as Stewart, opened an account with the bank. He produced a reference, and when the bank wrote to the address given they received a satisfactory reply, which had, however, been forged by the customer. The customer then paid in two cheques for large amounts drawn by the plaintiffs in favour of one Stewart, and later withdrew the money. *Held,* that the bank had been negligent in not making sure that their customer was the same Stewart as the man in whose favour the cheques had been drawn.

(*b*) A bank would be negligent in collecting a cheque for a customer where the cheque is drawn in favour of his employer and has apparently been endorsed to the customer. The bank is always presumed to know the names of the employers of their customers, and, indeed, in one case at least it has been held that they should know also the names of the employers of the husbands of customers who are married women.

Savory and Company v. *Lloyds Bank, Ltd.* The bank had collected for a woman customer cheques drawn in favour of her husband's employers, and apparently endorsed by them to her. The endorsement was a forgery by the customer's husband. *Held,* that it had been negligent for the bank to collect the cheque without making inquiries.

(*c*) It is similarly negligent for a bank to collect a cheque for a customer where the cheque has been made payable to him in a fiduciary capacity and he wishes it to be credited to his own account.

Marquess of Bute v. *Barclays Bank, Ltd.* X had been employed by the plaintiff as a farm manager. It was his job to make application to the Ministry of Agriculture for payments under the subsidy scheme for hill sheep farmers. When he left the plaintiff's service the Ministry were not informed, and they sent a cheque to him, payable to "X for the Marquess of Bute." The defendant bank collected the cheque for X's private account. *Held,* that they had been negligent to do so without making inquiries.

(*d*) The bank must study the customer's account from time to time to make sure that there are no unusual or special circumstances about the transactions which have passed through the account.

Nu-Stilo Footwear Company, Ltd. v. *Lloyds Bank, Ltd.* The plaintiffs employed one X as secretary and works accountant. Giving the name of Y, X opened an account with the defendants. He gave himself (X) as reference. The first cheque paid into Y's account had apparently been drawn by the plaintiffs in his favour, though it had been signed by X, who had authority to sign cheques. Further cheques were paid in, drawn by the plaintiffs in favour of third parties and apparently endorsed by them to Y. *Held,* that the bank was protected by Section 82 as far as the first cheque was concerned, but not in respect of the later cheques. Y had given as his occupation that of a freelance agent, and the bank should have queried cheques for large

G

amounts, passing through such an account. Furthermore, since all cheques were drawn by the employers of Y's referee, they should have investigated the connexion that existed between the plaintiffs and Y.

(*e*) Where a cheque is crossed 'account payee' the collecting bank has a heavy burden of proof to discharge if they collect the cheque for a person other than the payee. They will be deemed to be guilty of negligence unless they can show that they had satisfied themselves as to the title of the person for whom they collected the cheque.

House Property Company v. *London County and Westminster Bank.*
A cheque was drawn in favour of "X or bearer" and crossed "account payee." The cheque got into the hands of Y, who as bearer of the cheque paid it into his bank, and the bank collected it for him. Y had no title to the cheque. *Held,* that in view of the crossing of the cheque the bank had been negligent in collecting the cheque for Y.

It may just be added that the crossing 'not negotiable' does not affect either the collecting or the paying banker. As far as they are concerned, the cheque is crossed generally, with the normal results of such a crossing. The real importance of that crossing lies, as has been shown already, in the fact that it deprives the cheque of its quality as a negotiable instrument.

Section 4 of the Cheques Act, 1957, differs from Section 82 of the Bills of Exchange Act, 1882, which it has replaced, in two main respects :

(*a*) Section 4 grants protection to the collecting banker in respect of all cheques collected by him for a customer, while Section 82 applied to crossed cheques only.

(*b*) Section 4 states specifically that failure on the part of the collecting banker to concern himself with endorsements on an instrument should by itself not be taken as proof of his negligence. Failure to concern himself with endorsements may, however, be proof of negligence if there are other circumstances present which should have made the collecting banker suspicious of the instrument presented to him for collection.

Cheques Act, 1957. Section 3

This section has been passed in order to help businessmen making payments by cheque. Prior to the passing of the 1957 Act separate receipts were required for such payments, or a receipt clause had to be printed on the back of the cheque. The difficulties to which this practice could give rise have been commented on already. Section 3 now provides that an unendorsed cheque which appears to have been paid by the banker on whom it is drawn is evidence of the receipt by the payee of the sum payable by the cheque.

The passing of this section has not completely removed the necessity for giving receipts. The Stamp Act, 1891, has not been repealed, and this Act demands that a properly stamped (2d.) receipt must be given by the creditor on demand by the debtor, where the debt exceeds £2. All that the Cheques Act has done is to provide that the court will accept an unendorsed cheque which has passed through the creditor's bank account as proof of payment, but the debtor may still insist on a separate receipt, and such receipts will in any case be required where payment has been made in some other form.

PROMISSORY NOTES

A promissory note is defined by Section 83 (1882 Act) as "an unconditional promise in writing, made by one person to another signed by the maker, engaging to pay, on demand or at a fixed or determinable future time, a sum certain in money, to, or to the order of, a specified person or to bearer."

The maker of a promissory note corresponds to the acceptor of a bill of exchange, and the first endorser of such a note corresponds to the drawer of a bill.

All the provisions of the Act concerning bills of exchange apply equally to promissory notes, with the exception of the following:

(1) presentment for acceptance;
(2) acceptance;
(3) bills of exchange are occasionally issued in sets; promissory notes cannot be issued in this way;
(4) foreign bills which have been dishonoured have to be protested. This is not necessary in the case of promissory notes.

CHAPTER SIX

THE LAW OF PARTNERSHIP

DEFINITION

THE law of partnership is contained in the Partnership Act, 1890, and the Limited Partnerships Act, 1907. The Partnership Act, 1890, defines a partnership as "the relation which subsists between persons carrying on business in common with a view of profit." The relationship between persons carrying on business through a registered company is regulated by the Companies Act, 1948, and does not constitute a partnership. The main differences between partnerships and joint stock companies will be discussed in the next chapter.

A partnership must consist of at least two members, and it may not have more than twenty members (ten members, where the business is one of banking). Where more than twenty persons are associated for business purposes they must form themselves into a joint stock company.

A partnership will usually come into existence by an express agreement of the parties. No special form is laid down for such an agreement, though normally it will be in writing in the form of a partnership deed. While a partnership is based on the agreement of the parties, it is possible for a person to be treated as being another's partner for the purpose of being held responsible for that other party's business contracts. This is based on the principle of agency by estoppel, which we have discussed already in Chapter 3. Where a person, by words or conduct, holds himself out as being another's partner he will be treated as his partner (ostensible partnership), though only for the purpose of liability for the other person's contracts. None of the usual rights and duties existing between partners would exist between such ostensible partners.

In order to clarify the position concerning ostensible partners, Section 2 of the 1890 Act lays down certain important rules:

1. Joint ownership does not by itself create partnership. Thus where two or more persons happen to own jointly some property they are not necessarily partners in the sense of being liable on each other's contracts.

2. The sharing of the gross returns of a business is not by itself proof of the existence of a partnership between the persons sharing the returns.

3. The sharing of net returns or profits is *prima facie* evidence

of the existence of a partnership, but it does not as such make the persons sharing partners. In other words, though you are taking a share in the net profits of a business, you may still prove that you are doing so in some capacity which rules out the existence of a partnership. In particular, a partnership will not exist in the following cases:

(a) where a person is paid a debt or other fixed sum by instalments out of the profits of a business;

(b) where an employee is paid a share in the profits of the business;

(c) where a widow or child of a deceased partner receives a share in the profits of the business;

(d) where the seller of the goodwill of a business is repaid by a share in the profits, or where a person who has lent money to a business is paid a rate of interest on the loan which varies with the profits of the business. These arrangements must, however, be in writing to exclude the presumption of partnership.

The Firm Name

The name under which the partnership business operates is known as the firm name. The partners may choose any name they like for their business, provided that by doing so they are not pretending that the business is connected in any way with any other existing business. In this context it is necessary, however, to consider the provisions of the Registration of Business Names Acts, 1916–47.

These Acts provide that every firm in the United Kingdom carrying on business under a name which does not consist of the true surnames of all partners, without any addition other than their Christian names or the initials of these, must be registered. Registration takes place with the Registrar of Business Names in London, and he must be supplied with particulars concerning the name of the business, its nature, its principal place of business, the full names of all the proprietors, and their nationality. Registration must take place within a fortnight from the commencement of the business. The Registrar will issue a certificate which must be exhibited in some conspicuous place on the business premises. The full names and the nationalities (if other than British) of all proprietors of the business must also be shown on all notepaper, circulars, etc., issued by the business. Failure to register renders every person concerned liable to a fine of up to £50. Further, a firm which should have registered its name and has failed to do so will be unable to enforce by action any contract made, except when the court is prepared to grant relief to the firm on the ground that the failure was either accidental or that for some other reason it would be fair to grant relief.

The requirement concerning the registration of business names applies not only to partnerships but also to sole traders and joint stock companies where they are operating businesses under a name which does not consist of the name of the owner or owners, or in the case of a company, its registered name. Readers should make sure that they appreciate the difference between the registration of a business name, which is intended solely to give publicity to the identities of the owners of registrable businesses (the Register of Business Names being open to public inspection), and the registration of a company, which actually serves to bring a company into existence.

RIGHTS AND DUTIES OF PARTNERS

The rights and duties of the partners depend on the terms of the partnership agreement. Failing an express agreement, the rights and duties are specified in Section 24 of the Act as follows:

1. All partners are entitled to share equally in the capital and the profits of the business, and they must contribute equally to losses. The fact that a partner has in fact been drawing a larger than proportionate share of the profits would be taken as evidence of an agreement to that effect.

2. No partner is entitled to interest on his capital contribution prior to the ascertainment of profits.

3. No partner is entitled to remuneration for acting in the partnership business. Every partner, in the absence of an agreement to the contrary, must take part in the management of the affairs of the partnership.

4. No person can be introduced as partner without the consent of all the existing partners.

5. Differences as to the day-to-day running of the partnership business are resolved by a majority vote of the partners, but no fundamental change in the business may be made without the consent of all the partners.

6. A partner making a contribution to the partnership beyond the amount of his capital contribution is entitled to receive 5 per cent. interest on it.

7. The partnership books must be kept at the main place of business of the partnership, and every partner has a right of access to them.

8. Where a partner has incurred any expense on behalf of the

partnership he is entitled to be indemnified out of the partnership property.

THE ADMISSION AND RETIREMENT OF PARTNERS

We have stated already that a new partner may not be introduced without the consent of all existing partners. A partner may, however, assign his share in the partnership to another person. The assignee will not become a partner, but will merely be entitled to receive the share in the profits which would have gone to the assignor. Beyond this, he has no right to interfere in the management of the partnership.

A partner may not be expelled from the partnership by the other partners unless the partnership agreement provides otherwise.

THE RELATIONSHIP OF THE PARTNERS TO THIRD PARTIES

Every partner is deemed to be the agent of his fellow-partners. From this it follows that a contract made by a partner in connexion with the partnership business will be legally binding on his fellow-partners. The person with whom the contract has been made could then take action against the partnership even if the partner who made the contract had no actual authority to make it, since he is ostensibly authorized to make such contracts. Where, of course, the third party knew that the partner had no authority to enter into the contract, he could not proceed against the partnership.

The implied authority of a partner covers the following:

(1) to sell the goods of the partnership and to buy such goods as the partnership normally deals in;
(2) to receive payments of money owing to the partnership and to issue receipts;
(3) to engage employees for the partnership.

In a *trading* partnership, the partner has the following additional powers:

(1) to issue and accept negotiable instruments in the name of the firm;
(2) to borrow money on behalf of the partnership, and to pledge the firm's property for this purpose;
(3) to instruct a solicitor to represent the firm in an action brought against it.

A partner may not sign a deed on behalf of the partnership unless he has been authorized to do so by deed, and he may not without authority from his fellow-partners submit a dispute to arbitration.

The liability of partners for contractual obligations entered into on behalf of the partnership is a *joint* one. This means that the partnership creditors will have to join all partners in one action. If any partner has been omitted from the action—perhaps because his existence was unknown to the creditor—he may not be sued separately by a later action. Where, however, a wrong has been committed by the partnership, or by a partner acting on its behalf, the liability of the partners in an action for damages is *joint and several*. This means that the partners may be sued either jointly or individually.

Where a new partner is admitted into the partnership he does not become liable to the existing creditors for anything which happened before he joined the partnership. This is so even if the new partner agreed with his fellow-partners that he should take his share of the firm's liabilities. If his fellow-partners are sued they may ask him to contribute his share of what they had to pay, but the creditors cannot sue the new partner directly.

Where a partner retires from the partnership it is customary for the remaining partners to take over the assets and the liabilities and to pay out to the retiring partner his net share of the assets. This agreement between the partners is again not enough to prevent the creditors of the partnership from joining the retired partner in an action brought against the other partners for debts which originated from transactions entered into before his retirement, though in this case the retired partner could subsequently ask to be indemnified by his former fellow-partners for anything which he had to pay.

As far as debts are concerned which the partnership incurred after his retirement, the former partner will be responsible only where his liability can be founded on the doctrine of estoppel, or holding out. This assumes that where certain persons have dealt with the partnership before his retirement, the partner has been holding himself out as being in part responsible for the debts of the firm, and this presumption lasts for so long as he has not informed the persons in question of his retirement from the partnership. Persons who have not dealt with the partnership before his retirement cannot claim from him if he has either given notice to them of his retirement or if he has had a notice to that effect published in the *London Gazette*. In any event, no one who had no knowledge of his partnership can claim from him after he has ceased to be a partner.

Tower Cabinet Company, Ltd. v. *Ingram.* X and Y were partners. The partnership was dissolved, but no notice was given. Afterwards X, using the old stationery of the partnership, which also gave Y's name, ordered goods from the plaintiffs. The plaintiffs had never dealt with the partnership before, nor had they had any previous knowledge of Y being a partner. *Held,* that the plaintiffs' action against Y failed.

Where a partner has died, or has become bankrupt, his estate will be liable for debts incurred before the death or bankruptcy, but not for those incurred afterwards.

DISSOLUTION OF A PARTNERSHIP

A partnership may be dissolved in the following ways:

1. Where the partnership has been entered into for a fixed term it will be dissolved when that term has expired.

2. Where the partnership has been entered into for an indefinite period of time the partnership is a partnership at will, and may be dissolved by either partner giving notice to the others. No particular form of notice is required, except that where the partnership has been made by deed written notice will be required.

3. The death or bankruptcy of any of the partners will bring the partnership to an end, but the remaining partners may at once agree to enter into a new partnership agreement.

4. Where an event takes place which would render the partnership illegal the partnership will be dissolved at once.

5. The court may dissolve a partnership on the application of one of the partners in any of the following cases:

(*a*) when a partner is lunatic, or is, to the satisfaction of the court, of permanently unsound mind;

(*b*) when a partner becomes in any other way permanently incapable of performing his duties under the partnership agreement;

(*c*) when a partner has been guilty of conduct calculated prejudicially to affect the carrying on of the partnership business;

(*d*) when a partner wilfully or persistently commits a breach of the partnership agreement, or otherwise so conducts himself that it is not reasonably practicable for the other partners to carry on the business in partnership with him;

(*e*) when the business of the partnership can only be carried on at a loss;

(*f*) whenever the court thinks it just and equitable to dissolve the partnership.

It should be noted that an application under (*a*) above could be made on behalf of the partner affected, while in the other instances the partner guilty of the conduct in question could not apply for the dissolution of the partnership.

On a dissolution of the partnership each partner is entitled to have the partnership property sold and the proceeds applied for the payment of the partnership debts. If there should not be enough to pay the debts the partners would have to share the loss in the proportion in which they share the profits.

One of the most important assets of any business is its goodwill. This was defined by Lord Eldon as "the probability that the old customers will resort to the old place." Goodwill may be based either on the excellent location of a business (*e.g.,* a sweet-shop opposite a school) or on the special skill of the owners (*e.g.,* pastrycooks). The former type of goodwill (sometimes referred to as cat-goodwill, because it stays behind when the owners leave) is sold with the business, so that if a partnership is dissolved, and some of the partners wish to continue operating the business, they will have to pay the retiring partners not only for the tangible assets which they may take over but also for the goodwill. Goodwill based on personal skill (known also as dog-goodwill, because it follows the owners) cannot be sold unless the skill can be embodied in something such as a patent, or a recipe which could be sold with the business. Where, then, the goodwill of the firm has not been sold on the dissolution of the partnership each partner may use it for his own benefit, as long as he is not implying that he is still in partnership with his former partners.

Where the goodwill has been sold the seller may not represent himself as continuing the old business, nor may he in any other way take advantage of his acquaintance with the customers of the old business. He may, however, carry on a similar business, as long as he is not in any way implying any connexion between it and the business the goodwill of which he has sold.

LIMITED PARTNERSHIPS

Limited partnerships were set up by the Limited Partnerships Act, 1907, with a view to setting up a halfway-house between ordinary partnerships and limited companies. As it happened, they never took the fancy of businessmen, and no more than twenty or so of them exist at the present time.

The number of members is the same as in ordinary partnerships, but there must be among them always at least one general and one limited partner. The general partner or partners are entirely responsible for the management of the business, and they are also fully responsible for the debts of the partnership.

A limited partner contributes merely a fixed sum of money to the partnership, and his liability for the partnership's debts is limited to this amount. He may take no part in the management of the partnership business. If he did he would be treated as liable for the partnership debts in the same way as a general partner. He may inspect the partnership books, and may also, subject to the approval of the general partners, assign his share in the partnership business.

A limited partnership must be registered with the registrar of joint stock companies. The following details have to be sent to him:

(1) the name of the firm;
(2) the nature of the business;
(3) the principal place of business;
(4) the full names of all the partners;
(5) the term for which the partnership has been entered into;
(6) a statement that the partnership is limited, and an indication as to which partners are limited partners, stating in each case the sum contributed by the partner.

Whenever a change in any of these particulars occurs the entry in the register must be altered.

CHAPTER SEVEN

JOINT STOCK COMPANIES

FORMATION OF A JOINT STOCK COMPANY

IN order to form a joint stock company it is necessary to submit certain documents to the registrar of joint stock companies in London. If the registrar is satisfied that the documents are in accordance with the requirements of the Companies Act, 1948, he will issue a certificate of incorporation, and the company will have legally come into existence. The documents involved are the following:

1. *The memorandum of association.* The memorandum of association contains what is in effect the company's constitution, by which the relationship of the company to the outside world is determined. It must include the following points:

(*a*) The name of the company. The choice of the company's name rests with the promoters of the company, but the registrar may refuse to register any name which in his opinion is undesirable. This would apply particularly to any name which is already the name of another registered company. Whatever name may be chosen, the last word of it must be the word 'limited.' The Board of Trade may grant a licence to a company to dispense with the word 'limited' in its name. The Board must be satisfied that the purpose of the company is to promote "commerce, art, science, religion, charity or some other useful object" and that the company will not be paying out any dividends to its members. In practice, only companies limited by guarantee and without share capital will be able to take advantage of this provision.

(*b*) The registered office. Every company must have a registered office to which all official communications may be sent by the registrar. This office need not be the same one as that used by the company for its commercial activities. The memorandum need only state whether the office will be situated in England or Scotland (in which case the company would have to be registered in Edinburgh); the actual postal address of the office must be sent to the registrar within a fortnight of registration. The postal address of the office may be altered merely by informing the registrar; if the office were to be moved to another country it would be necessary to wind up the company in England and reform it in the other country (which could be Scotland).

(c) The objects of the company. The memorandum must state the objects for which the company is to be incorporated, and the company if formed may enter into such contracts only as are covered by its objects. Any other contract would be *ultra vires* the company, and therefore void. (*Cf. Ashbury Railway Carriage and Iron Company, Ltd.* v. *Riche*, page 21). A company may alter its objects. This would require a special resolution of the company's shareholders, and it must be for one of the following purposes:

    (i) to carry on the business more economically or efficiently;
    (ii) to attain its main purpose by new means;
    (iii) to enlarge its area of operation;
    (iv) to carry on some other business which may be conveniently combined with its existing one;
    (v) to curtail or abandon any of its existing objects;
    (vi) to sell the whole or part of the undertaking or to amalgamate with another company.

Where a resolution has been passed for the alteration of the company's objects, the alteration will become effective unless an application is made to the Court for its cancellation. The application must be made within twenty-one days after the date of the alteration by holders of not less than 15 per cent. in nominal value of the issued share capital of any class, or by holders of not less than 15 per cent. of the company's debentures entitling the holders to object to alterations of the company's objects. An application may not be made by any person who has assented to or voted in favour of the alteration.

(d) The memorandum must state whether the liability of the members of the company is limited.

(e) The memorandum must indicate the nominal capital with which the company will commence operations, and how this capital will be divided into shares, though the types of the shares need not be given at this stage.

(f) The memorandum ends with the association clause, by which the signatories to the memorandum ask to be formed into a company. Where the company is to be a private company there must be two signatories, while for a public company seven signatories would be required. Each signatory must state how many shares (with a minimum of one) he wishes to take up in the company, and the signatures must be witnessed.

2. *The articles of association.* While the memorandum acts as the constitution of the company, thus determining the company's legal

position in relation to others, the articles are the rules of the company, and they deal with the relationship between the shareholders and the company. Legally, the articles are a contract between the shareholders and the company. The articles must be signed by the same persons who sign the memorandum, and the signatures must again be witnessed.

A public company limited by shares need not submit their own articles to the registrar. If no articles have been submitted it is presumed that the company wish to adopt as their own the model set of articles which appears as Table A in the First Schedule to the Companies Act, 1948. Alternatively, the company may register with the registrar a short statement that they are adopting Table A with such alterations as may be specified in the statement. The contents of the articles are not laid down by law, as are those of the memorandum, but the subject-matters covered by Table A should be covered by the articles of a company since otherwise the relevant articles of Table A would prevail, except when the relevant articles of Table A are expressly excluded. The articles of a company are always subsidiary to the memorandum, so that in the event of a clash between the two the provisions of the memorandum would prevail.

A company may alter its articles by special resolution at a meeting of the shareholders, but the alteration must not clash with the provisions of the memorandum.

3. A list of directors, together with the consent in writing of each of the persons named to act as such, must be filed with the registrar by every company, other than a private one.

4. A separate statement of nominal capital must be filed so as to enable revenue authorities to assess the company for stamp duty. Stamp duty is payable at the rate of 10s. for every £100 of nominal share capital of the company.

5. A statutory declaration that all the requirements of the Companies Act have been complied with. This declaration has to be signed by a director and the secretary of the company.

TYPES OF COMPANIES

From the point of view of the liability of the members for the debts of the company, companies may be divided into:

1. Companies with unlimited liability, where each member is in the same position as to the company's debts as a partner is in a partnership. These companies are very scarce.

2. Companies with liability limited by guarantee. In such a company a member, when becoming a member, will accept responsibility for the debts of a company up to a fixed amount, his guarantee.

3. Companies with liability limited by shares. In these companies

every member is the holder of one or more shares, and his liability
to the company's creditors is restricted to the amount, if any, still
unpaid on the shares which he holds.

As companies with liability limited by shares represent the largest
number of all companies, our discussion in this chapter will be
restricted to them.

A further division of companies is that into private and public
companies. A private company is defined by Section 28 as one which
by its articles:

    (1) restricts the right of its members to transfer their shares;
    (2) limits the number of its members to fifty (exclusive of
         present employees and past employees who were and
         continued to be members of the company);
    (3) prohibits any invitation to the public to subscribe to its
         shares or debentures.

Any company which does not comply with these provisions is a
public company. Private companies may be further subdivided into
exempt and non-exempt private companies. A private company is
exempt if a director and the secretary certify that:

1. No corporation is a shareholder or debenture holder, and no
person other than the registered holder has any interest in any of its
shares or debentures.

2. The number of persons holding debentures does not exceed
fifty.

3. No corporation acts as director of the company.

4. No arrangement exists under which control over the company
is exercised by persons other than its directors, shareholders,
debentureholders, or their trustees.

Private companies unable to file such a certificate will be 'non-
exempt.'

Any company which does not satisfy the requirements for a
private company is automatically a public company.

This may be a convenient place to summarize the privileges which
a private company enjoys, and which are not extended to public
companies. The following privileges are extended to all private companies, exempt as well as non-exempt:

1. Only two persons are required to form a company, while with
public companies a minimum of seven must be maintained.

2. Private companies need not hold a 'statutory meeting,' and
they need not submit to the registrar of companies the preliminary
'statutory report.'

3. No prospectus or statement in lieu of prospectus is required.

4. Directors need not retire on reaching the age of seventy.

5. A public company may not commence business immediately on being registered; it has first to obtain a 'trading certificate' from the registrar of companies.

Exempt private companies (but not other private companies) enjoy the following additional privileges:

1. The annual return which has to be submitted to the registrar of companies need not have attached to it a copy of the last audited balance sheet and of other documents which have to be submitted with the balance sheet.

2. The auditor of an exempt private company need not be a qualified accountant. He may also be a partner or employee of an officer of the company.

3. An exempt private company may make loans to its directors.

A private company must send annually to the registrar a certificate signed by a director and by the secretary of the company, stating that the company is still satisfying the statutory definition of a private company.

A private company can convert itself into a public one simply by an alteration of its articles, excluding those provisions which must be found in the articles of a private company.

RAISING OF SHARE CAPITAL

The total amount of capital which a company wishes to raise by means of the issue of shares is stated in the memorandum. This represents the maximum which a company may raise, so that if it is intended to raise more the memorandum would have to be altered first.

The memorandum does not tell us, however, what types of shares will be issued by the company. This question is settled either by the articles, or it may be decided by a special resolution of the shareholders passed in a general meeting. While the exact distribution of the shares among the different classes, as well as the rights of the holders of these classes, will be fixed as stated above, the following general points may be considered:

1. *Preference shares*. The holders of these shares are entitled to a fixed rate of dividend, which is payable to them before any dividend is distributed to any other class of shareholders. Their preferential treatment extends in principle to the distribution of dividend only. Where the holders are to receive also preferential treatment in the repayment of their capital in the winding-up of the company, the articles of the company would have to make special provision for this. Even then, the holders of these shares would have no right to share in the surplus assets of the company. Preference shares differ from other classes of shares in that they may be made

redeemable (see below). The articles will also determine what voting rights, if any, preference shareholders possess. Generally speaking, they are entitled to be invited to meetings and to vote there only if their dividend has been in arrears for more than a certain length of time.

Preference shares may be divided into the following classes:

    (a) cumulative and non-cumulative preference shares;
    (b) participating and non-participating preference shares.

Preference shares are cumulative where the preference dividend, if not paid in one year, is carried forward to succeeding years in such a way that no dividend may be paid to other classes of shareholders in future years unless the accumulated preference dividends have first been cleared. Where the preference shares are non-cumulative, a dividend not paid at the proper date will not be carried forward, and will thus have been lost by the holders of the shares. Whether the preference shares are cumulative or non-cumulative will depend on the terms of issue, but if these fail to clear the point preference shares are always presumed to be cumulative.

Preference shares also may be participating in the sense that in addition to the fixed rate of dividend the holders would be entitled also to some further dividend in prosperous years. How the participating rights would work would be determined by the terms of issue, but unless the terms of issue clearly give participating rights to the preference shares the shares will be deemed to be non-participating.

Joint stock companies are not as a rule entitled to repay any of their share capital without deciding on this by a special resolution of the shareholders, which would have to be approved by the court. Preference shares represent an exception to this rule, in that a company may, subject to its articles, issue *redeemable preference shares*. Section 58 provides, however:

    (a) that the shares may be redeemed only either out of accumulated profits or out of the proceeds of a new issue of shares;
    (b) that the shares to be redeemed must be fully paid up;
    (c) that any premium payable on redemption must come out of the company's profits and
    (d) that where the shares are redeemed out of profits a sum equal to the value of the redeemed shares shall be transferred from the company's profits to a special reserve fund, known as the 'capital redemption reserve fund.'

2. The *ordinary shares* represent the bulk of the company's shares. They do not qualify for any fixed rate of dividend—their dividend will depend on how much their holders vote to themselves at the annual general meeting—but they cannot vote a dividend at a higher rate than that which has been proposed by the directors. The exact voting rights of ordinary shareholders will be regulated by the articles.

3. The *deferred or founders' shares* entitle their holders to a dividend which is payable in general only after the preference shareholders have been paid their fixed rate, and after the ordinary shareholders have received a dividend of up to a certain fixed maximum.

THE ISSUE OF SHARES

A person may become a shareholder in a company in various ways:

1. The persons who have signed the memorandum of association had to state how many shares they wished to acquire, and they will become holders of that number of shares as soon as the company has been registered.

2. When a company has been registered it will have to proceed seriously with the task of raising the capital which it will need for its operations. A public company will do so by issuing a prospectus to the general investing public. A prospectus is, legally, an invitation to make offers. The prospective shareholders send in their offers, and the directors of the company will decide which of the offers to accept. A private company may not issue a prospectus, since by definition it has agreed not to issue invitations to the general public to subscribe to its shares and debentures. The contents of the prospectus are laid down by the Act so as to ensure that prospective shareholders are given the fullest possible information about the affairs of the company. If a prospectus issued by a company were to contain untrue or misleading statements, a person who had bought shares from the company, trusting in the prospectus, would be in the position of one who had entered into a contract under a fraudulent misrepresentation. It is, however, not only the company as such that is responsible for the statements contained in the prospectus. All persons who have authorized the issue of the prospectus—and that includes all the directors of the company—will be personally responsible to anyone who may have suffered a loss by buying shares from the company while trusting in the prospectus. These persons would have to pay damages to the shareholder, except where they can prove that they honestly and on reasonable grounds believed

the statement in the prospectus to be true, or where it represented the views of experts whom they reasonably considered to be competent, or was the copy of some official document. A director who had withdrawn his consent to the publication of the prospectus before its issue would also be able to disclaim liability.

A copy of the prospectus must be filed with the registrar. Where a public company is issuing shares, but is not offering them to the general public, having placed them privately with some large buyers, the company will have to file with the registrar a *statement in lieu of prospectus* containing the same information as that which would have had to be given in the prospectus. Since the files of the company at the registrar's office are open to public inspection, any future buyer of the shares could study the company's financial and business position before committing himself.

Instead of a company issuing its shares directly to subscribers, the company may sell all the shares to an issuing house, and this financial institution will then offer the shares to the public by means of an 'offer for sale.' The company and its directors are, however, responsible for the contents of the offer for sale in the same way as for a prospectus issued directly by them.

Where a shareholder has applied for shares, and shares have been allotted to him by the company, he will be entitled to receive a share certificate, which must be issued within two months of his becoming a shareholder. The company may not, however, proceed to the allotment of shares unless it has received applications equal at least to the 'minimum subscription' the amount of which must be stated in the prospectus. The minimum subscription, as stated in the prospectus, is based on an estimate of the directors as to the minimum amount that will be required to pay for the purchase of fixed assets, for working capital, and for the expenses incurred in connexion with the formation of the company or with the particular issue of shares. If actual applications were to fall below the minimum subscription the applications would be void, and any monies sent in by applicants would have to be returned to them. Companies protect themselves against this contingency by having the share issue underwritten—*i.e.*, by agreeing with some financial institution that, in return for a commission paid to it, it will take up and pay for any shares not applied for by the general public.

3. A person may become a shareholder by shares being transferred to him by their existing holder or by the transmission of shares consequent upon the death of the previous holder. A transfer or transmission of shares will have to be registered by the company secretary. The transfer must be in writing, signed by the transferor, and it must be sent to the secretary together with the transferor's

share certificate. When the transfer has been registered a new certificate will be issued to the new holder.

Where the holder of shares disposes of less than his total holding he will understandably not be prepared to part with his share certificate. What he will do is to lodge his certificate with the company, and the company will then certify that a certificate for *x* shares has been lodged. This certificate will then take the place of the share certificate. When eventually the transfer is registered with the company the company will cancel the old certificate and will replace it by two certificates, one for the transferee covering the shares which he has bought and one for the transferor in respect of the part of his holding which he has retained.

A company limited by shares may, if authorized by its articles, issue a *share warrant* to a shareholder in respect of fully paid-up shares. A share warrant is a negotiable instrument which may be passed on by mere delivery without the need for the making out of a written transfer. When a company has issued a share warrant to a shareholder the name of that holder will be removed from the register of shareholders. Dividends are paid to holders of share warrants against coupons which are attached to the warrants, and which will be honoured by the company if a dividend is declared. If the holder of a warrant wishes to attend a meeting of the company he will normally be requested by public notice to deposit his warrant with the secretary of the company some time before the holding of the meeting. Since the company has no control over the transfer of warrants, private companies cannot issue share warrants without losing their status as private companies. It should be noted that share warrants have never been particularly popular with English companies, mainly because of the administrative complications which they cause to the company.

THE ISSUE OF DEBENTURES

Where the company requires additional funds for its purposes, and it cannot or does not wish to raise these funds by the issue of further shares, the company may raise the money by the issue of debentures. A debenture is an instrument issued by the company as evidence of a debt owed by the company. Debentures are thus loan certificates, and their holders are creditors of the company, and not, like shareholders, part-owners of the company. This is an important point to remember. The debentures carry interest at a fixed rate. Interest is a contractual payment which the company must make, irrespective of whether it has earned profits in the year. Shareholders, on the other hand, receive dividends. Dividends are shares in the profits, and presume, therefore, the existence of profits. If no profits have been earned by the company no dividends may be paid, though profits from one year may be carried forward to finance the payment of dividends in a later year. The company borrows by means of debentures rather than issues new shares, where the capital is required for a short time only, or where the shareholders in a profitable company do not wish to share their profits with further shareholders, and prefer to hire additional money through the issue of debentures.

In order to make debentures more attractive still to prospective lenders the company will secure them by means of charges on the company's property. In this way the holders are assured that, come what may, they will receive preferential treatment as against other creditors of the company in a possible liquidation of the company. The charges by means of which debentures may be secured may be either *fixed charges*, where specific assets of the company have been charged with the repayment of the debentures and the payment of interest on them, or they may be *floating charges*, where the company has charged all its assets for this purpose. There is a practical difference between these forms of charges. A fixed charge will immobilize the asset on which it has been established, in that the company may not dispose of it without the consent of the debenture-holders or of a trustee who is normally appointed to represent them for this purpose. Where the charge is a floating one the company may use and dispose of its assets as it likes, as long as it is maintaining interest payments on the debentures, and is also paying off any of them that fall due for repayment. It is only where the company is in default with one of its obligations to the debenture-holders that the charge is said to crystallize, and that means that the floating charge becomes converted into a fixed one.

All the charges must be entered in a register of charges to be kept by the company's secretary. If a charge has not been entered within twenty-one days it would become void as against the creditors or the liquidator of the company. The holders of the debentures are either registered in the same way as shareholders or they may at their request be given debenture warrants, which are payable to bearer, are transferable by delivery, and are treated as negotiable instruments.

When a company is in default the debenture-holder or holders have the following rights:

1. They may appoint a receiver, if permitted by the terms of the debenture issue. The receiver would take over the management of the company's affairs from its directors.

2. They may bring an action for the sale of the assets secured to them.

3. They could present a petition for the winding-up of the company.

THE BOARD OF DIRECTORS

The affairs of every company are controlled by a board of directors. A public company must have at least two directors; a private company could have a sole director. What, in fact, the actual number of directors of any one company is will depend on that company's articles. In practice, the articles fix some minimum and maximum number, the actual number falling between these limits. The directors do not act as individuals, but always as a board. This means that if the board is not properly constituted, having either fewer members than the minimum number laid down by the articles, or not having been properly convened, a decision of the board would be void, and not binding on the company.

The articles of the company will contain rules about the election of directors, their retirement, their powers, and their remuneration. Directors are generally elected for three years, one-third of their number retiring each year. There are no general qualifications for directorships, though an undischarged bankrupt or a person who has been convicted of an offence in connexion with the formation of a company would be disqualified from serving as a director. Indeed, unless the articles provide otherwise, a director need not even be a shareholder of the company which he is representing. Most articles demand, however, that a director should be possessed of a minimum number of qualification shares. If he does not possess that number when appointed he has to buy them from the company within two months. The company may not lend to a director the money for this purpose. If a director should fail to acquire the shares within the correct time he would cease to hold office as director.

The first directors of the company, unless named in the articles, are appointed by the subscribers to the memorandum. Subsequent elections take place at the annual general meetings of the company. A director is elected for a definite period, but he may be removed from office by an ordinary resolution of the shareholders before this period has expired. A director of a public company must retire at the annual general meeting next following his seventieth birthday, except where either the articles provide otherwise or where his election has been approved at a meeting at which notice has been given of his age.

The company must keep a register of directors and secretaries containing the full names, former names, and addresses of these officials and, as far as directors are concerned, also their nationalities, dates of birth, business occupations, and details of other directorships held by them. The registrar of companies must be informed of any change in the register of directors.

The directors act as agents of the company. Their authority is governed by the company's memorandum and articles, and by any changes made in them by resolutions of the shareholders. As copies of all these documents are available for public inspection at the office of the registrar of companies, every person contracting with the company is presumed to have knowledge of their contents. Where the articles restrict the directors' authority to contract on behalf of the company a third party could not rely on their ostensible authority as directors. This principle works, however, also the other way. Where the articles of a company provide that the board of directors may do certain things provided that they have been given the sanction of the shareholders in a particular case, a third party who has studied the articles may assume that the authority has been given in fact.

Royal British Bank v. *Turquand.* The directors of a company were authorized by its articles to borrow money, provided that the shareholders had agreed to it by ordinary resolution. They borrowed money without having secured the shareholders' agreement. *Held,* that the company was liable on the debt, as the lender was entitled to assume that the necessary sanction had been given.

It is important to appreciate the limitations to this principle. Where the sanction of the shareholders has to be given by a special resolution the principle would not apply, as such resolutions have to be filed with the registrar, and it would be possible, therefore, for an outsider to make sure whether they had been passed. Furthermore, the presumption only benefits a person who has actually relied on the company's memorandum or articles, and a person who had never consulted these documents could not be in this position.

Rama Corporation, Ltd. v. *Proved Tin and General Investments, Ltd.* A director of the plaintiff company and a director of the defendant company, each purporting to be acting on behalf of his company, entered into a contract. Although the articles of association of the defendant company empowered the board of directors to delegate any of its powers to one of its members, the board had not in the present case empowered its member to enter into the contract, and, in fact, when informed of the contract repudiated it. Although the director of the plaintiff company knew the director of the defendant company personally, he did not know of the existence of the defendant company until the date of the contract, and no attempt was made to consult the articles of that company. *Held,* that the plaintiffs could not rely on the provision concerning delegation in the articles of the defendant company.

COMPANY MEETINGS

1. *Statutory meetings.* A public company must hold a meeting of its members not earlier than one month and not later than three months from the time when it became entitled to commence business. At least fourteen days before the directors must send to every member a 'statutory report' detailing the number of shares that has been allotted to applicants, the amount of cash received for them, the preliminary expenses incurred in connexion with the formation of the company, and containing also a general abstract of receipts and payments so far. The report must also give the names and addresses of the most important company officials.

2. *An annual general meeting* must be held by every company at least once in every calendar year. Not more than fifteen months must have elapsed since the previous meeting.

3. *An extraordinary general meeting* has to be convened by the directors at the request of shareholders representing not less than one-tenth of the total paid-up share capital. The shareholders must state the objects of the meeting when asking for it to be convened.

The *business* at any company meeting may be either ordinary or special business. Any business which is not specifically mentioned by the articles as being ordinary business will be treated as special business. Most articles mention the declaration of dividends, the election of directors, the consideration of the accounts, and the receiving of the directors' and auditors' reports as ordinary business. Where special business is to be transacted at a meeting notice must be given of it on the agenda of the meeting. The length of notice that has to be given to shareholders when a meeting is to take place is twenty-one days for the annual general meeting and fourteen days for any other meeting. Twenty-one days' notice is also required for certain ordinary resolutions, such as the removal of a director or auditor.

The decisions of a meeting of shareholders are made by means of *resolutions*. There are three types of resolutions:

1. An *ordinary* resolution is passed by a majority of the members present and voting at the meeting.

2. Where an *extraordinary* resolution is to be passed it is necessary for notice to have been given to the shareholders of the intention to propose the resolution as an extraordinary one, and the resolution must be passed by a three-quarters majority of those present who are entitled to vote.

3. The procedure for the passing of a *special* resolution is the same as for an extraordinary resolution, except that, irrespective of the type of meeting at which the resolution will be proposed,

twenty-one days' notice has to be given to those entitled to attend.

The Winding-up of Companies

A company may be wound up in one of three ways—namely, by

(1) compulsory winding-up (or winding-up by the court);
(2) voluntary winding-up, and
(3) winding-up under the supervision of the court.

(Readers should note that the correct expression to use for the legal process by means of which a company is brought to an end is that of 'winding-up,' or 'liquidation.' Bankruptcy proceedings can be taken against individuals and partnerships only, and not against companies.)

Compulsory winding-up

The reasons for which a company may be wound-up by the court are:

1. The company has resolved by special resolution to be wound-up.

2. Failure to deliver the statutory report or hold the statutory meeting.

3. The company has suspended its business for more than a year.

4. The number of members has fallen below the legal minimum.

5. The company is unable to pay its debts.

6. The court is of opinion that it is just and equitable to wind up the company.

A petition for the compulsory liquidation of a company may be presented either by the company itself, or by a shareholder, or by a creditor of the company. The petition will be made to the county court in whose district the registered office of the company is situated where the nominal capital of the company is under £10,000, otherwise to the Chancery Division of the High Court of Justice in London.

When the petition for the winding-up of the company has been submitted the court will hold a hearing at which the decision will be made whether or not to order the winding-up of the company. If an order is made the official receiver (a court official) will become the provisional liquidator of the company. He will summon separate meetings of creditors and shareholders for the purpose of deciding whether an application should be made to the court to appoint a liquidator in place of the official receiver, and also whether an application should be made for the appointment of a committee of inspection. If the two meetings cannot agree the court will decide. If no outside liquidator is appointed the official receiver will act as liquidator.

As soon as the official receiver has been appointed he may approach the directors of the company for a statement of affairs, giving particulars of the company's assets and liabilities, a list of the company's creditors, and the securities which they hold. The official receiver will then report to the court on the state of the company, commenting particularly on the likely deficit, and on the reasons for its failure.

The primary task of the official receiver, or of the liquidator, where one has been appointed, is to realize the company's assets and to distribute them among the various interested parties in the sequence which will be discussed below. In a company where the liability of the members is limited by shares each member is liable for the debts of the company to an amount not exceeding the sum unpaid on the shares which he holds. As soon as possible after his appointment the liquidator will prepare a list of 'contributories.' Contributories are the present and past shareholders who have to contribute towards the deficit shown by the company in its liquidation. The list will be made up of two parts, part A and part B. In part A there will appear the names of the present members of the company, while in part B will be the names of persons who have ceased to be members of the company within a year prior to the commencement of the liquidation. The persons on list B cannot be called upon to contribute to the assets of the company unless the persons on list A holding the same shares have proved unable to pay the amount called upon to pay in full. Even where all shares issued by the company are fully paid up, the list of contributories may be prepared in order to ascertain the members who will be entitled to a return of some of their capital.

When the liquidator has collected a sufficiently large sum of money he may start his distribution among the creditors. He need not wait until he has converted all the assets into cash. The payment which the liquidator makes to the creditors is known as a dividend, and is expressed as being so much in the £ on the debts which are outstanding, and which have been proved. Before declaring a dividend the liquidator must, however, give two months' notice to the Board of Trade, and to such creditors of the company as have not yet proved their debts to him. The only creditors who may be paid are those who have proved the debts owing to them. Creditors prove the debts by making a sworn statement (an affidavit) and supporting the claim by such vouchers and other evidence as may be in their hands. It is up to the liquidator to examine the proofs that have been submitted to him, and to reject those which he finds to be insufficiently supported. The dissatisfied creditor whose proof has been rejected may appeal to the court.

Monies in the hands of the liquidator will be distributed in the following sequence :

1. The cost of winding-up, which includes the remuneration of the liquidator and the actual expenses of running the business of the company during liquidation.

2. Preferential creditors, namely:

> (*a*) rates and taxes assessed for the last complete tax year prior to the commencement of the winding-up;
>
> (*b*) wages and salaries of employees prior to the winding-up; but the amount claimable as a preferential debt may not exceed £200 per head, nor may it cover a period of more than four months;
>
> (*c*) unpaid contributions under the national insurance scheme;
>
> (*d*) accrued holiday remuneration, where employees acquire an entitlement to holiday pay by each week of work done during the year.

The various preferential debts rank equally, so that if there should not be enough money to pay them all they would share the available funds proportionately.

3. Ordinary creditors, being all creditors except preferential and secured creditors.

Secured creditors are, of course, in a much stronger position. They may claim to be repaid out of the proceeds of the sale of the assets secured to them, and the other creditors will receive for distribution only the surplus after the secured creditors have been paid. If the assets set aside for the secured creditors should prove insufficient to settle their claims they may claim for the balance with the other creditors.

4. Any surplus left over would be divided among the shareholders in proportion to the capital contributed by them. Unless the articles of the company provide otherwise, the preference shareholders would have no preference in the distribution of capital.

5. If all the share capital has been repaid, and there is still some surplus left over, it would be distributed among the ordinary shareholders and the deferred shareholders in the proportion stated by the articles.

Voluntary liquidation

A company is wound up voluntarily when the shareholders decide so by a special resolution. A voluntary winding-up may be either a members' voluntary winding-up or a creditors' voluntary winding-up.

The winding-up is a members' voluntary winding-up where the directors deliver to the registrar within five weeks before the resolution was passed a statutory declaration by which they confirm that the company will be able to settle all its debts in full within one year from the winding-up being started. In this case the shareholders would appoint and control the liquidator who is in charge of the winding-up.

Where the directors are unable to make the statement in the form required, the winding-up will be a creditors' winding-up. A meeting of the creditors must be called for the day after that on which the shareholders meet to resolve the winding-up. The shareholders and creditors will separately elect a liquidator, and if the same person is not elected by both, the creditors' choice will prevail.

Where the company has voluntarily resolved to wind up, the court may order that the winding-up should proceed under the supervision of the court, and for this purpose an additional liquidator could be appointed by the court.

COMPANIES AND PARTNERSHIPS

At this point it may be useful to summarize, without further comment, the main differences between partnerships and joint stock companies.

Partnerships	*Joint Stock Companies*
1. A partnership is not a legal person.	A company is a legal person.
2. The number of members must be between two and twenty.	A private company has at least two and no more than fifty members. A public company must have at least seven members, but there is no maximum.
3. Each partner is assumed to be the agent of his fellow-partners.	The member of a company is not the agent either of the company or of his fellow-members.
4. No formalities are required in the formation of a partnership.	A company comes into existence by registration, and the registrar of joint stock companies has to be informed about changes in the company's constitution.
5. A partnership may be dissolved by agreement of the partners or by a court order.	A joint stock company is wound up either by a resolution of the shareholders or by a court order.
6. A partnership exists for as long as its members are in existence.	The existence of a joint stock company is independent of the continued existence of its members.

7. A partner in a partnership may assign his interest in the partnership only with the consent of his fellow-partners.

A shareholder may freely assign his shares, subject to the stated reservation in respect of private companies.

8. The property of a partnership is the joint property of the partners.

The property of a joint stock company is not in any way the property of the members of that company.

CHAPTER EIGHT

COMMERCIAL ARBITRATION

WHERE a dispute arises in connexion with a commercial contract the parties may, instead of submitting the dispute to the jurisdiction of a court of law, submit their differences to arbitration. The reasons for the popularity of commercial arbitration are the following:

1. Arbitration may be quicker than court proceedings in obtaining a result, but opinions on this differ.

2. Arbitration is generally much cheaper for the parties.

3. The arbitrator selected by the parties can combine legal knowledge with a thorough understanding of the practical problems of a particular branch of commerce.

4. Arbitration proceedings may be conducted in private, and unpleasant publicity may thus be avoided.

The law concerning commercial arbitration (arbitration of disputes between employers and workmen will be discussed in Chapter 16) is now contained in the Arbitration Act, 1950. A matter may be referred to arbitration in any of the following ways:

1. The court may refer to arbitration any question arising in court proceedings which, in the opinion of the judge, is suitable for this treatment—*e.g.*, any issue which requires the study of technical, accounting, or similar specialized problems.

2. Certain Acts of Parliament provide for the submission of disputes to arbitration—*e.g.*, under the Patents Act, 1949, disputes between an employee-inventor and his employers would be dealt with in this way.

3. The parties may have agreed to submit a dispute to arbitration by means of an arbitration agreement. Such an agreement may be entered into when a dispute has actually arisen, or it may be made in respect of future disputes which may or may not arise.

ARBITRATION AGREEMENTS

Arbitration agreements may be made in any form, but the Arbitration Act, 1950, applies only to those which have been made in writing. The agreement itself will normally name the arbitrator, but his appointment may be left by the agreement to a third party —frequently a trade association. Where the agreement provides that each party may name an arbitrator the two arbitrators will have to appoint an umpire as soon as they have taken office. The arbitrator or umpire may examine the parties and witnesses on oath, and he may also call on the parties to produce before him all relevant accounts and other documents. Where there are two arbitrators, they will hear the dispute together, but if they inform the umpire in writing that they are unable to agree he will take over from them. The award made by the arbitrator or umpire is final, and there is no appeal from it. The arbitrator or umpire will also make an award as to the costs of the proceedings before him, and he may order one of the parties to pay the entire costs.

Where there exists an arbitration agreement, and one of the parties nevertheless commences court proceedings against the other, the court will, on the application of the other party, stay the court proceedings. The court will wish to be satisfied, of course, that the arbitration agreement covers the dispute that has been brought before the court. Furthermore, the party who is asking for the staying of the proceedings must have taken no part in the court proceedings, other than to ask for the staying of the proceedings.

PROCEDURE IN ARBITRATION

The arbitrator has the duty of resolving the dispute that has been submitted to him by making an award. Where the arbitrator does not feel competent to deal with the legal issues involved in the dispute he may employ a legal adviser to help him in drawing up his award. The arbitrator will fix the time and place at which he will hear the parties, and will inform them of this arrangement. If then one of the parties fails to attend, the arbitrator may proceed in his absence. If the arbitrator has personal knowledge of the practice of the trade in which the dispute originated he may—unlike a judge in the court—dispense with technical experts and use his own knowledge.

Where in the course of arbitration proceedings the most important point is one of law, the arbitrator may 'state a case' for the opinion of the court. This he does by explaining the facts of the case, and following this up by a number of questions on which the legal opinion of the court is required. When that has been obtained the arbitrator will apply the law to the facts of the case and give his award. Where the arbitrator has decided against stating a case for the court a party to the arbitration proceedings may ask the court to compel the arbitrator to do so.

Although, as has been shown already, the arbitrator's award is final, and no appeal from it is possible, the court may set aside the award on procedural grounds, This may happen for any of the following reasons :

1. Where the arbitrator has misconducted himself, or where the award has been obtained by improper means. Misconduct on the part of the arbitrator means that he has conducted the proceedings in an irregular manner, even though he did not do so for any improper reason. Examples of such improperly conducted proceedings are:

    (*a*) where the arbitrator has refused to hear one of the parties;
    (*b*) where he examined witnesses in the absence of one of the parties;
    (*c*) where he is in communication with one of the parties about the subject-matter of the reference.

2. The award may be set aside where it is vague, or where it has not finally disposed of the dispute.

3. The award may be set aside where the arbitrator has received bribes, or where he has some undisclosed personal interest in the subject-matter of the dispute.

4. It would also be a misconduct for an arbitrator to give an award on a contract which is illegal.

A properly given award may be enforced by the party in whose favour it has been given in the same manner as a court judgment, but the court's consent must be obtained before proceeding to enforcement.

CHAPTER NINE

THE LAW OF MASTER AND SERVANT

THE CONTRACT OF SERVICE

A contract of service is a contract between an employer and an employee or, using the old legal terminology, between master and servant. The essence of the contract of service is that one of the parties, the employee (servant), has agreed to render services to the other, the employer (master). There are, however, other relationships outside that of master and servant where one person renders services to another. The master-servant relationship differs from these other relationships in that the servant or employee is under the control of his employer, not only in respect of *what* he should do but also as regards the *manner* of his performance. We can therefore have a true master-servant relationship only where the employer is entitled to exercise a measure of control over the servant's performance of his duties. This distinguishes the present relationship from a very similar one which arises where a person contracts with some independent contractor for the rendering of services. Here the contractor is responsible for the final result which he has agreed to achieve, but he is not under the control of his customer-employer with regard to the method which he will employ in achieving it. If I employ a chauffeur for my car he will be my servant, as I am legally entitled to control how he should treat the car, even if in practice he may know far more about it than I do. On the other hand, if I hire a taxi the driver will not be my servant. He is under contract with me to take me safely to my destination, but how he gets there is a matter for him alone to decide. We call this latter type of contract, where a person contracts for the rendering of services by some independent supplier of services, a *contract for services* to distinguish it from the *contract of service* which is the one we are primarily interested in in this chapter.

THE IMPORTANCE OF THE CONTROL TEST

The control test (*i.e.*, whether control is exercisable over the work of another) is important for various purposes:

1. The employer is responsible for providing a safe system of work for those who are employed by him, but not for independent contractors.

I

2. The employer is responsible for the wrongful acts of his servants if they have been committed by them in the course of their employment. He is not responsible for the acts of independent contractors, except where he has been negligent himself in issuing to them negligent instructions or if he employs a contractor on or near a highway to do work which is intrinsically dangerous. In recent years, however, the control test has been supplemented for this purpose by another test, generally referred to as the 'organization test.' The idea behind this test is that a person who controls an undertaking is responsible not only for the negligence of the persons working for him under a contract of service but also for those employed under a contract for services, where damage or injury has been caused to a third party who had entrusted himself or his property to the care of the organization. Most of the cases in which this test has been applied have dealt with injuries caused to patients in hospital.

> *Cassidy* v. *Ministry of Health.* A patient lost the use of some fingers on his hand through the negligence of the resident surgeon in the hospital where he was receiving treatment. *Held,* that although the surgeon was not the servant of the Hospital Board, who could not exercise control over the way in which he, a qualified medical man, was administering treatment, the plaintiff was entitled to succeed, as he had entrusted himself to the hospital as an organization, and it was the duty of those in charge of the organization to ensure that careful treatment was given.

3. The National Insurance (Industrial Injuries) Act, 1946 (see Chapter 13), applies to persons working under a contract of service and not to those working under a contract for services.

4. The control test has also been used in dealing with the problem of the 'loaned employee.' If A, who is employed by B, is lent by B to C for some time, or for the performance of some tasks, and then during this period either A is injured or he, by his negligence, causes injury to another party, who will be responsible? Will it be B (A's general employer) or C (A's temporary employer)? The answer is that responsibility will fall on that one of the two employers who at the time when the accident occurred was actually controlling the servant's method of doing his work. Which one that will be will depend, of course, on the facts of the case, but where the general employer loans a servant, together with some valuable piece of equipment which the servant is to service, the presumption is that control is retained by the general employer. The same applies where the servant is a skilled man in his craft or occupation, and the temporary employer is not himself skilled in that field, and he does not employ anyone who could control the servant's performance of his

work. By and large, control is usually retained by the general employer, and special proof would be needed to show that it had passed to the temporary employer.

Mersey Docks and Harbour Board v. *Coggins and Griffith (Liverpool), Ltd.* The harbour authority hired a crane to a firm of stevedores and loaned to them a driver to operate it. The driver was paid by the authority. The stevedores were authorized to instruct the driver as to what work to do with the crane, but they were not entitled to instruct him how to operate the crane. Through the driver's negligence in operating the crane another worker was knocked down. *Held*, that the driver was still the servant of the authority.

Garrard v. *Southey and Company.* A firm of electrical contractors loaned two electricians to the defendants, who were installing electricity in a new factory. The electricians were paid by their general employers, who also retained the right of dismissal, but they were supervised by a foreman of the defendants who was himself a skilled electrician. The plaintiff, one of the electricians, was injured through the collapse of some steps which he found in the factory and used for his work. *Held*, that control over the electricians had passed to the defendants, who were therefore responsible to provide reasonably safe equipment for the workers.

It must be made quite clear, however, that when control over a servant has passed from his general employers to temporary employers the latter have not actually become his employers; they are only responsible for him and to him as if they were his employers. A contract of service is a contract of a personal nature, and as such it cannot be assigned as other contracts.

Denham v. *Midland Employers Mutual Assurance, Ltd.* A company engaged a firm of contractors to undertake some work on the company's land. The contractors provided the skilled labour, the company provided the service of a labourer who was paid by them. The labourer was killed through the negligence of the contractors' employees in circumstances where the contractors had to pay damages to his widow. The contractors were covered by two insurance policies with different companies, one covering liability to persons employed under a contract of service, the other all other liabilities. *Held*, that though control over the labourer's services had passed to the contractors so as to make them responsible for providing a safe system of work for him, they had not thereby become his employers.

FORMATION OF A CONTRACT OF SERVICE

The general rules about the formation of contracts (see Chapter 2) will have to be applied here. In particular, there must have been offer and acceptance, the parties must possess capacity to enter into contracts, and consideration will have had to be provided by the employer for the servant's promise to work for him. No particular form is required for contracts of service, except that under the Merchant Shipping Act, 1894, contracts with members of the crew of a ship and with apprentices to the sea must be in writing.

Contracts of apprenticeship were governed in the past by special rules, but to-day it appears best to regard a contract of apprenticeship as one where the consideration for the servant's promise to serve his employer is the employer's promise to teach the servant a craft or trade, irrespective of whether money is paid in addition to the teaching. The duty of the employer to teach forms the essence of apprenticeship. Apprentices could be persons of full age, though in practice, of course, they are generally infants. Where a master makes a contract of apprenticeship with an infant it is customary to join the infant's parent as a party to the contract. This will enable the master to sue the parent if the infant should fail to carry out his side of the contract. Contracts of apprenticeship must be made in writing, and quite often they are made by deed. The payment of a premium by the apprentice is not an essential part of a contract of apprenticeship, but where in a contract of service the servant has paid a premium the presumption will be that this is a contract of apprenticeship.

The Duration of a Contract of Service

A contract of service is entered into either for a fixed time or for an indefinite time. If it is entered into for a fixed time it will expire when that time has ended. A contract made for an indefinite time is presumed to be a *contract of general hiring*—that is, a contract from year to year. Such a contract may be terminated only by notice expiring on the anniversary of the day on which the contract was made. This presumption dates back to medieval days, when most contracts of employment related to farm work and it was deemed fair that a man who had been employed during the busy harvest-time should get the benefit of the easier employment during the off-season.

The presumption that a contract of service for an indefinite period is a contract of general hiring may be rebutted where it can be shown that this was not what the parties had intended. Proof of such intention to rule out a general hiring may be found either in the express words used by the parties, or in the nature of the employment, or in the basis on which the servant's pay has been agreed. Where the pay is calculated on some basis other than an annual one the presumption of general hiring would be rebutted. It would not matter, however, that a man is paid weekly or monthly, provided that his pay is fixed at an annual rate.

Avis-Bainbridge v. *Turner Manufacturing Company, Ltd.* The plaintiff had entered the services of the defendants in August 1945 as sales manager on a two-year contract. When the contract expired he stayed on without any agreement as to new terms. In February 1948 the defendants gave him one month's notice. *Held,* that there was nothing in the contract to rebut the presumption of a general hiring. According to that, the plaintiff could not be dismissed before August 1948, and he was entitled to damages for wrongful dismissal.

THE DUTIES OF THE EMPLOYEE

The duties of the employee will be ascertained from the contract which he has made with his employer. The following duties are those which a servant owes to his employer at common law. They apply in the absence of an agreement between the parties to the contrary:

1. The servant must render personal service. This means that he may not employ a substitute to do his work for him.

2. The servant must obey all legitimate orders given to him by his employer. Which orders are legitimate is a question of fact which depends on the exact nature of the employment and on the customs of the trade.

3. The servant must render careful service, and if through want of care he causes damage to the employer he must indemnify the employer.

Lister v. *Romford Ice and Cold Storage Company, Ltd.* L. was a driver employed by the company. His father assisted him as his mate. Through L.'s negligence in driving his lorry his father was injured, and was awarded damages against the company. The company claimed that L. should indemnify them. *Held,* that as the employee had failed to render careful service he was bound to compensate his employers for the loss which had resulted.

In *Lister's case* the servant had to indemnify the employers because he had broken his duty of careful service. Quite apart from that, however, an employer who has been held responsible for a wrong committed by his servant could claim that the servant should contribute to the damages which the employer had to pay. This principle—that where two persons are responsible jointly for a tort the one who had to pay damages may claim a contribution from the other—is based on the Law Reform (Married Women and Tortfeasors) Act, 1935.

Jones v. *Manchester Corporation and others.* A man who went to hospital for a minor operation died as a result of the negligent administration of anæsthetics. His widow claimed damages from the hospital authority. *Held,* that the hospital authority could claim a contribution from the doctor who had administered the anæsthetics.

4. The servant owes a duty of loyalty to his employer. This means that he must not make any secret profit, nor may he take bribes from customers, except where this is tolerated by custom (gratuities). In his own time the employee may do what he likes, but even then he may not do anything which could harm his employers.

Hivac, Ltd. v. *Park Royal Scientific Instruments, Ltd.* Some of the plaintiffs' employees used their spare time to help the defendants in their business. The defendants had set up in business in competition with the plaintiffs in the manufacture of hearing aids. *Held,* that the employees were in breach of their contracts, and the plaintiffs were entitled to an injunction against the defendants restraining them from employing the plaintiffs' servants.

The servant's duty of loyalty is of particular importance in connexion with inventions made by him and their possible patenting. The Patents Act, 1949, states that only the true and first inventor or his assignee may apply for a patent for the invention. The question arises then in connexion with an invention made by an employee at work whether he or his employer is the true and first inventor of the invention. If the invention is the result of guided research, where the employee merely carried out instructions given to him by his superiors, the employer will be the true and first inventor. In all other cases it will be the employee.

Even if the employee is the true and first inventor, this will not necessarily mean that the benefit of the invention will accrue to him. In his contract of service he may have agreed to assign to the employer the right to take out a patent to any invention he might make while employed by the employer. Even in the absence of such an agreement, the employer could claim that the employee-inventor who had patented an invention was holding the invention as trustee for the employer. This would happen where it would be contrary to the duty of loyalty for the employee to retain the benefit of the invention. An example of this would be where the employee is engaged in a research capacity, so that making inventions is his job, or where the inventions resulted as a by-product from other work which he was employed to do, or where the invention could not have been made without the use of the employer's facilities. Each case will, of course, have to be decided on its own merits.

British Syphon Company, Ltd. v. *Homewood.* H. was employed by the company as their technical adviser. He had never been asked to advise them about a soda-water dispenser, but he invented one in his spare time, and obtained a patent for it. *Held,* that it was not consistent with good faith between employer and employee for the latter, in view of his position as a technical adviser, to invent something relating to his employers' business and withhold it from them.

Where the position is one in which the employer and the employee appear to have equal beneficial rights in a patent the court or the comptroller of patents may divide the benefit of the patent between the parties in such proportions as they think fair in the circumstances. This applies, however, only where the benefit of the patent does not clearly belong to one of the parties, to the total exclusion of the other.

The position concerning the copyright in some literary work prepared by the servant is a similar one. The employer would be entitled to claim the copyright if it would be a breach of the duty of loyalty for the employee to take advantage of material which belongs really to his employers. The employers would not be entitled to the copyright of a literary work merely because it embodied the result of experience or know-how which the employee had acquired in the course of his employment.

Stevenson, Jordan, and Harrison, Ltd. v. *Macdonald and Evans.* The plaintiffs, a firm of management consultants, employed one H, first as an accountant and later as an executive officer. After leaving the plaintiffs' employment H wrote a text-book on budgetary control, and assigned the copyright in it to his publishers, the defendants. Part of the book consisted of the texts of public lectures which H had delivered while in the plantiffs' employment, while another part consisted of a report made by him to his employers in connexion with a work assignment. The plaintiffs asked for an injunction to prevent the publication of the book. *Held,* that they were entitled to an injunction only in respect of the part dealing with the report, because the report had been prepared by him as part of his service to his employers. They were not entitled to an injunction in respect of the remainder of the book, which was the product of know-how acquired by the servant during his service. As far as the lectures were concerned which H had given during his employment, they formed no direct part of his service, though they had been delivered at the request of his employers. It was no part of his duties to deliver lectures, though his employers may have found the publicity value of them quite useful.

5. The employee must maintain secrecy regarding any information which has been entrusted to him by his employer during the existence of the employment, provided that it was impressed upon him that the information was confidential. Where employers wish to protect secret processes or methods they would be advised not to rely on this duty, but to protect themselves by including a clause in the employee's contract, since it may be difficult to prove that the confidential nature of the information was sufficiently impressed upon the employee.

United Indigo Chemical Company v. *Robinson.* The company tried to restrain the defendant from using certain secret chemical processes of which he had acquired knowledge during his employment. *Held,* that an injunction would not be granted, as the employee had not been warned at the time that the processes were to be treated as secret.

6. Where the servant has received property belonging to the employer, or where he has used his position with the employer to obtain some benefits for himself, he will have to account to the employer for any gain which he has made.

Reading v. *Attorney-General.* R. while serving as a sergeant in the British Forces in the Middle East used to accompany in uniform lorries carrying smuggled goods through Cairo. For this he was paid large sums of money by the smugglers. *Held,* that being in the service of the Crown he had used his position to obtain a private gain for himself and he had to account to the Crown for the money which he had received.

RESTRAINT OF TRADE

In our discussion of contracts opposed to public policy (page 44) reference was made to contracts in unreasonable restraint of trade. These contracts have now to be discussed at greater length.

A contract in restraint of trade is a contract whereby a person's freedom of action in regard to the way in which he will do business, employ, or be employed is circumscribed. Restraints of trade are common in three situations:

1. Where the seller of a business, having been paid for the goodwill of the business, agrees that he will not start a similar business or be otherwise interested in it for an agreed time and within a fixed area.

2. Where some competitors agree to charge similar prices or to reduce their output or their sales (so-called cartel agreements).

3. In a contract of employment where an employee agrees that after leaving his employment he will not engage in or be interested in any business competing with that of his employer.

The position at common law was that all restraints of trade were illegal and void as being opposed to public policy. Commercial necessity forced on the courts a slight modification of the rule during the last two hundred years, and the position now is that a restraint of trade can be enforced by court action, provided that it is reasonable—and that means that it must both be reasonable between the parties and be reasonable from the point of view of the public interest as well.

Reasonableness between the parties will be considered on the following bases:

1. *The nature of the employment.* A restraint can be reasonable only if the employee was employed in a capacity in which he came into contact either with trade secrets or with trade connexions of his employer. The employer has a legal right to protect these aspects of what one judge called "objective knowledge" by insisting that a restraining clause should be included in the employee's contract of employment. Where, on the other hand, the employee acquires only skill and experience in his employment (subjective knowledge), and there are no trade secrets or trade connexions about his employment, a restraint of trade could never be reasonable, and would not be enforced by the court.

Herbert Morris, Ltd. v. *Saxelby.* The employee in this case had been employed as a works manager, and had signed a fairly far-reaching restraint of trade. *Held,* that as there were no trade secrets or trade connexions about his employment, and the only knowledge which he had acquired was that of how to organize a department, the restraint was not reasonable.

2. The employee must have received some valuable consideration for his promise. While in contracts the adequacy of consideration is generally of no importance, in restraints of trade the court will take into account the rate of pay of the employee, since if he has been paid a low wage or salary it does not behove the employer to claim that he was employed in some important capacity where essential secrets or connexions would be handled by him.

M. and S. Drapers v. *Reynolds.* The defendant was a collector-salesman employed by the plaintiffs, a firm of credit drapers, at a weekly wage of £10, and subject to a fortnight's notice. When he had entered their employment he had brought with him a fairly wide connexion in the trade. In his contract with the plaintiffs he agreed in the event of his leaving their employment not to canvass any customers on their lists for five years. *Held,* that the restraint was unreasonable, partly because it was too wide (see below) and partly because there was a discrepancy between the length of the restraint and the terms of the servant's employment.

3. The restraint must not be unreasonably wide. The 'width' of the restraint is its extent in area as well as its extent in time. The employer is entitled to a reasonable protection of his interests, but to no more. If reasonable protection of the employer's interests requires a long restraint such restraint could be quite reasonable.

Nordenfeldt v. *Maxim-Nordenfeldt Gun and Ammunition Company, Ltd.* N. was an inventor and manufacturer of armaments. He sold his business to the company for a substantial amount, and agreed in the contract of sale that he would not for twenty-five years engage in or be interested in any similar business anywhere in the world. *Held,* that because of the world-wide ramification of the type of business involved a world-wide restraint lasting for twenty-five years was reasonable.

Fitch v. *Dewes.* A promise by a solicitor's managing clerk that he would not engage in the practice of a solicitor within seven miles of Tamworth, where he had been employed, was *held* to be reasonable.

Each case must be judged on its merits, and we have to look at the area from which the employer draws his customers, as well as at the knowledge which the employee has acquired, and for how long that will be of any benefit to him.

Attention must be paid to the exact wording of the restraint. The servant could utilize his knowledge of his former employer's affairs in various ways; he could operate his own business, or own a business and have it run by some one else, or be employed in a similar business; and the restraint should be so drafted as to include all these possibilities.

Apart from being reasonable between the parties, the restraint must also be reasonable from the point of view of the public interest. This would seem to imply that a restraint might be reasonable between the parties but not from the point of view of the interest of the public. Cases of that type could easily be imagined (*e.g.,* an inventor being paid a large sum by a firm on condition that he would not make further inventions) but until recently no case has been reported in which a restraint reasonable between the parties has in fact been held to be unreasonable from the point of view of public interest.

Kores Manufacturing Company, Ltd. v. *Kolok Manufacturing Company, Ltd.* The plaintiffs and the defendants, who were engaged in the same line of business (the manufacture of carbon paper and other office accessories), occupied adjoining premises. In 1934 the parties had agreed by exchange of letters that neither of them would, without the written consent of the other, employ any person who, during the preceding five years, had been employed by the other party. *Held,* that this agreement was void because (1) no evidence had been submitted that the period of five years was appropriate to any particular category of employees, and (2) the agreement was also opposed to the public interest in that it restricted an employee's freedom of choice of employment without constituting a fetter which the employers reasonably required for their own protection.

Where a contract of service contains a restraint which is unreasonable, and therefore bad, the restraint will be void but the remainder of the contract will be good and enforceable. If part of a restraint is bad and part is good the court may sever the good from the bad, and enforce the former while refusing to enforce the latter. Such a severance of a restraint of trade is possible only where the restraint consists of a number of separate parts, so that, when removing the bad parts, what is left still makes sense without the necessity for making any additions. Thus, if an employee promises not to work in places A, B, and C after leaving his employment the court may say that the restraint is valid only in respect of A, but if the restraint referred to the country X, and the court felt that this was too wide, it would not restrict the restraint to some definite part of the county, as that would involve adding further words to the restraint. The court will not readily engage in a severance of a restraint where it relates to employment, as distinct from one concerned with the sale of a business.

> *Attwood* v. *Lamont.* The plaintiff was in business in Kidderminster as tailor, dressmaker, hatter, milliner, and haberdasher. The defendant was the chief cutter in the tailoring department, and he had agreed in his service contract that he would not after leaving his employment carry on the trades of tailor, dressmaker, etc., within ten miles of Kidderminster. *Held,* that the restraint was too wide, as the cutter's knowledge of his employer's business connexions was limited to the tailoring side of the business. The court refused to enforce the restraint even in regard to this trade because it felt that the purpose of the restraint was mainly to protect the employer from competition and not to protect him against the employee's abuse of information acquired during his employment.

Where a contract of employment contains a valid restraint of trade, and the employer commits a breach of the contract, the employee may, according to the general principles of the law of contract, treat the contract as discharged, and that will mean that the restraint will also cease to be applicable to him.

DUTIES OF THE EMPLOYER

The duties of the employer, in the same way as those of the employee, depend on the terms of the contract, but in the absence of any specific agreement the following duties will exist:

1. The employer must pay his servant the agreed remuneration. This means that remuneration is payable only where it has been agreed, whether expressly or impliedly. There is no implied agreement to pay a wage where a person works for a relation in a capacity which frequently is undertaken without pay. If the contract, expressly or impliedly, provides for payment, but the amount has not been fixed, the employer will have to pay a reasonable amount.

2. Generally the employer's duty is limited to the payment of wages, and the employee may not ask to be given his work in addition to receiving the pay. The employer would thus be entitled

to pay a man his wage, but insist that the employee should not come to work. There are two cases only where the non-provision of work by the employer would constitute a breach of contract on his part:

> (a) where the employee is engaged in a capacity where employment provides him not only with an income but also allows him to acquire a reputation which is essential if he is to get other employment later. This refers mainly to actors, journalists, writers, etc.

H. Clayton and J. Waller, Ltd. v. *Oliver.* An actor was engaged for a particular part in a show. The management then decided not to use him for this part, but they were prepared to pay him his agreed salary. *Held,* that in these circumstances the employers had either to provide the part or pay damages for breach of contract.

> (b) where the employee's remuneration depends on the amount of work which he is able to do for his employer.

Turner v. *Goldsmith.* An employer engaged a commercial traveller who was to be paid by way of commission for the custom introduced by him. *Held,* that the employer had to give him a reasonable opportunity to earn the commission.

3. The employer must indemnify the servant where he has incurred a liability while acting on the employer's behalf. This duty will not exist, however, where the employee knew that the act which he was doing was unlawful, or that the employer had no right to give him the order in question.

4. In principle, the employee is not entitled to a reference or testimonial. The employer is quite within his rights to refuse to give one, whether he is asked for it by the employee himself or by another employer. Where the employer does give a reference, however, he may become liable to the employee for defamation of character. The burden of proof that the statement which the employer has made was defamatory will rest on the employee. He will have to show:

> (a) that the statement was defamatory—*i.e.,* that it tended to lower his reputation in the eyes of right-thinking members of society;
>
> (b) that the statement referred to him;
>
> (c) that the statement was published—*i.e.,* that it was communicated by the person making it to at least one person other than the plaintiff himself. Where the employer hands an open reference to the employee the employee will be unable to sue for defamation, since if the statement came into the hands of a third party it must have done so through the employee's own act;

(d) where the statement was made verbally (that is to say, was slanderous), that he has either suffered some loss (*e.g.*, not obtained an appointment which he would have otherwise done), or that it imputes to him incapacity in his trade or profession or occupation. This proof is not required where the statement was made in writing—that is to say, was libellous.

If the employee can prove these four points he will succeed in his action, except where the employer is able to take advantage of one or another of the defences which are known to the law of defamation—namely:

(a) Justification. The employer could prove that the statement made was true in substance, but if he attempts to justify his statement and he fails the damages awarded against him will be higher than they would have been otherwise.
(b) A more useful defence is that of qualified privilege. This means that the statement has been made to a person who had a justifiable interest to receive it. It must have been made carefully (*e.g.*, by ensuring that it would not come to the knowledge of other parties not having such an interest) and honestly. A statement made by one employer to another would be privileged in this way. The employee can counter this defence only by showing that the employer made the statement maliciously—that is, for some motive other than that of providing honest information.

Apart from his liability to the employee for defamation of character, the employer may also be liable to the employer to whom the reference or testimonial has been addressed, but only where he made the statements knowing them to be untrue or not believing them to be true or recklessly, not caring whether they were true or not.

The property right in the testimonial (*i.e.*, in the piece of paper on which it is written) belongs to the person to whom it has been issued; to the employee where it has been given to him by his former employer, or to the employer where it has been sent to him by a former employer.

5. It is the employer's responsibility to provide for the safety of his employees. This duty is generally discussed under three headings:

(a) The duty to provide safe premises. As all the other duties which will be discussed below, the present one is not absolute. The employer is not absolutely responsible that the premises are safe in fact. All that is expected of him is that reasonable care should be taken to make the premises safe.

Latimer v. *A.E.C., Ltd.* Because of heavy rainfall a river overflowed and flooded factory premises. The flood-water got mixed with an oily cooling substance used in the factory, and when the waters subsided the floors were left in a slippery state. The management did what they could to spread sawdust and sand, but there was not enough of these, and parts of the floor had not been treated. The plaintiff slipped, and a trolley which he was pushing crushed his leg. *Held*, that the management had done what was reasonable in the circumstances. The only absolutely safe way of dealing with the emergency would have been to send every one home, but it would not have been reasonable to close down an entire factory because of a remote risk of injury.

Premises could be unsafe where the roof, the walls, or the floors are unsafe. Other examples of unsafe premises include cases of unsafe insulation or of bad ventilation of the premises.

(*b*) The employer must provide reasonably safe plant, tools, equipment, and materials. Again, all that is expected of him is to do what may be reasonably expected of him. The employer will have broken his duty under this heading where, for instance:

(i) He fails to provide suitable equipment altogether, and so compels his employees to improvise equipment;

(ii) He provides equipment but the equipment is defective. This must be so either to the knowledge of the employer or where the employer should have known about it had he undertaken a reasonable inspection of the equipment;

(iii) He fails to remedy defects in equipment which have been brought to his notice by his employees.

(*c*) The employer must provide a reasonably safe system of work. This is the most far-reaching of his safety obligations, and includes the following requirements:

(i) The employer must provide reasonably safe fellow-workers. He does not guarantee that the workers he employs are safe, but if he has reason to believe that there is a man employed by him who through negligence or intentionally may cause injuries to his fellow-workers, he should dismiss him.

Hudson v. *Ridge Manufacturing Company, Ltd.* The company employed a man who was well known for his liking for horse-play. He had been warned often about it by the management, but he had not been dismissed. On one occasion he tripped up the plaintiff, who fell and broke his wrist. *Held,* that the employers were liable because they continued employing a man who by his habitual conduct had proved to be a source of danger to his fellow-workers.

(ii) Where the work on which employees are employed is inherently dangerous the employer must devise a system which will reduce the danger to the absolute minimum. He must not be satisfied leaving it to the workmen, even if they are experienced men, to look after their own safety.

General Cleaning Contractors, Ltd. v. *Christmas.* The plaintiff was a window-cleaner employed by a company contracting to clean windows in blocks of offices. He was injured when he fell while standing on the outside of a window. This was the usual practice followed by the cleaners employed by the company. *Held,* that the employers were negligent in not devising some system of work which would avoid the danger of people falling.

While the employer must devise a safe system of doing the work and, where necessary, provide the necessary safety equipment (goggles, masks, special creams, etc.), he need not stand over an experienced worker who has been instructed in the use of the safety devices to make sure that the employee continually uses them.

Woods v. *Durable Suites, Ltd.* The plaintiff contracted dermatitis while working with synthetic glue. His employers had instructed him as to the measures to be taken to avoid dermatitis, but after a new foreman had taken over supervision had become slack. *Held,* that an employer was not bound to stand over experienced workmen of full age to see that they did what they were supposed to do.

Where the employer 'provides' safety devices he must make sure that they are available at the place where they are wanted. It is not enough that an employee could have obtained them at some distance from the place where he was working.

Finch v. *Telegraph Construction and Maintenance Company.* The plaintiff was employed in grinding metal. A fragment of metal broke off and flew into his eye. Goggles were made available by the employers, but the plaintiff had not been told where he could find them. *Held,* that the employers had failed to provide a safe system of work.

(iii) A safe system of work also includes the making of arrangements so that employees would choose the correct equipment for the particular task on which they are engaged.

Lovell v. *Blundells.* Workers who had to overhaul boiler tubes on a ship required planking. There was no one in charge to tell them where to get suitable planking. They chose some wood which they found lying about, but it was unsound, and the plaintiff was injured when it collapsed. *Held,* that the employers had not provided a reasonably safe system of work.

(iv) The general conditions in which the work is done must be suitable.

Russell v. *Criterion Film Productions, Ltd.* The plaintiff, who was a film extra in crowd scenes, suffered injuries to her eyes because she had to work under excessive lighting. *Held,* that the employers were liable.

(v) Where the safety of an employee depends on the effective co-ordination of the work of a number of departments the employers must ensure that there exists such co-ordination.

English v. *Wilson and Clyde Colliery Company, Ltd.* Workers on the morning shift in a coal-mine were about to leave the pit when the haulage system was allowed to operate. A lump of coal fell and injured the plaintiff. *Held,* that the employers had failed in their duty to ensure the co-ordination between the departments involved.

The following general comments concerning the employer's duty to provide for the safety of his servants should be noted:

1. The employer is not responsible for the state of premises which are not under his control.

Cilia v. *H.M. James and Sons.* A plumber's mate was killed by electrocution in premises in which he was helping to instal new plumbing. His death was due to a defective electrical circuit in the building. *Held,* that his employer was not in breach of his duty, since the building was not in the occupation of the employer.

2. The employer is responsible to do what in the circumstances is reasonable to provide for the safety of his servants. If he follows the normal practice in the industry he will normally have fulfilled his duty, but there are exceptions even to that. The legal position has been stated by Lord Dunedin in a much-quoted pronouncement in *Morton* v. *William Dixon, Ltd,* as follows: "Where the negligence of the employer consists of what I may call a fault of omission, I think that it is absolutely necessary that the proof of that fault of omission should be one of two kinds, either to show that the thing which he did not do was a thing which was commonly done by other persons in like circumstances, or to show that it was a thing which was so obviously wanted that it would be a folly in anyone to neglect to provide it."

This means that where the employer has failed to provide some form of safety device which could have prevented an accident the proof that it was unreasonable of him not to provide it may be based either on the fact that he was acting against the practice of his trade or that it was folly not to provide it. In other words, even where an employer has followed the practice of his trade, he may still be in breach of his duty if he acted in a way which the judge (or jury) consider to be a folly.

It should be noted, however, that Lord Dunedin's formula must not be applied slavishly. The real issue is whether the employers have done what in the circumstances is reasonable, and if the judge (or jury) are of opinion that a practice commonly followed does not provide the employee with reasonable protection, damages may be awarded to him. This was the position in a recent House of Lords case:

Cavanagh v. *Ulster Weaving Company.* The plaintiff fell while carrying a bucket of cement down a ladder on a sloping roof. Following common practice no handrail had been provided. The House of Lords refused to upset a finding by the jury in the plaintiff's favour and *held* that an existing trade practice alone was not conclusive proof that an employer had met his obligations at common law.

In deciding whether it would be folly to omit providing some form of safety device the employer must take into account, not only the likelihood of danger if the device is omitted, but also the likely gravity of injury that may be suffered, and relate these to the cost and inconvenience of providing the safety device. It would be a folly to stint on a device costing perhaps a few shillings where the omission to provide it may endanger the life of a person. On the other hand, it would be reasonable for an employer not to buy a device costing many thousands of pounds in order to rule out a one in a million chance of some one being injured.

Paris v. *Stepney Borough Council.* The defendants employed a man as a fitter in a garage. He had only one good eye, and he lost that when a piece of metal flew up from some bolts which he was hammering and entered the eye. The defendants proved that it was not the custom for goggles to be provided for persons engaged on this kind of work. *Held,* that the defendants were liable, as they should have realized the much greater risk which the plaintiff faced, and they should have taken, therefore, precautions which would be unnecessary in the case of other employees, not similarly handicapped.

3. The employer's duty to protect his employees does not extend as such to other persons, such as independent contractors, who come to work in his premises. To them he has only the same duty as any occupier has to persons coming on his land by his permission, whether expressed or implied. The Occupiers' Liability Act, 1957, states that an occupier owes to such persons a "common duty of care." This duty is defined by the Act as "a duty to take such care as in all the circumstances is reasonable to see that the visitor will be

K

reasonably safe in using the premises for the purposes for which he is invited or permitted by the occupier to be there." It stands to reason that whether or not the occupier has discharged his "common duty of care" will have to be decided on the facts of each case. The Act adds, however, that "an occupier may expect that a person, in the exercise of his calling, will appreciate and guard against any special risks ordinarily incident to it, so far as the occupier leaves him free to do so." The meaning of this clause is that where the occupier employs an expert contractor (*e.g.,* a window-cleaner) it is not the occupier's duty to guard the contractor or the contractor's men against those dangers normally incident to their work.

The Act also states that where injury is caused to a visitor through faulty execution of some work of construction, maintenance, or repair by an independent contractor employed by the occupier, the occupier will not be held responsible if (*a*) it was reasonable to entrust the work to an independent contractor and (*b*) the occupier had taken reasonable steps to satisfy himself that the contractor was competent.

Similarly, it has been held in *Davie* v. *New Merton Board Mills, Ltd,* that where the employer has to supply tools he fulfils his legal obligation by obtaining these tools from a reputable manufacturer or dealer. If the tools turn out to be defective the employer will not be liable in damages to the employee who may have been injured.

4. The employer's duty to provide for the safety of his employees extends to their persons only, and not to their personal property.

Edwards v. *West Herts Hospital Committee.* The personal property of a resident surgeon at a hospital was stolen from his room. The hospital authorities had not provided him with a key, nor was anyone on duty in the hostel where he lived to prevent strangers from getting in. *Held,* that the employers had no responsibility for the safety of personal property belonging to their employees, not even if the employee had to live in.

THE TERMINATION OF A CONTRACT OF SERVICE

A contract of service, as any other contract, will be terminated in the ways which have been already discussed in Chapter 2. Here we shall be considering only some ways of terminating this kind of contract which are peculiar to it and are not found with other contracts.

1. Unless a contract provides that it is made for life (which would be rare) it may be terminated by either party giving notice to the other. The length of notice to be given may be contained in the contract. Where this is not so the length of notice will depend on what is customary in the trade or industry in question for persons

of the employee's position. If there is no custom that can be ascertained reasonable notice will have to be given, and what that means will depend on such factors as the position occupied by the employee, the intervals at which he is being paid, and on whether the employment was or was not intended to be permanent.

2. The employer may terminate the employee's engagement by paying him his wages in lieu of notice. The employee will receive the wages for the period of notice to which he is entitled. Where in addition to money wages the employee has also been receiving benefits in kind—e.g., board and lodging, he will be entitled to the money wages only, and the employer who wishes him to leave at once is not bound to compensate him for the loss of the benefits in kind. The employee has no corresponding right to terminate his employment by paying his own wages to his employer.

3. A contract of employment may be terminated summarily by either party where the other party has been guilty of a 'total breach' of the contract by doing something which undermines the essential purpose of the contract. The following instances are the most important ones where the employer may summarily (i.e., without notice and compensation) discharge the employee:

(a) Where the employee has been guilty of serious misconduct. Misconduct means any kind of behaviour which is inconsistent with the performance of the employee's duties under the contract of employment. To specify such behaviour would be impossible, but it should be remembered that what is misconduct will largely depend on the nature of the employment and on the position occupied by the employee. The higher his position, or the more closely he comes into personal contact with the employer, the higher will be the standard of conduct that the employer may rightly expect of him. Misconduct outside working hours can be ground for summary dismissal only where it is likely to have repercussions on the usefulness of the employee to the employer.

(b) The employee may be summarily dismissed where he shows wilful disobedience to lawful orders given to him by his employer or where he is guilty of wilful negligence in the performance of his duties. Wilful neglect by the employee means that he fails to do something which he should have done, knowing very well that this neglect may have serious consequences (e.g., the cashier leaving the office without locking up the safe).

Laws v. *London Chronicle*. The plaintiff had been summarily dismissed when she followed her immediate superior, who left a meeting after a quarrel with the managing director. The managing director had ordered the plaintiff to stay. *Held,* that a single act of disobedience was insufficient to warrant summary dismissal unless in the circumstances it indicated that the employee wished to terminate the contract.

(*c*) The servant may be dismissed on the grounds of incompetence where he obtained his employment on his claim that he was capable of doing a certain kind of work. If it should be discovered that he is not capable he may be dismissed summarily. A person cannot be dismissed summarily if he is unable to perform tasks which he never claimed that he was able to perform.

(*d*) Illness is a ground for summarily terminating the servant's employment, but only where the illness has frustrated the commercial purpose of his employment. For this purpose it is necessary to consider the nature of the servant's employment (*i.e.,* whether his work could be easily done by some one else or whether it is necessary to find a substitute at once), the length of his engagement, the time which has elapsed since the engagement started, and the expected duration of his illness. It is not often that the court will find that illness has frustrated the commercial purpose of a contract of service.

Storey v. *Fulham Steel Works Company.* A works manager employed on a five-year contract fell ill after two years and was away from work for five months. After four months the employers informed him that his services would no longer be required. *Held,* that in the circumstances the employers had no right to treat the contract as discharged.

This may be a suitable place for a general discussion of the effects of illness on contracts of service. It must be pointed out at once that the law is in a rather unsettled state, and that some of the authorities at our disposal are directly conflicting, but the position appears to be as follows:

(i) The contract of service may contain express provisions as to the effects of illness, particularly as far as the employee's right to payment is concerned.

(ii) If the contract is silent there may still be a custom in the trade or industry from which help could be obtained.

(iii) In the absence of express agreement or custom, the employee's right to be paid during sickness appears to be undeniable, except where the court is prepared to imply in the contract of employment that wages should not be payable.

Orman v. *Saville Sportswear, Ltd.* The plaintiff, who was acting as production manager in the defendants' skirt factory, had been off work for some ten weeks. *Held,* that a term could be implied in the contract only if the issue was one which was so obvious that the parties did not bother to mention it. As it could not be argued that the plaintiff would have agreed to lose his pay during illness if the matter had been raised when he contracted to work for the company, no term to that effect could now be implied.

It is sometimes suggested that a term ruling out payment during sickness will be implied in a contract of service where the consideration for the pay is the *actual performance* of work rather than the mere *willingness* to work. The difficulty rests, of course, in deciding under which heading a particular contract falls. It would probably be true to say that piece-workers and hourly paid workers will not be entitled to payment during absence from work, but in view of the decision in *Orman's case* even this may be open to doubt.

(iv) The fact that the employee is drawing sickness benefit, whether under the national insurance scheme or from a friendly society, has by itself no bearing on his right to pay. If he is entitled to pay, then, in the absence of a definite agreement to the contrary, he may claim his pay in addition to the sickness benefit. It is for this reason that most employers who pay wages during sickness insert a clause in service contracts that they will only make up a man's pay by supplementing the sickness benefit which he may be receiving.

(e) The employer will also be entitled to discharge the employee summarily where for some other reason it has become impossible for the employee to perform the duties of his employment—for instance, because of his having been sentenced to a term of imprisonment.

The position of the employee is in many ways similar to that of the employer. The employee may also in certain circumstances treat the contract of service as discharged and leave his employment without giving notice. Naturally, not all the reasons for which the employer may treat a contract of service as discharged will apply also to employees. The main reasons applying to employees will be:

(a) The employer's misconduct, such as where an employer has made improper advances to a female employee.

(b) The employee's own sickness would entitle him to treat the contract as discharged if he could not continue the employment without serious danger to his health.

(c) The wilful neglect of the employer to carry out his duties under the contract of service, such as paying the employee's wages at the agreed time or making the requisite provision for the employee's safety.

4. The death of either party will terminate a contract of service.

5. Where an employee is employed by a partnership the dissolution of the partnership or a change in the persons of the partners will be a breach of contract as far as the employee is concerned. This will entitle him to claim damages from the partnership, but, on the principle of minimization of loss, if the new partners or the persons continuing the partnership business offer him re-engagement on his old terms of employment he could refuse re-engagement only at the risk of being awarded no substantial damages. Similarly, the compulsory liquidation of a company operates as a dismissal of all employees, though the liquidator may offer re-engagement to some or all of them. If they accept re-engagement they will now be employed by the liquidator, and their pay will be part of the liquidation costs. A resolution of the shareholders for the voluntary liquidation of a company does not operate as a notice of dismissal to the employees.

The fact that an employer has sold the business does not mean that the contracts of service with his employees will have become discharged, and the employees will be entitled to pay for the period of their contractual notice. Whether or not they will in addition be entitled to damages for the employer's failure to provide them with work will depend on considerations which have been discussed already. The employer who sells a business cannot assign the benefit of the contracts of service with his employees to the buyer of the business, as a contract of service, being a contract of a personal nature, is not assignable.

Nokes v. *Doncaster Amalgamated Collieries, Ltd.* Two colliery companies had been amalgamated, with the effect that all the assets, liabilities, duties, etc., of one had been transferred to the other. N. had been employed by the company which had been merged into the other. He absented himself from work, which would represent a breach of contract if he had become an employee of the new company. *Held,* that his contract of employment had not been automatically transferred by the merger of the two companies.

REMEDIES FOR BREACH OF CONTRACT OF SERVICE

1. The main remedy for the breach of a contract of service is a claim for damages. Where the employee has been unjustifiably dismissed he may claim damages from the employer. The damages will not be restricted to the amount of pay which he would have received if he had been given the appropriate notice. If his loss has been larger he may claim more than the mere wages, but, of course, he must try to minimize his loss by accepting suitable alternative employment if it is offered to him. The dismissed employee is not entitled to damages for the hurt to his feelings where he has been

peremptorily dismissed without a good reason. The employer has similar rights against the employee where it is the employee who has broken the contract, but an employer cannot sue an infant apprentice, though the apprentice's father or guardian could be sued, if he has been made a party to the contract.

2. Neither party will be able to obtain a decree for the specific performance of a contract of service, as such a decree is never granted in respect of a contract of a personal nature. The employer may, however, get an injunction against an employee who is breaking a promise in his contract of service, such as by working for another employer.

> *Lumley* v. *Wagner.* A theatrical promoter had engaged a German opera singer to appear exclusively in his opera performances. The singer was about to break this agreement by appearing in an opera staged by a competitor. *Held,* that the promoter was entitled to an injunction both against the singer and against the rival promoter.

It is an essential condition for the granting of an injunction that the contract which is to be enforced in this way should have contained a clause expressed in negative terms. Thus, where A promises to work for B and then goes to work for C, B will not be able to get an injunction to restrain him, though he could recover, of course, damages for breach of contract. If, however, A promises to work for B, and for no one else, B could get an injunction if A should start working for C. As with all other remedies of equity, an injunction is discretionary, and the court will award it only if in the circumstances it appears a fair thing to do.

3. Where the employee has broken a term of his contract the employer may, if the breach of contract is a 'total' one, treat the contract as discharged, and dismiss the employee summarily. The details of this remedy have been discussed already. In the absence of any agreement or of a trade custom he may not, however, 'suspend' the employee, in the sense of telling the employee that his services will not be required for a certain time (*e.g.*, three days), and that he will not be paid for this time. Where the accepted custom of a firm is to suspend workers for certain breaches of discipline a worker who enters the employment of that firm will be deemed to have done so subject to accepting the possibility of suspension if he should commit a breach of his service contract.

4. Breaches of contracts of apprenticeship may be dealt with by the court of summary jurisdiction (the court of magistrates) under the provisions of the Employers and Workmen Act, 1875. The court may in appropriate cases order that the apprenticeship agreement should be rescinded, and where the apprentice has paid a

premium the repayment of part or all of the premium may also be ordered. The court may instruct the apprentice to carry out his side of the bargain, and where he wilfully refuses to do so he may be sent to prison. It should be noted, however, that the jurisdiction of the court of summary jurisdiction extends to apprenticeship agreements only where the premium does not exceed £25.

5. Where a person has rendered services to another in circumstances where it was understood that the services would be paid for, but there was no valid contract in existence between the parties, the employee will be entitled to a *quantum meruit* (Latin for 'as much as he deserves')—*i.e.*, he will be entitled to the payment of a reasonable sum. This applies also where the employee was to be paid for the completion of a certain task, but he was unable to complete it because of the fault of his employer. In that case he cannot claim the agreed reward, because that would have become due only on the completion of the task, but he may claim payment for what he has done already.

THE MASTER'S LIABILITY FOR THE WRONGFUL ACTS OF HIS SERVANT

Where the employee by his wrongful (tortious) act has caused damage or injury to a third party the third party will, of course, be entitled to claim damages from the servant. In addition, however, the third party may also claim damages from the employer where the employer is vicariously responsible for the act of the servant. This is an important right of the third party, as the servant may well be financially unable to satisfy the court award of damages, while the master is usually in a financially sounder position to do so. The master's liability may arise under one of the following two headings:

1. Where the master has expressly authorized the servant's wrongful act. In this case the master is not really vicariously responsible for the servant's wrong; he is responsible for his own wrong in issuing the wrongful instructions to the servant.

2. Where the master has not instructed the servant to do the wrongful act, but the servant has committed it while acting in the course of his employment. Much has been written about the nature of the master's liability in these circumstances. Some writers assume that the master is liable because he has impliedly authorized the servant to do all those things which are connected with his employment. This is hardly the right way of dealing with the problem, since it is accepted that the master is responsible also for such acts of the servant done in the course of his employment which the master has expressly instructed him not to do. The better view appears to be that the master is responsible for the servant's act, because by

employing him he has made it possible for him to commit the wrongful act, so that the financial consequences of the servant's wrong should be treated as part of the overall costs of the employer which the employer will cover by insurance.

The real question is, then, what is meant by 'acting in the course of his employment.' The master is responsible for the acts of the servant where the servant has done something which he is employed to do, even though he has done it in a wrongful manner.

L.C.C. v. *Cattermoles Garages, Ltd.* The garage proprietors employed X as a garage hand. His duties included the pushing away of cars which blocked the entrance to the garage. As X did not possess a driving licence, he was instructed to push by hand only, and not to drive offending vehicles. On one occasion, however, he got into a car and drove it on to the highway with a view to parking it elsewhere. On the highway he collided with a vehicle belonging to the L.C.C. *Held,* that his employers were liable for the damage, as he had done what he was employed to do, although he was doing it in an unauthorized manner.

Where the employee does something for his own benefit which he is not actually employed to do, even though his employers may have consented to his doing it, and causes damage to a third party, the employers will not be liable.

Crook v. *Derbyshire Stone, Ltd.* A lorry-driver employed by the defendants in the transport of stone was allowed by them to break his journey for refreshments. He stopped the lorry opposite a road café, and while crossing the road was involved in a collision with a motor-cyclist, the plaintiff, as a result of which the plaintiff suffered injuries. It was not denied that the collision was due to the driver's fault. *Held,* that the employers were not liable, as the act of the employee (crossing the road in search of refreshments), although tolerated by his employers, was not part of his duties of employment.

Warren v. *Henlys, Ltd.* The plaintiff suffered injuries when assaulted by a pump attendant employed by the defendants with whom he had quarrelled about payment. *Held,* that the defendants were not liable, as the employee was acting outside the scope of his employment when he engaged in fisticuffs with a customer.

If, however, the employee does something which he is employed to do it does not matter:

(1) that he was acting against express instructions of his employer.

Limpus v. *London General Omnibus Company.* The omnibus company had expressly forbidden their drivers to race other buses through the streets of London. One of their drivers disregarded these instructions, and when taking a corner at high speed upset the plaintiff's bus. *Held,* that the employers were liable because the driver was doing what he was employed to do—namely, driving a bus—even though he was doing it in an unauthorized manner.

(2) that he was committing a criminal offence.

Lloyd v. *Grace, Smith, and Company.* The managing clerk in a solicitors' office instructed a client, an old lady, to sign certain papers. By doing so she was transferring some of her property to the clerk, though she did not, of course, realize that at the time. *Held,* that the solicitors were liable in damages for the act of their managing clerk as he was doing what he was employed to do—namely, advise a client—though his motive was to enrich himself at the client's expense. The clerk was, of course, liable to a criminal prosecution.

LIABILITY OF THIRD PARTIES TO THE EMPLOYER

The general rule of law is that the existence of a contract between A and B does not concern C, who does not acquire any rights, or become subject to any liabilities, on a contract to which he has not been a party.

The existence of such a contract is, however, of some importance, in that it is wrong for the third party to interfere in it without legal justification. In particular, the third party would be liable to the employer in damages in the following cases:

1. Where he causes injury to the servant, and thus deprives the employer of the servant's services. The right of action of the employer is independent of the employee's own right to sue for the injuries which he has suffered. Naturally, the third party will be liable only if the causing of the injury has either been a tort (a wrongful act) or if it has constituted a breach of contract made between the employer and the third party. The damages which the employer could claim would compensate him for his personal loss in the shape of the wages which he had to pay to the servant during his illness, or in the loss of business which he might have suffered where the employee was irreplaceable. No action would lie, however, where the employee has been killed, because of an old rule of common law that no action will arise out of the death of a human being. This principle will be further discussed in Chapter 12.

The action which we are discussing here is in many ways anomalous under modern conditions, and courts to-day will not readily grant damages to the employer under this heading.

Inland Revenue Commissioners v. *Hambrook.* An established civil servant was injured in a motor accident caused by the negligent driving of the defendant. The civil servant was off work for ten months, during which time he was paid his full salary. The Inland

Revenue Commissioners sued the defendant for damages. *Held*, that the action could not succeed, because it lay only where the servant could be regarded as a member of the employer's household, a menial servant, and not in respect of other employees.

It appears, then, that the action will lie to-day only in respect of employees giving personal services. In practice it is employed to-day where a married woman is injured and her husband claims damages from the party responsible for the loss of his wife's personal services, even though these services are not rendered by her on a contractual basis.

2. It is an actionable wrong for a third party without justification to induce a servant to break his contract of employment. A clear distinction must be drawn between an inducement to break a contract of employment and one to terminate a contract by proper notice, or not to enter into a contract at all. Inducing a servant not to enter into a contract or to terminate a contract by proper notice is actionable by the employer thus deprived of the employee's services only where unlawful means have been used to persuade him, such as violence or threats.

A person who induces a servant to break a contract of employment will be liable in damages where he acted with knowledge of the existence of the contract, and where he had no justification for acting in this way. Self-interest would be no justification, but where the third party acted in pursuance of a moral, social, or legal duty he would not be liable to the employer. Thus, a father may persuade his daughter to leave a job where he fears her morals might be in danger, and a similar persuasion might also be justifiable if used by a trade union official.

3. It has been shown already that inducing a person not to enter into a contract of service, or to terminate his contract by proper notice, is actionable only if it has been done by unlawful means. It is, however, one of the features of English law that where a number of persons combine to do something which will cause harm to another party they will be guilty of the tort of conspiracy even though the means which they have employed would have been perfectly legal if pursued by one person acting on his own. Thus, if I threaten that I shall not talk to Bill Jones again unless he quits his job with Charles Brown, and Jones does quit in fact, Brown will have no action against me. If the warning to Jones has been issued, however, by a number of persons acting in combination this would be conspiracy, and Brown would have an action against every one of the persons participating in the agreement. Naturally, this situation is one which is likely to arise fairly often when trade unions or other representatives of workmen wish to exercise pressure on an

employer. Here we shall be discussing only the attitude to such action as shown by the common law; the special position prevailing under the trade union legislation will be discussed in Chapter 15.

The original stringency of the law has been much softened by developments during the last century, and the position as it prevails to-day is best illustrated by the statement of the law given by Lord Cave in *Sorrell* v. *Smith.* Lord Cave laid down two rules:

1. A combination of two or more persons wilfully to injure a man in his trade is unlawful, and if it results in damage to him is actionable.

2. If the real purpose of the combination is not to injure another but to forward or defend the trade of those who enter into it, then no wrong is committed, and no action will lie, although damage to another ensues.

Everything depends, then, on the predominating motive of those who entered into the combination. If they acted out of personal spite the combination will be actionable, but if they intended mainly to protect their own interests the combination will not be actionable.

Crofters Hand-woven Harris Tweed Company v. *Veitch.* The island of Lewis is a centre of cloth-weaving. The yarn used for this purpose is either imported from the mainland of Scotland or it is spun on the island. The large mills used yarn which was spun on the island, while the crofters used imported yarn. The workers employed in the mills were asking for higher wages, but their employers were able to satisfy them that they could not be paid more, as the cloth would otherwise be under-sold by that produced by the crofters. The mill-workers were members of a union to which also belonged the dockers handling imported goods. The defendants, who were officials of the union, persuaded the dockers not to handle any further supplies of imported yarn, and the crofters' organization sued them for conspiracy. *Held,* that the defendants were not liable, because their action was motivated by their desire to protect the living standards of their members.

A more recent decision has shown that procurement of a breach of contract will be actionable only if the defendant, with knowledge of the existence of a contract, directly induced a breach of it.

D. C. Thomson and Company, Ltd. v. *Deakin and others.* A dispute had arisen between the plaintiff company and some of its employees about a work rule by which employees were restrained from becoming members of trade unions. The union which wished to organize the plaintiffs' employees appealed for help to other unions, among them the union of which the first defendant was the general secretary. He agreed that all possible help should be given. Local officials of D.'s union intimated to a paper manufacturer who supplied the plaintiffs under contract with paper that a difficult situation might arise if their members—lorry-drivers—were to be instructed to deliver paper to a place which had been declared 'black.' The manufacturer decided to stop further paper deliveries to the plaintiffs. Subsequently, the lorry-drivers voted not to carry any paper to the plaintiffs. The plaintiffs asked for an injunction to prevent the trade union officials from interfering with their contract for the supply of paper. *Held*, that the injunction could not be granted, since the manufacturer had himself decided to break the contract without having been unequivocally persuaded to do so by the defendants.

4. It is an actionable wrong for a third party to 'harbour an employee' who has broken his contract of employment with an employer. Harbouring an employee means employing him with knowledge of the existence of his previous contract of employment, and of the fact that he has broken it. This wrong is committed when the new employer either knows of the breach when he engages the employee or finds out about it later and continues the employment of the employee. In order for the action to lie the former employer must prove, however, that he has suffered a loss as a result of the harbouring of his ex-employee.

Jones Bros. (Hunstanton), Ltd. v. *Stevens.* A fish-frier employed by the plaintiffs had decided for personal reasons that he did not wish to work for them any longer under any circumstances. He obtained employment with the defendant as an assistant cook. The defendant found out later that his cook had left his previous employment without notice, but he continued to employ him. *Held,* that the action failed as the plaintiff had not suffered a loss through the defendant's action, the court being satisfied that his employee would not have returned to him even if the defendant had not given him employment.

CHAPTER TEN

STATUTORY CONTROL OF WAGES

INTRODUCTION

THE fixing of wages is left in general to the process of bargaining between the employer on the one hand and the employee, or his union or professional organization, on the other. It is only in those cases—nowadays fortunately rare—where Parliament believes that employers might take advantage of the bargaining weakness of their employees that statutes have had to be passed to control the process of wage-determination. With the growing strength of trade unionism in this country the need for such measures has declined, and it is perhaps not wrong to assume that many of the measures discussed in this chapter will be abolished or amended in our own lifetime.

The four main problems to which legislation has addressed itself are that of the form of wage-payment; the amount of wages payable; the conditions under which deductions from wages are to be permissible; and the ascertainment of the amount payable by way of wages.

THE TRUCK ACTS

By the term 'truck' we understand the payment of wages in kind, a practice which is reprehensible, because it forces the wage-earners to find buyers for the wage goods before being able to spend their wages. Buyers may often be found only by offering the goods at lower prices, thus leading to a reduction of the real wages earned. The first-known attempts by Parliament to deal with the problem of truck date back to the fifteenth century, but the modern law is based on the Truck Acts, 1831, 1887, 1896, and 1940 as amended by the Payment of Wages Act, 1960.

The main purpose of the Truck Act, 1831, was to prevent the payment of wages in kind, and to make illegal the operation of 'tommy shops'—i.e., shops owned by employers where their workers were compelled to spend part of their wages. The effect of the 1887 Act was to extend the classes of persons to whom the Truck Acts were to apply. The 1896 Act made provision for deductions from wages on account of fines or of bad workmanship. Lastly, the 1940 Act was passed in order to fill a gap in the law discovered in the House of Lords decision in *Pratt* v. *Cook*. In the following we shall describe the law as it exists to-day, without referring specifically to its historical development.

The Truck Acts do not apply to all employees, but only to 'work-men' as defined in Section 10 of the Employers and Workmen Act, 1875. The essence of the definition is that a 'workman' must be a servant engaged in *manual* labour. Domestic or menial servants are specifically excluded from the application of the Acts. The definition refers to manual *labour*, not to manual *work*, and this means that the employment in question must be one requiring some physical effort, and not just involve working with one's hands. There exists a wealth of case law as to who is to be included under the definition. The following have been held to be 'workmen': framework-knitters, a bus-driver who was also responsible for making repairs to the vehicle, a packer in a warehouse, a girl working a sewing-machine and responsible also for ironing dresses. On the other hand, the following occupations have been held not to be those of 'workmen': professional footballers, bus conductors, hairdressers, and grocers' assistants. It can be readily seen that the line of demarcation is by no means a clear-cut one.

Domestic or menial servants are those whose main function is that of catering for the personal comfort or personal wants of people in a household or residential establishment.

Cameron v. *Royal Ophthalmic Hospital.* A stoker employed by a hospital to look after its central heating system was *held* to be a domestic servant for the purposes of the Truck Acts.

The Truck Acts provide that a contract of service between an employer and a 'workman' is illegal if it allows the payment of wages in any form other than in legal tender, or if it imposes any condi-tions on the workman as to where or how he should spend his wages. Where the contract itself contains no such provision, but the em-ployer has paid part or all of the workman's wages in any other form (whether or not the workman agreed), such payment will be null and void, and the workman may ask to be paid again in legal tender. The employer cannot in such a case make any charge for the goods which he has supplied in an attempted part-payment of the workman's wages.

While, in general, the payment of wages in kind is illegal, there exists an exception in favour of agricultural workers. Farmers may supply their farm-workers with food and drink (not intoxicating), a cottage, and similar allowances in addition to a money wage. This wage must not be less than the minimum laid down by the Agricul-tural Wages Board, though deductions may be made for the fair value of the benefits in kind received by the farm-worker.

The 1887 Act makes provision for the practice of 'subbing'—*i.e.*, the making of advances on wages. Whenever a workman is entitled by agreement or custom to receive an advance on his wages in anticipation of the payment of the full amount it would be illegal for the employer to withhold such an advance or to impose any charge for making it.

Originally, under the 1831 Act, the only deductions from a workman's wages that were permissible were those in respect of medicine and medical attendance; fuel; materials and tools provided by the employer; the rent of a house let by the employer to the workman; and for meals prepared and consumed on the employer's premises. Some of these deductions will now be obsolete. The deductions for fuel, tools, and materials apply only to workmen engaged in mining. As far as the deduction of rent is concerned, the employer may deduct it only if the house is occupied by the worker himself.

> *Penman* v. *Fife Coal Company.* P.'s father, a retired miner living in a house belonging to his former employers, was in danger of eviction because of non-payment of rent. P. agreed with his employers, who owned the house, that he would pay his father's rent, and that it should be deducted from his wages. *Held,* that the deduction was an unlawful one.

In all the cases mentioned above, in addition to the deduction being one for the named purposes, it must also be based on a written agreement, signed by the workman, consenting to the deductions. This applies also to deductions for meals prepared and consumed on the employer's premises. Doubts had existed whether this was so, but the matter has now been settled by the Truck Act, 1940.

There is nothing in the Truck Acts to prevent a workman from asking his employer to make deductions from his wages in favour of a third party—*i.e.,* some person other than the employer himself.

> *Hewlett* v. *Allen.* An agreement by a workman to have 2½d. weekly deducted from his wages in favour of a sick club was *held* to be valid.

Thus, we find sometimes workmen asking their employers to make deductions in favour of their wives, where they are under an obligation to pay a separation allowance to them. Similarly, workmen might ask their employers to deduct trade union subscriptions from the wages. A written agreement would, however, be required in all these cases.

The general rule being that an employer may not deduct anything from the workman's wages (subject to the above exceptions), the employer may not even deduct wages which he has over-paid in a past period. Where such over-payments have taken place the employer may ask for the return of the money, and if the workman refuses the employer would have to sue him. Deductions in favour of employees' clubs are permissible if these clubs are entirely independent of the employer (Shop Clubs Act, 1902). If the club is one run or controlled by the employer the deduction of a workman's contribution from his wages would infringe the Truck Acts.

There is nothing to prevent the employer from paying bonuses to such workmen who comply with the conditions (*e.g.*, those concerning regular attendance) laid down by the employer. If the workmen do not comply the bonus will not be paid, but this is not a 'deduction' from wages, as the bonus has never been earned. Should, however, certain bonuses be paid regularly (*e.g.*, Christmas bonuses), the bonus may become an implied part of the workmen's wages, and its non-payment would then constitute an illegal deduction. Where such bonuses have become established as regular payments they would also have to be paid in legal tender and not in kind, such as in the shares of the employing company.

The workman may always enter into an independent contract with his employer for the purchase of goods or shares or anything else, provided he is not compelled by his contract of service to do so, and provided that any payments due from him are not directly deducted from his wages.

Deductions from wages by way of fines or for bad workmanship are governed by the 1896 Act. As far as fines are concerned, the Act applies also to shop assistants, who do not otherwise come under the heading of 'workmen.' A fine may be deducted only where there either exists a written agreement with the workman providing for this or where the employer has publicized the fact that he intends to charge fines by means of a notice clearly exhibited in the workroom where the workmen in question are working. Some employers who are in the habit of handing out works rule-books (containing the terms of the contract of service, apart from other information) to new employees insert a detachable sheet in the book, and the employee is requested to sign and return the statement appearing there that he agrees to the deduction of the fines for the disciplinary offences which are detailed in the handbook. It is important that the agreement or notice specifies the acts or omissions for which fines will be imposed, and that these acts or omissions are such as are likely to cause loss or damage to the employer, or as will hamper the conduct of his business. The amount of a fine must be fair and reasonable, having regard to the circumstances of the case, and written particulars of the fine must be given to the workman when it is imposed. Similar provisions apply also to the making of deductions for spoilt work or damaged goods, except that the deduction must not exceed the actual or estimated damage or loss caused to the employer by the act or omission of the workman.

L

An employer who enters into a contract with a workman, where the contract is proved to be illegal under the Truck Acts, or who makes a payment of wages otherwise than in the form of legal tender, or who makes any illegal deduction from a workman's wages, is guilty of an offence, and will be liable on conviction to a fine. In addition to the fine, the workman may also recover from the employer any part of his wages which has not been paid in legal tender. The provisions of the Limitation Act, 1939, apply to the recovery of wages paid in kind, so that the action has to be brought within six years from the date when payment was due. Where illegal deductions from wages have been made proceedings must be taken within six months from the date of the deduction (Truck Act, 1896). Where the workman has consented to or acquiesced in the deduction he will be able to recover only the excess of what has been deducted over the amount which, in the opinion of the court, would have been fair and reasonable in the circumstances. If there has been no acquiescence the full deduction may be recovered.

The enforcement of the provisions of the Truck Acts is the responsibility of the Factories and Mines Inspectors, who may institute criminal proceedings against offending employers. The inspectors are entitled to demand the production of any contracts in writing entered into with workmen providing for the making of deductions. Where such deductions have been made details must be recorded in a register of fines, and these registers are also open to inspection by the inspectors.

THE PAYMENT OF WAGES ACT, 1960

The Truck Acts prohibit the payment of wages in any form other than legal tender. The 1831 Act permitted the payment of wages by bearer cheque, provided that it was drawn on a bank within a radius of fifteen miles from the place of payment. The worker had to be in agreement, and the bank had to be one entitled to issue its own notes. Since such banks have now disappeared, this provision had in fact become obsolete.

The economic condition of workers has improved to such an extent that many of them have their own bank accounts, and the application of the rigid rule demanding payment of wages in legal tender had become an obstacle to increased mechanization in the wages departments of large companies. In addition, the weekly movement of large sums of money from the banks to the employers has dangers of its own which need hardly be elaborated. In order to simplify the legal position, while still retaining an essential protection of the worker's rights, the Payment of Wages Act was passed in 1960.

The Act provides that an employer may, at the written request of a worker, employ any of the following methods of wage payment:

1. Payment into a bank account or an account with a savings bank standing in the name of the worker.

2. Payment by postal or money order.

3. Payment by cheque made payable to the worker. This method of payment will not become permissible until a date to be fixed by the Minister of Labour.

No special deduction may be made from the wages as a consideration for using any of the above methods of payment. The worker must also be given at the time of payment a written statement detailing his gross pay and any deductions made from it. Fixed deductions, which do not change from week to week (*e.g.*, national insurance contributions), may be shown each week as a single deduction without having to be individually specified.

Irrespective of whether the employee has consented to his wages being paid in one of the forms mentioned above, the employer is entitled to post the wages to the employee by money order or postal order (but not in the form of a cheque) where the employee is absent from work due to sickness or injury or where he is working away from the place where wage payment would normally take place. The employee must, however, be sent a written statement specifying the way in which his wages have been calculated. The employer is not entitled to use this method of wage payment where the employee has given written notice to him that he does not wish his wages paid in the aforesaid manner.

It should be noted that the Payment of Wages Act applies to those workers only to whom the Truck Acts apply. (See page 159).

The Ascertainment of Wages

The ascertainment of wages represents a special problem in those industries where workers are paid by results, and where doubts may exist in their minds as to whether they have been fully credited with the results of their work. Special provisions exist in all branches of the mining industry to meet this situation, and these provisions have also been extended to some other industries by the Checkweighing in Various Industries Act, 1919. This Act applies to the following four industries:

(1) the production and manufacture of iron and steel;

(2) the loading and unloading of goods from or into vessels;

(3) the getting of chalk or limestone from quarries;

(4) the manufacture of cement and lime.

The Minister of Labour and National Service may, by regulations, extend the provisions of the Act also to other industries, but no regulations have been made so far.

The main effect of the Act is that the workers employed in the named industries, in so far as they are paid by results, may appoint checkweighers to check the weights used by their employers, and to be present at the process of weighing. The checkweigher, who is paid by the workmen on whose behalf he is acting, must be accorded facilities by the employer to be present when the weighing is done. It would be an offence for the employer to prevent the checkweigher from doing his job, but the checkweigher for his part must not interfere with the weighing itself, or with the general conduct of the employer's operations. The employer cannot remove or dismiss a checkweigher, but if he believes that a checkweigher has exceeded his authority, and has impeded work or has done anything else to the detriment of the employer, the employer can complain to a court of summary jurisdiction who may order the removal of the checkweigher.

Where the majority of the workmen paid according to output agree the employer may deduct from their wages their contributions towards the payment of the checkweigher without committing thereby an offence under the Truck Acts.

WAGES COUNCILS

Wages councils, as introduced by the Wages Councils Act, 1945, are the successors of the trade boards which were set up for the first time in 1909 for the purpose of fixing minimum wages in the so-called 'sweated trades.' On the passing of the 1945 Act all the existing 52 trade boards became automatically wages councils. The law relating to wages councils has now been consolidated in the Wages Councils Act, 1959.

New wages councils may be set up by the Minister of Labour and National Service by means of a 'wages council order.' The Minister will make such an order if he is of opinion that no adequate machinery exists in the industry or trade concerned for the effective regulation of the remuneration of workers engaged in it, and if he considers in the circumstances the establishment of a wages council to be expedient. An application may be made to the Minister for the creation of a new wages council, either by a joint industrial council or similar joint body in the industry or, jointly, by organizations of employers and workers which claim to be habitually participating in wage bargaining in the industry. The ground for an application must be the present or future inadequacy of the existing negotiating machinery. On receiving the application the Minister has to decide whether the applicants are truly representative bodies of employers and workers. If he has doubts about this he may either reject the application or ask other organizations in the industry for their observations before proceeding further. When he is satisfied that the application is supported by a fair proportion of the employers and workers in the industry the Minister will refer the application to a commission of inquiry whose task it is to investigate the situation in the industry. If the commission feel that a case has been made out for the establishment of a new wages council they will address a 'wages council recommendation' to the Minister.

The Minister may seek the commission's advice even where no application has been received from the two sides in the industry, provided he feels that industrial relations in the industry would benefit from the appointment of a wages council. Before making a 'wages council order' the Minister has to publish the proposed order in draft form, and invite observations from interested parties. A time limit for the receipt of these will be fixed, and the Minister will make the order only after having considered such communications as he may have received.

The Minister may, by order, dissolve an existing council if he believes that the need for it no longer exists, and he may also in a similar fashion vary an existing order—*e.g.*, by altering the constitution of the council.

A separate council is appointed for each trade or industry in respect of which a wages council order has been made. The exact composition of each council is outlined in the order establishing it, but it always consists of an equal number of persons representing employers' and workers' interests respectively, together with three independent members, one of whom is appointed chairman of the council. All members of each council are appointed by the Minister, who will, when considering the selection of the representative members, seek the advice of the most important workers' and employers' organizations in the trade or industry.

The functions of a wages council include the making of proposals to the Minister as to:

1. The remuneration to be paid by employers to workers in the industry, either generally or for particular work. Special rates may be fixed for male and female workers, for young workers and for learners, and also for workers employed in different parts of the country.

2. Holidays and holiday remuneration of workers employed in the industry.

The council may also consider and report on any other matter (*e.g.*, the payment of guaranteed wages) concerning the conditions prevailing in the industry if asked to do so by the Minister.

It should be noted that a wages council does not actually fix wages. What it does is to submit proposals ('wages regulation proposals') to the Minister, who will either refer the proposals back to the council for reconsideration or will make a wages regulation order, giving statutory effect to them The Minister may not make an order deviating from the proposals.

The council will arrive at their proposals after conducting such investigations as they deem necessary. Before submitting proposals to the Minister, notice of the proposals must be given to all known employers in the industry, who will have to post a copy of the proposals at some convenient place in their works where it may be studied by their employees. A notice of the proposals is also inserted in the *London Gazette*. A period is fixed within which employers and workmen may submit representations to the council. These representations will be further considered by the council at another meeting, and the original proposals will then be either approved or amended, and the final draft is then sent to the Minister.

The proposals of a wages council are decided upon by a majority of votes, and as the employers' and workers' representatives are equal in numbers, the independent members possess, in fact, a casting vote.

When the Minister has made an order fixing wages or holidays in a specified industry it will be an offence for any employer in that trade or industry to pay less or to allow shorter holidays. The Minister appoints special officers (wages inspectors) to see that the provisions of the Act are complied with. These officers may start criminal proceedings against defaulting employers (who are liable to a fine of up to £20), and they may also take action in a civil court on behalf of a worker for the recovery of underpaid wages. Employers must keep records about their wage payments, which must be open to inspections by the officers of the Ministry.

In some cases workers suffering from some physical or mental infirmity would find it impossible to secure employment if their employers had to pay them full wages. An employer of such a handicapped person may apply to the appropriate wages council for a permit to employ him at a lower wage. Where this is granted it is limited to the specified worker, and is given for a limited period only.

No deductions may be made from the wages fixed by the Ministerial order, except for the following purposes:

(1) deduction of income tax under the P.A.Y.E. scheme;
(2) for contributions under the national insurance scheme;

STATUTORY CONTROL OF WAGES 167

(3) at the written request of the worker for contributions to superannuation or thrift schemes, or for any other purpose in which the employer has no beneficial interest;

(4) under a written contract as provided for in the Truck Act, 1896.

OTHER FORMS OF STATUTORY WAGE REGULATION

The Catering Wages Act, 1943, provided for the setting up of a Catering Wages Commission. The functions of the commission, whose members were appointed by the Minister of Labour and National Service, included the making of inquiries into the existing arrangements in the catering industry for the regulation of remuneration and of working conditions of persons employed in the industry. If the existing facilities were considered to be inadequate the commission could recommend to the Minister that a wages board be set up with powers similar to those of a wages council. Five wages boards were set up to cover five branches of the catering industry. The Terms and Conditions of Employment Act, 1959 converted these wages boards into wages councils.

Agricultural wages are fixed by the Agricultural Wages Board for England and Wales. The board also determines what holidays should be given to agricultural workers. There exist separate agricultural wages committees for the various counties, but their functions are limited to-day to the granting of exemption permits to handicapped workers, the valuation of cottages provided in part-payment of wages, and similar matters.

THE FAIR WAGES CLAUSE

Our discussion of official wage control would be incomplete if no mention were made of the Fair Wages Resolution of the House of Commons. The resolution was first passed in 1891, at a time when 'sweated labour' was still a serious social problem. The resolution was intended to ensure that at least one class of employers—namely, Government contractors—should pay 'current wages.' It was hoped that this would not only help directly to raise certain sub-standard wage rates, but that it would also serve as an example to be followed by other employers. The House of Commons resolved, therefore, that it was the duty of all Government departments to insert certain conditions (fair wage clauses) in contracts handed out by them to contractors.

The original resolution was amended in 1909, and again in 1937, and was replaced eventually by a resolution adopted by the House on October 14, 1946, which is still in force. This resolution demands that fair wage clauses should be inserted in all Government contracts, and that these clauses should provide that:

1. The contractors should pay rates of wages and observe hours and conditions of labour not less favourable than those commonly accepted in the district where the work is to be carried out. If there are no such commonly accepted conditions the contractor should grant terms of employment equal at least to those observed by other employers in the industry whose general circumstances are similar to his.

2. The contractor must comply with the provisions of the clause in respect of all his employees, and not merely those directly engaged on the Government contract. Before being placed on the list of firms invited to tender for Government contracts, the contractor must satisfy the department concerned that he has complied with the conditions stated above for at least the preceding three months.

3. The contractor must recognize the freedom of his work-people to be members of trade unions.

4. A copy of the resolution must be displayed in every workplace used by the contractor during the continuance of the contract.

5. The contractor must also accept responsibility for the observance of the resolution by sub-contractors employed by him in the execution of the contract.

Should any question arise as to the observance of the terms of the resolution the matter, unless it has been disposed of otherwise, must be referred by the Minister of Labour and National Service, acting on behalf of the Government department concerned, to an independent tribunal for arbitration. In practice, this generally means that, if an amicable solution has not been reached, the matter will be submitted to the Industrial Court for arbitration.

CHAPTER ELEVEN

FACTORY LAW

WHAT IS A FACTORY?

THE law concerning employment in factories is contained in the Factories Act, 1961, which has consolidated the earlier factory legislation. Any reference to 'the Act' in this chapter should, unless otherwise stated, be construed as a reference to the Factories Act, 1961.

Section 175 of the Act contains both a general definition of 'a factory' and an enumeration of certain premises which are to be treated as factories for the purposes of the Act, whether or not they would also be covered by the general definition.

A factory, in general, means any premises in which or within the precincts or curtilage of which persons are employed in manual labour in any process for or incidental to any of the following purposes—namely:

(1) the making of any article or part of any article; or
(2) the altering, repairing, ornamenting, finishing, cleaning, or washing, or the breaking-up or demolition of any article; or
(3) the adapting for sale of any article;

being premises in which or within which the work is carried on by way of trade or for purposes of gain, and to or over which the employer of the persons employed therein has the right of access or control.

Section 175 (6) further states that, where a place situate within the precincts forming a factory is solely used for some purpose other than the processes carried on in the factory, that place will not form part of the factory, but if it otherwise would be a factory it shall be deemed to be a separate factory.

The following comments will help in understanding the definition:

1. In order that the premises should qualify as a factory persons must be employed there by way of manual labour. The meaning of manual labour is the same as that which we have described already in connexion with the definition of 'workmen' under the Truck Acts. The essential question is whether manual labour represents a substantial (as distinct from a merely incidental) part of the employment of the people working there. The employment of merely one

person by way of manual labour does not make the premises concerned a factory.

> *Joyce* v. *Boots Cash Chemists (Southern), Ltd.* A man was employed in a Boots shop to deal with the carrying of crates and similar heavy jobs. While it could not be doubted that he was engaged in manual labour, it was *held* that this did not make the shop a factory even though things were being made there, since the employment of one person by way of manual labour was not enough.

2. 'Adapting for sale' means increasing the saleability of goods by some process. 'Packing' goods does not as such constitute adapting for sale, but 'packaging' does. The difference is that with packing goods are placed in containers mainly for purposes of protection, while with packaging they are placed into containers because that would increase their saleability. Thus, placing chocolates into boxes would be adapting for sale, as a box of chocolates is commercially a different article from the same quantity of chocolates sold loose.

3. It is essential that the work should have been undertaken either by way of trade or for purposes of gain. The engineering workshop of a technical college would thus not be a factory.

4. The employer of the persons must have the right of access or control over the premises in which the work is being conducted. This rules out from the definition private homes in which out-workers are doing work which has been sub-contracted to them.

5. Where any place within the general factory precincts is used for some purpose other than a factory purpose it will not be treated as part of the factory. The factory purposes include, however, not merely the main purposes (*e.g.*, the making of some articles) but also everything which is ancillary to this main purpose—*e.g.*, the feeding of the workmen or the repair of the machinery.

> *Luttman* v. *Imperial Chemical Industries, Ltd.* A factory contained within its precincts a canteen which was used for the purpose of feeding and entertaining people working in the factory. *Held,* that the canteen formed part of the factory, since the feeding and entertaining of work-people was a process incidental to that of manufacture.

> *Thurogood* v. *Van den Berghs and Jurgens, Ltd.* A repair shed had been erected within the precincts of a factory manufacturing margarine. Equipment used in the factory which was in need of repair was taken to the shed. *Held,* that the shed formed part of the factory.

The connexion between the place in the factory precincts and the main factory must be one based on the main productive purposes of the factory. Thus, a part of a factory which is used solely for administrative purposes or for the feeding or entertainment of persons engaged in administrative duties is not a part of the factory in the legal sense.

Thomas v. *British Thomson Houston Company, Ltd.* A separate building standing in factory grounds was used as a directors' canteen. One of the rooms was also used occasionally for meetings between the management and the shop stewards. *Held,* that the building did not form part of the factory, because it was used for a purpose which was not essential for the welfare of the *industrial* workers employed in the factory.

The health, safety, and welfare of persons employed in offices is governed by the Offices Act, 1960, which came into operation on January 1st, 1962. This Act is an enabling Act, which means that it merely creates conditions for the making of regulations by the Minister of Labour, and the exact nature of the obligations which employers of office workers will have to meet will depend on these regulations.

The premises enumerated specifically in Section 175 as being factories include the following:

(1) yards and dry-docks used for the construction and repair and breaking-up of ships;
(2) premises in which articles are sorted as a preliminary operation for the work of a factory;
(3) premises in which bottles or other containers are filled or washed where this is being done incidentally to the purposes of a factory;
(4) laundries, carried on incidentally to the purposes of another business or of a public institution;
(5) premises used for the construction or repair of loco-motives where the operation is incidental to the purposes of a transport undertaking;
(6) premises in which printing or bookbinding is carried on, whether for trade or incidentally to the purposes of another business;
(7) premises in which dresses and other equipment are made or repaired in connexion with the production of cine-matographic or theatrical performances;
(8) film studios.

GENERAL HEALTH PROVISIONS IN FACTORIES (PART I)

1. *Cleanliness* (Section 1). Every factory must be kept in a clean state, and free from effluvia arising from any drain or sanitary convenience. Accumulations of dirt must be removed daily from floors,

benches, and passages. The floors of workrooms must be washed, or otherwise cleaned effectively, at least once a week.

All inside walls and partitions, and all ceilings and tops of passages, must either be washed with hot water and soap every fourteen months or, where they are kept painted in a prescribed manner, be repainted at intervals of not more than seven years as may be prescribed, and be also washed as above every fourteen months. Where the walls, etc., are whitewashed the whitewashing must be renewed every fourteen months.

2. *Overcrowding* (Section 2). A factory shall not while work is carried on be so overcrowded as to cause risk of injury to the health of the persons employed there. A factory is presumed to be over-crowded if at any time the number of persons employed in a workroom is such that there is less than four hundred cubic feet of air-space per person. In calculating the total amount of floor-space available no space more than fourteen feet above floor-level shall be taken into account. Unless the district inspector of factories provides otherwise, a notice must be kept posted in every work-room specifying the number of persons who may be employed there.

It should be noted that a factory may be overcrowded even if there is the requisite quantity of cubic space per person, such as where a large part of the floor of the workroom is taken up by machinery and other equipment.

3. *Temperature* (Section 3). Effective provision must be made for securing and maintaining a reasonable temperature in each work-room. No method of heating may be employed which would allow the escape into the workroom of any dangerous fumes.

In every workroom in which a substantial proportion of the work is done sitting, and does not involve any serious physical effort, a temperature of less than 60 degrees would not be deemed after the first hour of work to constitute a reasonable temperature. At least one thermometer must be maintained in such a workroom.

The Minister of Labour may prescribe for particular factories special standards of 'reasonable temperature.'

4. *Ventilation* (Section 4). Effective and suitable provision must be made for securing and maintaining by the circulation of fresh air in each workroom the adequate ventilation of the room, and for rendering harmless, so far as is reasonably practicable, all fumes, dust, and other impurities which may be generated in the course of the process of work. The Minister may prescribe by regulations a standard of adequate ventilation for particular classes of factories.

5. *Lighting* (Section 5). Effective provision must be made for securing and maintaining sufficient and suitable lighting, whether

natural or artificial, in every part of a factory in which persons are working or passing.

The Factories (Standards of Lighting) Regulations, 1941, made by the Minister under powers granted to him by the Act prescribe standards of lighting for various factory purposes.

The Act also provides that all glazed windows and skylights used for the lighting of workrooms must, so far as is reasonably practicable, be kept clean on both sides, except that they may be whitewashed or shaded in order to avoid glare.

6. *Drainage of floors* (Section 6). Where any process is carried on which renders the floor liable to be wet, and the wet may be removed by drainage, effective provision for such drainage must be made.

7. *Sanitary conveniences* (Section 7). Sufficient and suitable sanitary conveniences must be provided for the persons employed in the factory. They must be kept clean, and effective provision must be made for lighting them. Where persons of both sexes are employed in a factory separate accommodation for the two sexes must be provided.

The Minister of Labour has made regulations (Factories (Sanitary Accommodation) Regulations, 1938) by which standards are laid down as to the number of conveniences to be provided in relation to the average number of persons employed in a factory.

It may be noted that the responsibility for the enforcement of the provisions concerning sanitary accommodation rests with the local health authority—*i.e.*, the councils of county boroughs and boroughs and the councils of urban and rural districts. The same authorities are also responsible for the enforcement of the other health provisions of the Act, but only in respect of factories in which mechanical power is not used (Sections 8–9).

8. *Medical supervision* (Section 11). The medical examination and supervision of persons employed in factories is not generally required by the Act, but the Minister may insist on it by special regulations in respect of factories in which cases of illness have occurred which he believes to be due to the nature of the work done there, or where he feels that there may be danger to the health of persons employed in a factory because of the materials used in their processes, or where young persons are employed in work which causes risk of injury to their health.

GENERAL SAFETY PROVISIONS (PART II)

The Act demands that certain kinds of machinery must be securely fenced. They are:

1. Every flywheel directly connected to a prime mover and every moving part of a prime mover (Section 12).

2. Every part of transmission machinery (Section 13).

3. Every dangerous part of any machinery (Section 14).

These provisions of the Act are of great importance, because they have given rise to the largest amount of litigation. The following explanatory comments should therefore be carefully noted:

1. Prime movers (machinery from which power originates) must be securely fenced, and no alternative is provided for, except in respect of electric generators and flywheels connected to them, which are subject to the same rules as shown in paragraph 2 below.

2. Transmission machinery and any dangerous part of any machinery must be securely fenced unless it is in such position or of such construction as to be as safe to every person employed or working on the premises as it would be if securely fenced. Thus, transmission machinery (*e.g.*, belts) would not need to be fenced if running along the ceiling of a workroom as long as no person employed comes within reaching distance of the machinery. If some one does come close—*e.g.*, in connexion with the decoration of the premises—the machinery at once would be subject to the duty to fence.

3. Prime movers and transmission machinery have to be fenced even if they are not dangerous, while other machinery must be fenced only in so far as it is dangerous. When is machinery dangerous, then? The answer has been given by Du Parcq, J. in his much-quoted statement in *Walker* v. *Bletchley Flettons, Ltd*, where the learned judge said: "A part of machinery is dangerous if it is a possible cause of injury to anybody acting in a way in which a human being may be reasonably expected to act in circumstances which may reasonably be expected to occur."

Carr v. *Mercantile Produce Company, Ltd*. A girl employed in working a machine used for making macaroni put her hand into the interior of the machine. To do this she had to force the hand through a narrow opening. Her fingers were injured. The occupiers of the factory were prosecuted for not fencing the opening to the machine. *Held,* that the machine was not dangerous, as the type of accident which had happened was one which could not have been reasonably foreseen.

4. Where the duty to fence exists the duty is an absolute one. This means that it is no excuse for the employers to plead that it was not practicable to fence the machine. If the machine cannot be fenced securely and still be used, then it should not be used at all, and if the occupier of the factory uses it he does so at his risk.

John Summers and Sons, Ltd. v. *Frost.* A fitter's thumb was injured when it came into contact with a revolving grindstone. The upper part of the machine was guarded and there was a tool rest at the bottom, but a portion of the stone was unguarded, since otherwise it could not have been used. *Held,* that the duty to fence was an absolute one, and that impracticability was no excuse.

Where an important type of machine could not be legally used because it could not be securely guarded and still be workable, the Minister may by regulations made under powers granted to him by Section 53 lay down a standard of guarding which would be sufficient for legal purposes even though it might not securely guard the machine. As an example we might quote the Woodworking Machinery Regulations which deal with the type of guard to be fitted to a circular saw.

5. Where the Minister has laid down a standard of fencing for a particular machine the occupier who satisfies the requirements of the regulations need not also satisfy the provisions of the Act. The regulations take the place of the Act. It should be noted, however, that where the regulations demand the provision of a certain type of guard for a dangerous part of a machine, the provision of this guard does not exempt the employer from also guarding securely any other dangerous part of the machine.

Benn v. *Kamm and Company.* A horizontal milling machine had been guarded in accordance with the provisions of the Horizontal Milling Machine Regulations, 1928, which provide for the guarding of the cutters of the machine. The worker operating the machine was injured by another moving part of the machine which had not been guarded. *Held,* that the regulations did not supersede the general safety provisions of the Act dealing with other parts of the machine.

Automatic Woodturning Company, Ltd. v. *Stringer.* S. was the operator of a power-driven circular saw used to cut lengths of timber into convenient sizes for chair-legs. It was her job to remove off-cuts by means of a push stick. Her hand came into contact with the saw, and she was injured. The machine had been guarded in accordance with the Woodworking Regulations, and the question was whether Section 14 of the Act also applied. *Held,* that it did not because the removal of the off-cuts was an essential part of the industrial operation of cutting lengths of timber, and the regulations provided how the persons engaged in this operation should be protected.

6. Where a machine has to be guarded the guard must be a secure one, and not merely one which is somewhat secure. The standard adopted in deciding whether a guard is secure is the same as that which is used in deciding whether a machine is dangerous—namely, that of reasonable foreseeability. If the guard was sufficient to deal with all foreseeable contingencies, then it is secure, even if some

one happens to get injured on the machine in circumstances which could not have been foreseen.

> *Burns* v. *Joseph Terry and Sons, Ltd.* The transmission machinery behind a cocoa-grinding machine was fenced underneath and on the sides but not above. A young man employed in the factory tried to clear cocoa beans from a shelf at the top of the machine. Without turning off the machine, he placed a ladder against it and climbed up. The vibration of the machine moved the ladder, and when he tried to get hold of something to avoid falling his hand came into contact with the moving belt and was pulled against a pinion and crushed. *Held,* that the machine had been securely guarded, as the possibility of this kind of accident could not have been reasonably foreseen.

7. For some time it was believed that the duty to fence related to all foreseeable dangers, including the possibility of parts of the machinery flying out, so that the guard had to be effective against all these dangers. This is no longer true. In *Sparrow* v. *Fairey Aviation Company, Ltd,* Devlin, L. J. explained Section 14 as follows: ". . . the employer does not owe an unlimited duty to the employee to protect him from all injury caused by the machine, but only from injury caused by or through contact between him and the machine." This reasoning has subsequently been approved of by the House of Lords in *Close* v. *Steel Company of Wales.*

There is no general liability to guard materials which may be dangerous while in the machine, but the Minister may make regulations requiring that the materials should be fenced (Section 14 (6)).

> *Bullock* v. *G. John Power (Agencies), Ltd.* A workman was killed by being struck on the head by a length of wire which was being reduced in diameter by being pulled through a die under pressure and then wound round a revolving drum. The drum had a guard to prevent the wire from flapping out at the side, but it must have ridden over the top of the guard. *Held,* that the wire was material in the machine, and as such it had to be guarded only if provided for by regulations. None had been made.

8. The duty to fence applies only to machinery which is being used in the factory as part of its productive equipment and not to machinery which is either made in the factory or which has been sent there for repair.

> *Parvin* v. *Morton Machine Company, Ltd.* P., a boy of seventeen, was injured while cleaning a dough-brake made in his employers' factory. The machine had not been fenced. *Held,* that as it had been manufactured in the factory, the duty to fence did not apply.

9. All fences and guards must be of substantial construction and

must be maintained in good order and kept in position while the parts of the machine which are to be guarded are in use or motion, except when they are necessarily exposed for lubrication or adjustment. New machines sold must be already equipped with a secure guard, and any person who sells or hires out such machines which are not equipped in this way is guilty of an offence and liable to a fine of up to £200 (Section 17).

Special Safety Provisions

1. Every vessel containing dangerous liquids, the edge of which is less than three feet above the ground, must be either securely covered or securely fenced up to at least that height. Where neither method is practicable all other possible steps must be taken to prevent any person from falling into the vessel (Section 18).

2. Every hoist or lift must be of good mechanical construction, sound material, and adequate strength and must be properly maintained. It must be thoroughly examined by a competent person at least every six months. A report on the examination must be entered into or attached to the general register within twenty-eight days. A copy of the report has to be sent to the District Inspector of Factories (Section 22).

Hoistways and liftways must be properly enclosed so as to prevent people from falling down or coming into contact with the lift.

A gate to the liftway must be efficiently protected by interlocking or similar devices to prevent it from being opened when the lift is not at the landing. On every hoist or lift there must be marked conspicuously the maximum working load which it is allowed to carry. Lifts and hoists used for the carriage of persons must be equipped with devices to prevent overrunning (Section 23).

Similar provisions as to construction and maintenance apply also to cranes, except that they need be inspected only once every fourteen months. If any person is employed near the wheel-track of an overhead crane, or in any place where he might be struck by the crane, effective measures must be taken to warn the driver of the crane or otherwise ensure that the crane does not approach within twenty feet of that place (Section 27).

3. All floors, steps, stairs, passages, and gangways must be of sound construction and must be properly maintained and shall, so far as is reasonably practicable, be kept free from any obstruction and from any substance likely to cause persons to slip (Section 28).

A substantial handrail must be provided for every staircase. Where one side is open the handrail must be on that side. Where a staircase, because of its construction or for other reasons, is specially

M

likely to cause accidents there must be handrails on both sides (Section 28).

All openings in the floor must be securely fenced, except where the nature of the work renders this impracticable. All ladders must be soundly constructed and properly maintained.

4. There shall, so far as is reasonably practicable, be provided and maintained safe means of access to every place at which any person has at any time to work and every such place shall, so far as is reasonably practicable, be made and kept safe for any person working there (Section 29).

It should be noted that this provision benefits not only workers who are employed by the occupier of the factory, but also independent contractors, (e.g., electricians or window-cleaners), who happen to be working in the factory.

The occupier's duty to provide safe means of access is governed by the words 'so far as is reasonably practicable,' so that where it has not been practicable to provide safe means of access the employer will not be in breach of his duty.

> *Thomas* v. *Bristol Aeroplane Company, Ltd.* A ramp leading down to the entrance to a factory had become slippery when snow which had fallen during the night froze. A worker coming to work early on a Monday morning slipped and injured himself. Normally the company used some of the maintenance men on the night shift to deal with any snow that had fallen during the night, but as this happened on a Monday morning no night shift had been on duty. *Held*, that in the circumstances the occupiers had not failed in their duty to do what was reasonably practicable to make the means of access safe.

The safe means of access once provided must be maintained by the employer, and he should therefore have a system in operation for the removal of obstacles that might make transit through passages more difficult. It would be too much to expect, however, that all obstacles might be removed at once.

> *Levesley* v. *Thomas Firth and John Brown, Ltd.* A worker returning to his workshop, after having taken refreshment in the canteen, tripped over a piece of metal packing used for levering heavy objects from the floor. The packing must have dropped off a lorry which was standing in the gangway, and had not been there when the worker went to the canteen. *Held*, that Section 29 (1) has not been broken if the obstruction is one of a transient or exceptional nature.

5. Where work has to be done in some confined place, such as a tank or chamber, in which dangerous fumes are liable to be present, the confined space must, in the absence of any other means of egress, be provided with a manhole of suitable size. No person may enter

the confined space unless all practicable steps have been taken to remove all the fumes and to prevent the access of further fumes, and it has been ascertained that the space is free from fumes. In addition, the man entering the space must wear a suitable breathing apparatus. The man entering the confined space must have received permission from a responsible person and, where practicable, he must wear a belt with a rope attached (Section 30).

6. Every steam boiler shall have attached to it:
   (a) a suitable safety valve to prevent the boiler being operated at a pressure larger than the maximum permitted one;
   (b) a suitable stop valve connecting it to the steam pipe;
   (c) a correct steam-pressure gauge;
   (d) at least one water gauge of transparent material;
   (e) where the boiler is one of a number, a distinctive number must be attached to it.

No person should enter a boiler which is one of a range unless first all inlets have been blocked so as to prevent hot water or steam from entering the boiler. Steam boilers and their parts and fittings must be properly maintained, and must be inspected by a competent person at least once every fourteen months. This examination should consist of two parts, one involving an examination of the boiler when it is cold and the other when it is under normal steam pressure (Section 32).

Fire escape

The provisions of the Act dealing with precautions against fire risk (Sections 40–52) apply to the following factories:
   (1) all factories in which more than twenty persons are employed;
   (2) factories built or converted after July 30, 1937, in which more than ten persons are employed above ground-level or factories built before that date in which more than ten persons are employed above the first floor or more than twenty feet above ground-level;
   (3) factories in or under which explosive or inflammable materials are stored or used.

As far as these factories are concerned, a certificate has to be obtained from the local fire authority to state that the available fire escape facilities are adequate in the circumstances. It would be an offence to operate such a factory without having obtained a certificate. The certificate shall specify precisely and in detail the means of escape provided, and shall contain particulars as to the maximum number of persons to be employed in the factory, and as to any explosive or inflammable material to be stored there (Section 40).

All means of fire escape must be properly maintained and kept free from obstruction. While any person is in the factory the doors of the factory and any doors affording means of exit from the rooms in which the persons are employed must not be locked or fastened in such a way that they cannot be easily opened from the inside. Doors, with the exception of sliding doors, shall be so constructed as to open outward. Every hoistway and liftway shall be completely enclosed with fire-resisting material, and at the top only by some material easily broken by fire. Every door or window or other exit affording a means of escape in the event of fire, other than the ordinary means of exit, should be clearly marked by a notice printed in letters of adequate size. Where more than twenty people are employed in a factory as well as in any factory in which explosive or inflammable substances are used, effective provision for the giving of fire-warning clearly audible through the factory should be made. The contents of any room in which persons are employed shall be so arranged that there is a free passage-way for people wishing to escape in the event of fire.

Where in a factory there are more than twenty people employed above the first floor, or where explosive or inflammable substances are used, effective steps must be taken to ensure that all persons employed there are familiar with fire drill.

The Minister may make special regulations indicating the means of fire escape to be provided in factories or in particular classes of factories. Where fire accidents have been frequent in a factory or in a particular class of factories the Minister may by regulations compel the occupier or occupiers to instal special supervisors to deal with these risks (Section 53).

The Minister may make special regulations as to the measures to be taken to reduce the risk of fire breaking out in any factory or of fire or smoke spreading, and such regulations may prescribe requirements as to the internal construction of a factory and the materials to be used in construction (Section 50).

In every factory there shall be provided and maintained appropriate means for fighting fire, which shall be so placed as to be readily available for use. The Minister may by regulations specify the particular means to be provided for particular classes of factories (Section 51).

The Minister may by regulations extend the provisions regarding fire-warning and fire drill (see above) to other classes of factories (Section 49).

Fire-warnings shall be tested at least once every three months, or at such shorter intervals as the Minister may direct. A note about the result of every test must be entered in the general register (Section 52).

GENERAL WELFARE PROVISIONS (PART III)

1. *Drinking-water* (Section 57). An adequate supply of wholesome drinking-water must be provided at suitable points throughout the factory, where it would be conveniently accessible to all persons employed there. The supply of water should either come from the public main or from some other source approved by the local health authority.

Where the supply of water is not laid on it must be contained in suitable vessels, the contents of which must be renewed daily. The supply of drinking-water must always be clearly marked as such. Except where the water is provided in an upward jet, one or more suitable cups must be provided, together with facilities for rinsing them in drinking-water.

2. *Washing facilities* (Section 58). Adequate and suitable facilities for washing shall be provided for the employed persons. These shall include the supply of soap and clean towels (or other means of cleaning and drying) and the provision of hot and cold running water, and the facilities shall be conveniently accessible and kept in a clean and orderly condition. Standards of the facilities to be provided may be laid down by the Minister by regulations.

3. *Accommodation for clothing* (Section 59). Adequate and suitable accommodation for clothing not worn at work must be provided. Where it is reasonably practicable arrangements must also be made for drying such clothing. The Minister may again prescribe standards of accommodation by means of regulations. In considering whether accommodation is adequate account has to be taken also of the possibility of theft.

McCarthy v. *Daily Mirror, Ltd.* A workman's clothes had been stolen from a peg provided for him by his employers. *Held,* that this did not form adequate accommodation.

4. *Sitting facilities.* Earlier legislation demanded only the provision of sitting facilities for the use of female workers whose work is done standing so as to enable them to take advantage of any opportunities for resting. This has now (Section 60) been extended to all workers, male as well as female. It is further stated that, where a substantial proportion of the work may be done sitting, a seat shall be provided for every person thus employed, the seat to be of a design, construction, and dimension suitable for the worker

and the work. Together with the seat. a foot-rest should be provided on which the worker can readily and comfortably support his feet.

5. *First Aid* (Section 61). A first-aid box or cupboard of a prescribed standard must be provided, and be readily accessible. Where more than 150 persons are employed at any time there must be one box for every 150 persons employed. Each box must be placed under the charge of a responsible person. In a factory where more than 50 persons are employed this person must be trained in first aid. The Minister may lay down the type of training required. A notice affixed in every workroom must give the name of this person.

Where a factory contains an ambulance room, and arrangements are made for all injuries occurring in the factory to be treated there, the chief inspector of factories may by a certificate exempt the factory from all or some of the general provisions concerning first-aid boxes. In some classes of factories the Minister has by regulations prescribed the setting up of an ambulance room.

6. *Welfare regulations* (Section 62). In addition to the general welfare requirements detailed above, the Minister may by regulations specify the detailed facilities that have to be provided for the persons employed. In addition, he may also make regulations concerning the supply of the following: arrangements for preparing, heating, and taking of meals; protective clothing; ambulance and first-aid arrangements; the use of seats in workrooms; rest rooms; the supervision of persons employed.

SPECIAL HEALTH, SAFETY, AND WELFARE PROVISIONS (PART IV)

1. In every factory in which in connexion with any process there is given off any dust or fume or other impurity of such a character or to such an extent as to be likely to be injurious or offensive to the persons employed, or any substantial quantity of dust of any kind, all practicable measures shall be taken to protect the persons employed against inhalation of the dust or fume, and to prevent its accumulation in any workroom (Section 63).

The measures to be taken are those which are practicable. This means that the employer fulfils his obligation by following the practices of the most advanced firms in the industry. If it is later proved that there existed a better method, but that method was not known at the time, it would not have been practicable for the employer to adopt it.

Richards v. *Highway Ironfounders* (*West Bromwich*), *Ltd.* R. had been employed by the defendants as iron-moulder from 1929 until 1952. During the 'knocking out' process which forms part of the moulding operation substantial quantities of dust are raised. It was not known before 1950 that the dust concerned contained invisible particles which might cause silicosis. The plaintiff had not been provided with a mask. It was shown that only one type of mask (a so-called Mark IV mask) could have protected the worker against the dangerous invisible particles. Since the danger was unknown before 1950 the defendants would not have provided this mask, since it was uncomfortable, and the employees would not have used it if it had been provided. The plaintiff had become ill with silicosis in 1946, and had left the employment of the defendants in 1952. *Held,* that there was no breach of Section 47 (1)[1] because in the relevant period the provision of masks was not a practicable measure to protect the persons employed, since the defendants did not know of the danger.

2. Where poisonous substances are used in a workroom in a way which is likely to give rise to dust no person may partake of food or drink in that room, nor may he stay there during his meal interval. The Minister may by regulations prescribe certain additional processes which are to be treated in a similar fashion (Section 64).

3. The Minister may prescribe by regulations certain processes which involve a particular risk to the eyes of the persons employed in them, and the employers of these persons will then be compelled to provide them with goggles for the protection of their eyes (Section 65).

NOTIFICATION AND INVESTIGATION OF ACCIDENTS AND INDUSTRIAL DISEASES (PART V)

The district inspector of factories must be immediately informed of the happening of any of the following accidents:

1. Accidents involving personal injuries, where a worker is killed, or is disabled for at least three days from earning full wages at his usual work (Section 80);

2. Accidents in which no person is injured, provided that the necessity of notification has been prescribed by the Minister (Section 81). The list of the accidents in question is now contained in the Dangerous Occurrences (Notification) Regulations, 1947. Among the many types of dangerous occurrences enumerated there, the following are the most important ones:

   (a) the bursting of a revolving vessel or grindstone;
   (b) the collapse or failure of a crane or hoist;
   (c) explosion or fire causing damage to any room, and leading to the suspension of work for at least five hours;
   (d) electrical short circuit or the failure of electrical machinery attended by explosion or fire causing damage and leading to suspension of work for at least five hours;

[1] This refers to the Factories Act, 1937, now Section 63 (1) of the 1961 Act.

(*e*) explosion of a container used for the storage of any gas at a pressure greater than atmospheric pressure.

Every medical practitioner who is attending a patient whom he believes to suffer from lead, phosphorus, arsenical, or mercurial poisoning or anthrax contracted in any factory, must at once inform the Chief Inspector of Factories in London, giving full details about the case. The employer of a person suffering from any of these diseases must similarly inform the district inspector and the appointed factory doctor (Section 82). The provisions of the Act have been extended by regulations to cover also other forms of poisoning, including toxic jaundice, chrome ulceration, manganese poisoning, and others.

Where the coroner holds an inquest on the body of a person whose death may have been caused by an accident or disease, of which notice has to be given under the above provisions, the inquest must be adjourned unless a representative of the factory inspectorate is present.

The Minister may order the holding of a formal inquiry into any case of accident or disease contracted in a factory. For this purpose he would appoint a competent person to hold the inquiry, and if he does not possess legal qualification a legal assessor would be appointed to assist him. The hearing would take place in open court, and the court would have all the powers of a court of magistrates in summoning witnesses or in entering buildings for inspection, as well as in demanding the production of books and other records. On completing the hearing the court would report to the Minister on the causes and circumstances of the accident, and add any observations which they think fit to make (Section 84).

The Employment of Women and Young Persons (Part VI)

The Act defines young persons as being persons of either sex under the age of eighteen. Women are defined as female persons over the age of eighteen.

Women and young persons may not clean any part of a prime mover or transmission machinery while it is in motion, or any part of any machine if the cleaning thereof would expose them to risk of injury from any moving part (Section 20).

Regulations made by the Minister have prescribed certain machines as 'dangerous machines,' and a young person may not work at such a machine unless he has either received sufficient training in this work or he is under the supervision of some experienced person (Section 21).

A person may not be employed to lift, carry, or move any load so heavy as to be likely to cause injury to him. The Minister may by regulations prescribe the maximum weights that may be shifted by persons employed in factories (Section 72).

The Act also contains provisions prohibiting the employment of female young persons in certain processes in the glass-making industry, and of women and young persons in connexion with lead-manufacture or in processes involving the use of lead compounds (Sections 74–75).

Part VI of the Act deals with the hours of work and the holidays of women and young persons. The following provisions should be noted (Section 86):

1. The total hours of work (excluding time spent on meals and rest) must not exceed 9 in any day or 48 in any week (44 for young persons under the age of sixteen).

2. The period of employment (*i.e.*, the time between starting work and finishing work) must not exceed eleven hours in any day. It must not commence before 7 A.M. nor end later than 8 P.M. (6 P.M. where young persons under the age of 16 are concerned). On Saturdays work must end by 1 P.M.

3. The maximum length of a spell of work is $4\frac{1}{2}$ hours, but if during the spell a rest period of at least ten minutes is granted the spell of work may extend to 5 hours. After every spell of work an interval for a meal of at least half an hour must be given.

4. The time of starting and finishing work and the intervals for meals must be the same for all women and young persons employed in the factory, except that young persons under sixteen may finish earlier than the others.

5. No woman or young person shall be employed during a meal interval.

6. No work is to be done on Sundays. Christmas Day, Good Friday, and Bank Holidays are to be given as holidays. The management may substitute other days, but three weeks' notice of their intention of doing so would have to be posted in the factory, and, in any case, half the holidays thus given would have to fall in the period between the 15th of March and the 1st of October.

7. A notice of hours and mealtimes must be posted up in the factory. The arrangements may not be changed more often than once in every three months. The district inspector of factories must be informed of every change (Section 88).

Certain exceptions exist to the above rules in the following cases (Section 100 ff.):

1. Where the factory operates a five-day week an extra hour may be added to the hours of work as well as to those of employment,

but the limits within which employment may take place are not affected.

2. It is possible for the management to fix different times for starting and finishing work, meal intervals, etc., for different days of the week.

3. The morning spell of work for male young persons over the age of sixteen may be 5 hours if they work with men and their continuous employment is necessary.

4. Meal intervals need not be simultaneous where the work has to be continuous, or where the employer's canteen would not accommodate all persons at the same time.

5. Where it is possible under the above rule for different persons to have different times for meals those who are not actually having their meal interval may stay in the workroom while others are having their meals.

Women and young persons may work overtime—*i.e.*, work in excess of 48 hours a week—but only subject to the following provisions (Section 89):

1. No young person under sixteen may work overtime.

2. The total number of hours of overtime is 100 in a year and 6 in any one week. Overtime may be worked in 25 weeks of the year only. It is important to note, however, that the above overtime ration is a ration for the factory, and not for individual women and young persons. Whenever any woman or young person is employed on overtime that counts towards the ration, and it does not matter how many of them are working overtime simultaneously.

3. The hours of employment, including overtime, must not exceed 10, or $10\frac{1}{2}$ in five-day-week factories.

4. The maximum period of employment is twelve hours a day, and it must fall within the usual limits. Women may, however, be employed on overtime until 9 P.M.

5. The Minister has power to relax certain of the provisions concerning overtime. In factories where it is customary for workers to be employed on overtime individually, rather than in whole departments, he may replace the factory 'ration' of overtime by a personal ration. That ration must not exceed, however, 75 hours for women and 50 hours for young persons. He may also increase the permitted daily maximum of overtime for a period of up to eight weeks in factories engaged on work which is subject to special seasonal pressure (*e.g.*, fruit-canning). On the other hand, the Minister may reduce the overtime ration or abolish it completely in any industry where he is satisfied that it will not cause a serious loss.

6. The Act also makes provision for shift-working by women and young persons. This is covered by Section 97, which allows the Minister to sanction such a scheme for women and young persons over 16 on the application of the occupier of a factory, provided the working hours fall between the hours of 6 A.M. and 10 P.M. and each shift does not exceed eight hours. The factory occupier will have to secure the approval of the employees affected by a ballot held among them.

It is important to reiterate that the above provisions apply to women and young persons only, and not to adult men. Their hours are a matter for agreement between them or their unions and the employers. The provisions do not apply either to women employed in managerial positions or in the cleaning of the factory, and to male young persons over sixteen who are members of the factory's regular maintenance team.

The Minister has power under Section 96 of the Act in the event of an unforeseen emergency by order to suspend as regards any factory the provisions of the Act dealing with hours and holidays, but only insofar as it is necessary to avoid serious interference with the ordinary working of the factory. Under Section 117 the Minister may also grant exemptions from the provisions regulating hours of employment where this is necessary in the public interest for the purpose of increasing industrial efficiency. Under this section the Minister may exempt the employment of persons over the age of 16 from the provisions of Part VI of the Act (except those sections dealing with the medical examination of young persons) and from the provisions of certain other Acts which deal with the employment at night of women and young persons. The Minister must be satisfied that it is desirable in the public interest to grant the exemption. The exemption may be general, or may refer to particular classes of persons or factories only. Exemptions applying to particular persons or factories are given by a so-called "special exemption order," while a general exemption would necessitate the making of "general exemption regulations." A special exemption order must not be made for more than one year at a time.

No general exemption regulations may be made except on:

1. the application of a joint industrial council or similar body
2. the application of a wages council;
3. the joint application of organizations representing employers and workmen in the industry;
4. the application of either of the organizations mentioned under (3) and after consulting the other side.

Not later than seven days after taking a young person into

employment, the occupier of the factory where the young person is employed must send a notice to the appointed factory doctor. The appointed factory doctor will then arrange for the young person to be medically examined, with a view to issuing a certificate of fitness for factory employment. It would be illegal for the employer to continue the employment of the young person for more than fourteen days without having him medically examined (Section 118).

The certificate issued by the appointed factory doctor may be a provisional one which is operative for a stated period of time only. This will be so where he requires further information before being able to certify the young person as fit for factory employment. The certificate when issued may either apply to all factories occupied by the same employer or only to some of them, and it may also be conditional as to the type of work which the young person may undertake. The doctor may insert a further condition to the effect that the young person must be re-examined after a specified time. A certificate issued is valid only for one year or such shorter period as may be prescribed by the regulations of the Minister, and after the expiration of this period the young person has to be re-examined.

The examination of young persons takes place in general at the factory where they are employed, except where not more than three young persons are employed at the factory. In that case the examination will be held at a place fixed by the Chief Inspector of Factories. Where the examination is held at a factory the occupier must provide the exclusive use of a room, properly cleaned, warmed, and lighted, and a screen, a table with writing materials, and chairs. The appointed factory doctor must also be given full facilities to inspect any process of work in which a young person is to be employed.

If the factory inspector has doubts about the suitability of a particular process of work for young persons he may request the factory occupier to discontinue the employment of young persons on that process until the young persons concerned have been examined by the appointed factory doctor, and have been passed as fit for that particular operation (Section 119).

PARTIES RESPONSIBLE FOR THE OBSERVANCE OF THE ACT

The responsibility for the observance of the provisions of the Act rests primarily on the occupier of the factory. The occupier is the person who actually runs the factory, irrespective of whether he is also the owner of the factory building. Generally speaking, he will be the employer of the persons employed in the factory. Where the occupier contravenes a provision of the Act he will be guilty of an offence for which he may be prosecuted before the local magistrates. He will be exempt from liability where he is able to show that the offence has in fact been committed by another person, and that he (the occupier) (i) has used all due diligence to enforce the execution of the Act; and (ii) that the other person has committed the offence without his consent, connivance, or wilful default (Section 161). This would apply, for instance, where the machines used in the factory do not actually belong to the occupier, but have been hired from a third party on whom the duty to guard the machines would fall.

In addition to the occupier, the persons employed in the factory would also be guilty of an offence where they have wilfully interfered with or misused any means, appliances, conveniences, or other things provided in pursuance of the Act for securing their health, welfare, or safety. The Act also provides that no person employed in a factory shall wilfully and without reasonable cause do anything likely to endanger himself or others (Section 143).

It should be noted that the employee is guilty of an offence only where he is misusing some equipment, etc., which his employer is compelled by the Act or by regulations made under the Act to provide. He is not guilty of an offence where he misuses or fails to use equipment which the employer has provided without legal compulsion.

We shall see in the next chapter that where an employee acts in such a way he will, when suing the employer in damages for personal injuries, lay himself open to the defence of contributory negligence.

The parent of a young person employed in a factory in contravention of the provisions of the Act would also be liable to a fine of up to £10 unless he can satisfy the court that the contravention occurred without his consent, connivance, or wilful default.

The Enforcement of the Provisions of the Act

The responsibility for enforcing the provisions of the Factories Acts rests primarily on the members of the factory inspectorate. Factory inspectors are appointed by the Minister of Labour. Apart from the district inspectors who exercise general supervision over working conditions in the factories in their district, there are also specialized inspectors at the regional offices of the inspectorate who may be called in by the district inspectors for specialized inquiries. The general supervision over the work of the inspectorate falls on the chief inspector, who also makes out an annual report which is submitted to Parliament by the Minister of Labour.

An inspector of factories has the following powers (Section 146):

1. He may enter, inspect, and examine a factory at all reasonable times of day and night when he has reasonable cause to believe that anyone is employed there.

2. He may enter by day any place which he has reasonable cause to believe to be a factory.

3. He may take with him a constable if he has reasonable cause to apprehend any serious obstruction in the execution of his duty.

4. He may require the production of the registers and other documents which have to be kept in pursuance of the Act.

5. He may make such examinations and inquiries as may be necessary so far as respects the factory and any young persons employed there.

6. He may require any person he finds in the factory to give such information as he can give as to the identity of the occupier.

7. He may examine, either alone or in the presence of another person, any person he finds in the factory, or anyone whom he has reasonable cause to believe to have been employed in the factory within the preceding two months, and obtain a signed declaration from such person.

8. Where the factory inspector is a duly qualified medical practitioner he may undertake such medical examinations as he considers necessary.

9. He may conduct or defend proceedings before a court of summary jurisdiction even though he is not a qualified solicitor or barrister, provided that he has the authority in writing of the Minister of Labour (Section 149).

10. He may exercise such other powers as may be necessary for carrying the Act into effect.

It would be an offence for the occupier of a factory to obstruct an inspector in the discharge of his duties.

The Chief Inspector of Factories may appoint a sufficient number of medical practitioners to act as appointed factory doctors for each division of the factory inspectorate. A person who is the occupier of a factory, or who is directly or indirectly interested in one, would not be qualified to act in this capacity (Section 151).

The appointed factory doctor may inspect the general register of a factory at all reasonable times. If directed by the Minister he has to make a special inquiry into the conditions of work at any factory. The fees for the services of the appointed factory doctor in connexion with the medical examination of young persons have to be paid by the occupier of the factory. The scale of fees has been laid down by Ministerial order.

Reference has been made already (pages 173, 179) to the powers of the local health and fire authorities in enforcing certain provisions of the Act.

MISCELLANEOUS PROVISIONS

Every factory must keep a *general register* (Section 140) in which must be entered all important events affecting the factory, in particular the following:

(1) prescribed particulars about young persons employed in the factory;

(2) particulars as to washing, whitewashing, and painting of the factory;

(3) particulars as to every accident and case of industrial disease occurring in the factory of which notice has to be sent to the inspector;

(4) particulars about special exceptions (young shift-workers, etc.) of which the occupier of the factory has availed himself;

(5) reports about inspections of hoists, lifts, cranes, steam-boilers, gas-holders, and air-receivers;

(6) particulars about such other matters as the Minister may prescribe;

(7) a copy of the certificate from the local health authority concerning means of fire escape must be attached to the register.

The inspector of factories may require the occupier to send to him from time to time extracts from the register in a prescribed form. The register and the records kept in connexion with it must be preserved for at least two years after the date of the last entry.

Not less than one month before the occupier begins to occupy a building as a factory he must serve a written notice on the district inspector of factories giving him particulars of the address and of the nature of the work that will be performed in the factory. A similar notice has also to be given before mechanical power is used for the first time in a factory (Section 137).

Certain notices must be kept posted at the principal entrance to a factory (Section 138):

(1) the prescribed abstract of the Act (copies may be bought from H.M. Stationery Office);

(2) a notice of the address of the district inspector and of the superintending inspector for the division;

(3) a notice of the name and address of the appointed factory doctor;

(4) a notice specifying the clock, if any, by which the times of work and of intervals will be regulated;

(5) a copy of the special regulations, if any, applying to the particular type of factory.

CHAPTER TWELVE

THE LAW RELATING TO INJURIES TO WORKMEN

INTRODUCTION

WHERE an employee is injured at work it is upon him to prove that the injury was due to some fault of his employer. He could either claim that the employer was guilty of common law negligence in having failed to observe the common law duties which an employer owes to those employed by him (see pages 141 *ff.*), or he may found his action on a breach by the employer of his statutory duties of care for the safety of the persons employed by him. The employee's rights under the National Insurance (Industrial Injuries) Act, 1946, will be discussed in Chapter 13.

BREACH OF COMMON LAW DUTY

Where the servant's action is based on a breach of the employer's common law duty he will have to prove that the employer has failed either to provide reasonably safe premises, or to provide reasonably safe machinery, materials, and other equipment, or that he has failed to instal and to maintain a reasonably safe system of work. The employer is also responsible for injuries caused to his servant by the negligence of a fellow-servant. The meaning of these duties has been discussed already. Attention must be drawn again to the fact that the employer's duty is not an absolute one; the extent of his duty depends on what a reasonable person would have done in his circumstances.

Watt v. *Hertfordshire County Council.* A fireman was travelling by lorry to an emergency where a woman had been trapped under a heavy vehicle. The lorry carried some lifting gear, although it was not specially equipped for this. In the course of the journey the gear, a large jack, shifted and caused serious injuries to the plaintiff. *Held,* that though the fire authority were bound to provide safe equipment for their servants, they were not negligent in asking their fireman to take some risk in order to save life. In the course of his judgment Denning, L. J., said: "It is well settled that in measuring due care you must balance the risk against the measures necessary to eliminate the risk. To that proposition there ought to be added this : you must balance the risk against the end to be achieved."

The plaintiff must prove, then, not only that there existed a duty on part of the defendant, but that the defendant owed the duty to

N

him (that is, that he was a servant), and that the defendant had failed to carry out his duty by not behaving in the way in which a reasonable employer should have behaved in that situation.

BREACH OF STATUTORY DUTY

Where an Act of Parliament imposes certain duties on an employer, and the employer has failed to observe them, it is always a question of construction as to whether the remedy is for the injured party to bring an action for damages or whether the employer is merely liable to a fine in a criminal prosecution. Under the Factories Act, for instance, it has been held that a breach of the welfare provisions (as distinct from the safety provisions) is visited solely by a criminal sanction, and that an employee who claims that an injury which he has suffered is connected with a breach of the welfare provisions will not be able to found an action on that, though, of course, he might have a claim at common law.

> *Clifford* v. *Challen and Sons, Ltd.* A workman employed in a factory suffered dermatitis because of the inavailability of water with which to wash off from his hands the synthetic glue. *Held,* that no action would lie under Section 42 of the Factories Act, 1937, because this was a 'welfare section,' and not one concerned with safety, but the employee recovered damages for breach of the common law duty to provide a safe system of work.

An action for breach of statutory duty is similar to one for breach of the common law duty, except that the standard of care to be observed by the employer is not necessarily that of a 'reasonable employer.' What standard of care should be expected from the employer depends on the wording of the relevant statutory provision. The employee-plaintiff will have again to prove (*a*) that there existed a duty imposed on the employer-defendant by statute; (*b*) that the defendant had failed to carry out the provisions of the duty; and (*c*) that the plaintiff has as a result suffered some injury. The injury must have resulted from the breach of duty, and it does not necessarily follow that, because there has been a breach of a statutory duty and the plaintiff has been injured, the injury necessarily followed from the breach.

> *Bonnington Castings, Ltd.* v. *Wardlaw.* A steel-dresser contracted pneumoconiosis in the course of his employment. At his work he was exposed to silica dust emanating from the pneumatic hammer at which he worked, as well as from swing grinders used elsewhere in the workshop. At that time there existed no known method of preventing the escape of the dust from the pneumatic hammers. Dust

from the swing grinders could have been made harmless, but the plaintiff was able to show that the swing grinders were not kept free from obstruction, and that this constituted a breach of Section 1 of the Grinding of Metals (Miscellaneous Industries) Regulations, 1925. The question was whether this breach of the regulations caused the plaintiff's disease. *Held,* that the burden of proof rested on the plaintiff to show that at least on the balance of probabilities the breach materially contributed to the injury which he had suffered.

It has been shown already that, where an Act provides that certain things have to be done, it is no excuse for the employers to claim that it is not practicable to do so. Similarly, the employer's liability is not affected by delegation. This means that once an Act imposes certain duties on an employer it is up to him to ensure that the duties are carried out. If he employs others for this purpose the risk of any negligence on their part will still fall on him, even if he has employed the best experts available. The only exception to this principle is where the employer has delegated the duty to carry out the provisions of the Act to the man for whose protection the duty was imposed and he is injured through his own negligence in failing to carry out the employer's instructions. It is essential, however, that the man to whom the performance of the duties has been delegated is some one who is sufficiently experienced and responsible, so that it was reasonable for the employer to delegate the duties to him.

Johnson v. *Croggan and Company, Ltd.* The employers, following the custom of their trade, had delegated to the plaintiff, a foreman steel-erector, the task of selecting suitable gear for the work. The plaintiff used a slight fruit-picking ladder for a job, although he should have known that it was quite unsuitable. The ladder collapsed, and he was injured. *Held,* that the defendants had rightly delegated the duty to the plaintiff, and that the accident was caused entirely by his own negligence.

Although some writers treat delegation as a separate defence in an action for personal injuries, it is probably better to look upon it as a special case of contributory negligence (see below).

The Employer's Defences

Apart from the obvious defence of a denial that the employee's injury was connected with his employment, or that it had been caused by the employer's breach of one of his duties, the employer has the following further defences:

1. In an action for breach of common law duty (but *not* in an action for breach of statutory duty) the employer may plead *volenti non fit injuria*. This means that the employer contends that the employee freely accepted the risk of injury when he entered the

employment. This defence can be used only where the employment is one of a known dangerous nature (such as that of steeplejacks) and the employee has clearly shown—for instance by accepting danger money—that he was prepared to take the risk of injury upon himself. It is not enough for the employer to prove that the employee knew of the risk as long as he had not actually accepted it. If the employee has protested about the danger, and has been only with difficulty persuaded into facing it, he will not be deprived of his remedies if he should get injured.

> *Bowater* v. *Rowley Regis Corporation.* A road-sweeper was per-suaded by his foreman to take out a horse for his cart, although he knew the horse to be nervy in traffic. The horse bolted when he was leading it through the town, and he was thrown off and injured. *Held,* that the employee was not prevented from claiming that he had been given unsafe 'equipment' to work with, since he had not volunteered to face the extra danger.

The reason why *volenti non fit injuria* is not a defence in an action for breach of statutory duty is that the purpose of statutes containing safety provisions is to protect the very people who are employed in dangerous occupations.

2. The other defence which the employer may use is that of contributory negligence. Here the employer does not deny that he has been negligent himself, but he contends that the employee has been negligent as well. The Law Reform (Contributory Negligence) Act, 1945, provides that, where the court is satisfied that there has been contributory negligence, it will divide the loss suffered by the plaintiff between him and the defendant in proportion to their respec-tive degrees of negligence.

The standard of care which the worker must take for his own safety is not as high as that which a person has to take for the safety of others.

> *Staveley Iron and Chemical Company, Ltd.* v. *Jones.* A workman co-operating in the moving of heavy metal cores by a crane suffered personal injuries, partly through the negligence of the crane-driver and partly through his own want of care. *Held,* that although the plaintiff had been careless, his want of care for his own safety was not bad enough to justify a finding of contributory negligence.

FATAL ACCIDENTS

At common law the position was that 'the death of a human being could not give rise to an action in law.' This meant that the depen-dants of a worker who had died as the result of an injury at work could not bring an action against the employers although the employers might have been liable to the worker himself if he had not died.

A significant change in the law was brought about by the Fatal Accidents Acts, 1846 and 1864. These Acts (as amended by the Fatal Accidents Act, 1959) provide that where a person is killed (not necessarily as the result of an industrial accident) in circumstances where he would have had a right of action if he had not died, an action for damages may be brought by his dependants. The persons who may bring such an action are the surviving spouse, parents, grandparents or step-parents, children, grandchildren, or step-children, assuming in each case that the plaintiffs suffered some financial loss through the death of the deceased. The 1959 Act has extended the list of dependants to include also brothers, sisters, uncles, aunts, and their issue. Adopted children are treated in the same way as natural-born children. Illegitimate children may claim in the event of the mother's death or the death of the reputed father. The action is based entirely on financial loss, and no non-financial losses, such as personal grief, will be taken into account. The plaintiffs must bring into account any financial benefit which they have derived from the death of the deceased (e.g., the value of property inherited from the deceased), with the sole exception of insurance moneys, pensions, gratuities, or benefits received under the national insurance scheme. One action only may be brought on behalf of all the dependants, and if the court awards damages to them the total awarded will be shared out by the court among the plaintiffs in proportion to the losses suffered by them.

The financial loss for which the action is brought includes the loss of the earnings of the deceased in so far as he contributed to the family pool and, in the case of young people, even their potential future contributions to the family pool, provided that it would be reasonable to expect that they would have made such contributions. The cost of the deceased's funeral may also be included, as well as the cost of employing a house-keeper where the deceased has been a woman keeping house for her dependants.

It is essential to remember, however, that the action will lie only if the deceased could have claimed himself if he had not died. Any defence which the defendant could have used against the deceased if he had sued may similarly be employed against the deceased's dependants—e.g., contributory negligence or *volenti non fit injuria*.

Even where the dependants are able to claim damages for the financial loss which they have suffered, the defendant would still be better off than if the victim of the accident had survived and had brought an action in person, since the injured person could have claimed not only for loss of earnings but also for such personal losses as the pain and suffering caused to him by the injury, the loss of expectation of life, and the loss of certain amenities of life resulting from the accident. In order to deal with this situation a further Act was passed, the Law Reform (Miscellaneous Provisions) Act, 1934. Before this Act was passed the rule was that a personal action died with the person. The Act altered this by stating that all causes existing in favour of or against a person shall survive him, and shall exist in favour of or against his estate. It is thus possible now for the estate of a deceased worker to sue his employer for damages for loss of expectation of life, pain, etc.

This action is one brought on behalf of the estate of the deceased. Where the deceased has not left a will appointing executors of his estate it is customary for the widow to have herself appointed by the court administratrix of her late husband's estate and to bring then two actions: one in that capacity under the Law Reform Act and the other on her own behalf and on behalf of her children under the Fatal Accidents Acts. Any damages which the estate may recover under the Law Reform Act will be taken into account as a financial benefit when assessing the damages to be awarded under the Fatal Accidents Acts, though, of course, this will affect only those dependants who have derived some benefit from the deceased's estate.

The Law Reform (Limitation of Actions) Act, 1954, has laid down a period of limitation of three years for all actions arising out of personal injuries, whether they are brought by the injured party himself or by his estate or his dependants.

CHAPTER THIRTEEN

THE NATIONAL INSURANCE (INDUSTRIAL INJURIES) ACT, 1946

HISTORICAL INTRODUCTION

AN employee who has suffered an injury at work may claim damages from his employer if he can prove that the injury has been caused by the employer's negligence in circumstances which have been discussed in the preceding chapter. There are, however, many instances when a person may suffer injury at work without the employer being negligent, and because of the injury the worker's earnings may cease, and, indeed, his working capacity may be permanently reduced. It was to deal with these cases—particularly important in industries which are inherently dangerous, such as coal-mining—that the first Workmen's Compensation Act was passed in 1890. The idea behind the Act was that an employee who was injured in the course of his employment should be entitled to some compensation for the resulting loss of earnings, even if the employer was not liable to pay damages. Compensation was payable by the employer, who would add the cost of it (generally covered by an insurance policy) to his costs of production. The amount payable by way of compensation was always a proportion of the lost earnings, subject to a fairly low ceiling.

The Workmen's Compensation Act was amended on a number of occasions, and its regime lasted until July 1948, when the National Insurance (Industrial Injuries) Act, 1946, came into operation and took its place. The workmen's compensation legislation had been unpopular for the following reasons:

1. The benefits (compensation) provided under the Acts were rather low.

2. If the employer (or his insurance company) was not prepared to acknowledge liability lengthy court proceedings followed, and many injured workers settled for less than they would have been awarded by the court because they could not afford to wait for the end of the proceedings.

3. Compensation was payable only for loss of earnings, so that a man who was seriously injured in an accident had little incentive to try to train for another trade, since if he succeeded in becoming proficient at that trade, and earned as much or more than he had earned before he suffered his injury, the compensation would end.

4. Employers also had the right under certain circumstances to discharge their liability to an injured worker by paying him a lump sum of money in lieu of the weekly compensation payments. Many recipients of these lump sum payments invested them unwisely, lost everything, and then became a burden on public assistance.

5. A final objection to the workmen's compensation scheme was its cost. Most employers covered their liability by insurance, and the amounts which they had to pay far exceeded the total sums paid out in compensation to injured workers.

It was for these reasons that Lord (then Sir William) Beveridge recommended in his famous war-time report on social insurance that the workmen's compensation scheme should be replaced by a national insurance scheme. The details of the scheme had been worked out during the War, and it was passed by Parliament in 1946.

Liability for insurance

The National Insurance (Industrial Injuries) scheme (to be referred to in the following for short as the industrial injuries scheme) is operated in conjunction with the general national insurance scheme which will be discussed in the next chapter. Most people are insurable under both schemes, and pay their contributions by means of a stamp which is attached to the insured person's insurance card. There are, however, some persons who may be insurable under one but not under the other scheme.

In principle, all persons in insurable employment are compulsorily insured. Insurable employment may be identified with employment under any contract of service or apprenticeship in Great Britain. Thus, persons who are self-employed, even if they are working for others under a contract for services, would not be insurable. Insurability exists irrespective of the sex or age of the person in insurable employment. The number of hours worked is also immaterial where insurance against industrial injuries is concerned. Married women in employment are insurable.

Some people, although working under a contract of service, are excepted from insurance. The Act contains a list of these employments, the most important of which are:

(1) employment of a casual nature, not for the purposes of the employer's trade or business. Note the reference to 'casual' employment, which is not the same thing as part-time employment;

(2) employment by one's husband or wife;

(3) employment by a relative in connexion with household duties.

What is an insured person insured against?

An insured person is insured against two kinds of risks:
  (1) A personal injury caused by accident arising out of and in the course of his employment;
  (2) a prescribed disease or personal injury not caused by accident, but due to the nature of the insured person's employment.

Personal injury caused by accident

An insured person is covered against personal injuries which he may suffer. The injuries may be physical or mental, but they must be injuries to the person, as distinct from injuries to property. The Act does not make it a condition for a claim for benefit that the insured person's capacity to work should have been affected by the injury; even injuries which have no effect on earning capacity will entitle the insured person to some benefits.

It is essential, however, that the injury should have been caused by 'accident.' This means not only that the injury must not have been designed by the insured person himself (though the intentional act of a third party may still be an accident from the point of view of the victim), but also that it followed instantaneously from the event causing it. We must, therefore, distinguish carefully between personal injuries caused by accident and those which are the result of a process, such as lengthy exposure to some unfavourable working conditions. Where the injury was caused by a gradual wearing down of the insured person's resistance to it it has been caused by a process and not by accident, and no benefit could be claimed there.

The personal injury by accident must have arisen "out of and in the course of" the insured person's employment. These words, which have been taken over from the old workmen's compensation legislation, have given rise to a great deal of case law. An accident arises 'out of' a man's employment if it was connected with the doing of something which formed part of his employment. It arises 'in the course of his employment' if it happens during the time when he is following his employer's business. The first statement relates, then, to the issue of causation, while the second deals with the much simpler time-factor. The Act has introduced a presumption in Section 7 (4) which is of great help to the claimant for benefit. It is provided there that an accident arising in the course of an insured person's employment shall be deemed, in the absence of evidence to the contrary, to have arisen out of that employment. If, then, the claimant is able to prove that he suffered an accident during the time while he was acting in the employer's business the presumption is that the accident arose directly out of something which he was employed to do, and it will be for the insurance officer to prove that it arose from some other cause if he wishes to deny benefit to the claimant.

It will be best, then, to discuss first when the 'course of employment' commences and when it ends. Strictly speaking, it should commence only when the employee starts on his duties and should end when he leaves his duties (e.g., clocks out). In fact, however, the course of employment may begin earlier and last longer. Where, for instance, the employee reaches his employer's premises before the start of the work so as to put his outdoor clothes away, or where he stays for some time after the end of the work, he will still be in the course of his employment. Similarly, if he returns to the employer's premises after working hours for some purpose connected with his employment he will when he gets there still be in the course of his employment. It is quite possible, then, that during a day the 'course of employment' is on and off a number of times.

It is accepted that the employee is not in the course of his employment while on his way to or from work. He is there not subject to any special risk which is not shared equally by all other persons who are using the roads or the various forms of public transport. Even if the employee is travelling in his own vehicle, and the employers have sanctioned the use of it, he is not in the course of his employment until he reaches his destination, except where the travelling forms part of his employment, such as with a commercial traveller. When the employee approaches his employer's premises he will be treated as being in the course of his employment as soon as he gets on some private road or other means of access to his employer's premises on which he would not be if it were not for his employment. This means that, as soon as he leaves the public highway and reaches some place which is reserved for the use of those who have business to do at his employer's premises, he is in the course of his employment.

Under the Workmen's Compensation Acts it was accepted that where an employee was *compelled* by his contract of employment to use a certain means of transport to get to or from work he was in the course of his employment as soon as he got on it. The Industrial Injuries Act has enlarged this principle in its Section 9, which provides:

"An accident happening while an insured person is, with the express or implied permission of his employer, travelling as a passenger by any vehicle to or from his place of work shall, notwithstanding that he is under no obligation to his employer to travel by that vehicle, be deemed to arise out of and in the course of his employment, if:

(*a*) the accident would have been deemed so to have arisen had he been under such an obligation, and

(*b*) at the time of the accident the vehicle

(i) is being operated by or on behalf of his employer or some other person by whom it is provided in pursuance of arrangements made with his employer, and

(ii) is not being operated in the ordinary course of a public transport service."

Where an employee is on emergency call, so that he may be called to work at any hour of day or night, and he is called in such a way, and suffers an injury on his way to work, the injury will be treated as having been caused by accident arising in the course of the employment, as in these circumstances the course of employment commences when the worker leaves home and not when he reaches his place of work.

The course of employment is not interrupted when the employee does something which, though he is not employed to do it, is reasonably incidental to his work, such as having a meal in the works' canteen. Of course, if he were to leave work to go home for the meal his course of employment would have terminated, and would start again when he returned to work.

We have already shown that where the accident is proved to have arisen in the course of the insured person's employment it will be deemed to have risen out of it in the absence of evidence to the contrary. It is then for the insurance officer to prove that the accident has not arisen out of the insured person's employment. The Act itself deals with two situations where doubts might possibly arise as to whether an accident in the circumstances described had arisen out of the employment.

Section 8 provides that an accident shall be deemed to arise out of and in the course of an insured person's employment, notwithstanding that he is at the time of the accident acting in contravention of any statutory or other regulations applicable to his employment, or of any orders given by or on behalf of the employer, or that he is acting without instructions from his employer, if:

(*a*) the accident would have been deemed to have so arisen had the act not been done in contravention or without instructions as the case may be, and

(*b*) the act is done for the purposes of and in connexion with the employer's trade or business.

Thus, for instance, where an underground colliery worker decided to ride on a tub (though this was strictly forbidden), and was injured, it was held that he was entitled to benefit. If there had been no rule about not riding on tubs the accident would have been one arising out of and in the course of the collier's employment, since at the time he was doing what he was employed to do—namely, trying to leave the mine after finishing his work—though he was doing it in a wholly unauthorized manner.

Section 10 provides that an accident happening to an insured person in or about any premises at which he is for the time being employed for the purposes of his employer's trade or business shall be deemed to arise out of and in the course of his employment if it happens while he is taking steps, on an actual or supposed emergency at those premises, to rescue, succour, or protect persons who are, or are thought to be, injured or imperilled, or to avert or minimize serious damage to property.

Assume that an electrician is sent by his employer to do some work on a farm. While he is there another man falls down a well, and the electrician attempts to rescue him and is injured himself in the attempt. If it were not for Section 10 the electrician could not claim benefit, as he was not when he was injured doing something which he was employed to do, or something which even was incidental to his employment.

Beyond giving us a decision for these two types of situations, the Act does not further describe when an accident is to be deemed to arise out of a person's employment. The only possible way of dealing with it is, then, to enumerate certain cases where accidents have been deemed not to arise out of the insured person's employment, bearing in mind always that each case will be decided on its own merits, subject to the general interpretation of the phrase given earlier.

1. Where an insured person is injured as a result of a quarrel with another worker during working hours the decision will depend on whether the quarrel was connected with the work. Thus, where a foreman was assaulted on his way to the canteen by a worker whom he had reprimanded earlier the foreman's injury was held to entitle him to benefit.

2. Where the injury is the result of a frolic of the worker, quite unconnected with the work, such as playing football in the workshop, the accident has not arisen out of the employment.

3. Where an apprentice or other young worker suffers injuries at a technical school which he is attending during working hours the accident will be deemed to arise out of the employment only if it is a condition of his employment that he attends the school. If he attends without being compelled to do so he will not be able to claim benefit, even if the employers have encouraged him to attend to the extent of paying him for the time spent at school. The same

applies where an employee is injured playing games. Unless he had to play, he will not be able to claim.

4. An accident of a kind which a person could have suffered anywhere will not be an accident arising out of the employment, unless the employment has predisposed him towards it. Thus, an injury by a wasp-sting would not entitle the worker to claim benefit, except where wasps formed a particular occupational risk—*e.g.*, in a sweet factory.

PRESCRIBED INDUSTRIAL DISEASES

An industrial disease does not qualify as a personal injury by accident where it is the result of a gradual process, as, indeed, most industrial diseases will be. It is for this reason that Section 55 authorizes the Minister of Pensions and National Insurance to "prescribe" certain industrial diseases for particular classes of employed persons. He may do so if he is satisfied that:

(1) it ought to be treated, having regard to its causes and incidence and any other relevant considerations, as a risk of their occupations and not as a risk common to all persons, and

(2) it is such that, in the absence of special circumstances, the attribution of particular cases to the nature of the employment can be established or presumed with reasonable certainty.

The National Insurance (*Industrial Injuries*) (*Prescribed Diseases*) *Regulations*, 1959, mention forty-two industrial diseases, but the Minister may, of course, further add to this list. In each case the disease is coupled with one or more occupations, and the insured person who wishes to claim benefit must prove not only that he suffers from the disease, but also that he has been in the employment bracketed with the disease in the regulations within the time stated by the regulations. Naturally, the diseases which have been prescribed are those which, according to Section 55, represent a definite occupational risk, and before adding to the list the Minister has to be fairly sure on sound medical evidence that it is possible to establish a causal connexion between the employment specified and the disease.

BENEFITS

Since the Act came into operation insurance benefits have been increased practically at two-yearly intervals. The details about the benefits are in any case of limited interest only to the student of law, who is more concerned with the principles on which they are awarded. In order to avoid the information contained in this book becoming stale even before the printer's ink has dried, it is probably better not to refer to benefit rates at all. Readers of the book are recommended to call at their nearest office of the Ministry of Pensions and National Insurance and ask for a pamphlet containing the latest benefit rates. They will be able to obtain one free of charge.

The Act provides for three basic benefits, together with various supplements. The basic benefits are the following:

1. *Industrial injury benefit.* This benefit is payable for every workday (*i.e.*, not for Sundays) for which the insured person is incapable of work. The benefit will terminate when the insured person becomes again capable of work or, in any case, at the end of 156 days. No benefit is payable for the first three days of incapacity, except where the incapacity lasts for twelve days or more.

2. *Industrial disablement benefit.* An insured person can claim this benefit either when his injury leaves some lasting effects without his becoming thereby incapable of work (so that he has not been entitled to injury benefit) or where at the end of the period for which he has been receiving injury benefit there remains some lasting effect of the injury. The amount of benefit payable is not a set figure as for injury benefit, but varies according to what the Act calls "the degree of loss of mental or physical faculty." This means that the insured person will have to submit to a medical examination to ascertain the gravity of the effects of the injury. The degree of loss of faculty will be expressed in percentage terms, the scale of disablement benefit for 100 per cent. loss of faculty (*e.g.*, loss of both eyes or both legs) being the same as that for injury benefit. Proportionately lesser amounts will be payable for a lower percentage loss of faculty. In order to standardize the awards the Minister has provided for a scale of assessments to be applied to the more frequent types of disabilities. The medical board will have to rate other disabilities by fitting them into the scale according to their gravity. Account will be taken of the insured person's state of health and of existing disabilities, but not of his occupation.

Disablement benefit takes the form of a disablement pension if the degree of loss of faculty has been assessed at 20 per cent. or more. If the degree of loss of faculty is assessed at less than 20 per cent. the claimant will receive a lump-sum payment as a 'disablement gratuity.' Provision is made, however, for the claimant to choose a small pension instead of a gratuity where he believes himself to be entitled to one of the supplements mentioned below.

3. *Industrial death benefit.* This benefit is payable normally to the widow of the insured person, though where the husband of an insured woman has been dependent on her he may claim this benefit

as well. In exceptional cases the parents of the deceased person may also claim death benefit if they have been substantially maintained by him or her. For the first thirteen weeks of widowhood a widow would receive a widow's allowance at a slightly higher rate, which is intended to help her to adjust her life to the new situation. Afterwards a widow receives a widow's pension at one of two rates. The higher rate is payable where the widow is or becomes over fifty years old, where she is incapable of self-support, or where she has the care of a child of school age. The pension is paid as long as the widow remains unmarried. If she should remarry the pension would cease, but she would be paid a gratuity equal to one year's pension.

SUPPLEMENTS TO INSURANCE BENEFITS

Insurance benefits may be supplemented in the following ways:

1. Industrial injury benefit may be supplemented by an allowance for an adult dependant and by further allowances for the children of the insured person. The allowance for the adult dependant is subject to an earnings limit. Where the adult dependant earns herself or himself more than £2 a week the allowance would not be paid.

2. Industrial disablement benefit is supplemented in the following form:

(*a*) Where the person in receipt of disablement benefit has become unemployable (which means that he is unlikely to be able to earn more than £52 a year) he will qualify for an unemployability supplement.

(*b*) A special hardship allowance is payable to a person in receipt of disablement benefit where:

(i) he is incapable, and is likely to remain incapable, of following his regular occupation, and
(ii) he is also incapable of following suitable employment of an equivalent standard.

The total amount payable to a person by way of disablement benefit and special hardship allowance may not exceed what would be payable for 100 per cent. disablement.

(*c*) Where the disabled person is in need of constant attendance which he is not receiving in hospital he may claim a constant attendance allowance. It does not matter whether he is attended by some person whom he pays or by a member of his family, since in the latter event the member of the family will be unable to undertake other paid employment.

(*d*) Where a person in receipt of a disablement pension of less than 100 per cent. has entered hospital for treatment he will, while the treatment lasts, have his pension increased to the level corresponding to 100 per cent. disablement. The purpose of this provision is to encourage disabled persons to enter hospital.

(e) A person in receipt of disablement benefit will also qualify for the dependants' and children's allowances, but only where he is in receipt of an unemployability supplement or where he is in hospital as an in-patient.

THE ADMINISTRATION OF THE INDUSTRIAL INJURIES SCHEME

The responsibility for administering the industrial injuries scheme rests with the Minister of Pensions and National Insurance. The Minister appoints inspectors whose main task it is to secure enforcement of the Act. They may enter premises in which persons are employed and question anyone they find there. They may ask for the production of wages books and of other records so as to see that all insurable persons have in fact been insured.

The day-to-day administration of the scheme falls to the local offices of the Ministry. In each of these offices there is one or more insurance officers whose responsibility it is to deal with claims for benefit. The insurance officer may either grant benefit, or he may refuse it, or, in exceptional cases, he may refer the claim to the local appeal tribunal. Where, however, the claim involves what is called by the Act a 'special question' the insurance officer will have to refer it for decision either to the Minister or to the local medical board.

The following questions have to be referred to the Minister:
   (1) whether a person is or was in insurable employment;
   (2) whether a person is exempt from paying contributions;
   (3) who has to pay contributions as the employer of an insured person;
   (4) what rate of contribution is payable;
   (5) where there is more than one person claiming industrial death benefit, to whom payment should be made;
   (6) when constant attendance allowance is claimed how much should be paid, and for how long;

Where the Minister has decided a question under 1-4 above the dissatisfied claimant may appeal against the Minister's decision on a point of law to a judge of the High Court. Decisions of the Minister under points 5 and 6 are final.

The local medical board will have to pronounce on the following:
   (1) whether the accident has resulted in a loss of faculty for the claimant;

(2) whether this loss of faculty is likely to be permanent, and

(3) what the degree of loss of faculty is.

The dissatisfied claimant may appeal from the decision of the medical board to a medical appeal tribunal, consisting of a chairman and two other members who are medical practitioners. It is possible to appeal from the tribunal to the Industrial Injuries Commissioner, but only on a point of law and subject to obtaining leave from the tribunal or the Commissioner.

From a decision of the insurance officer an appeal lies to a local appeal tribunal. Such a tribunal consists of one or more members representing employers and an equal number of members representing work-people, together with an independent chairman. All members are appointed by the Minister who will choose the representative members from panels set up by nominations from representative organizations of employers and workers. The tribunal, apart from dealing with appeals from decisions of insurance officers, also deals with claims directly, where they have been referred to the tribunal by the insurance officer.

Provision is made by the Act for a further appeal. For this purpose the Crown has appointed an Industrial Injuries Commissioner and a number of Deputy Commissioners, who must be barristers with a minimum of ten years' professional experience. Since the Family Allowances and National Insurance Act, 1959, there is no need to obtain leave to appeal. The appeal will be heard either by the Commissioner or by one of his deputies, sitting on his own, or by a tribunal consisting of the Commissioner and two of his deputies sitting together. This latter method is used where the Commissioner feels that the appeal involves a question of some legal difficulty.

An appeal from the decision of a local appeal tribunal may be made either by an insurance officer or by the claimant or by a trade union of which the claimant (or the deceased in the case of a claim for death benefit) was a member. The decisions of the Commissioner and of the tribunal are published by H.M. Stationery Office, and insurance officers are expected to note the reasoning behind them. There exists, therefore, a kind of national insurance case law.

Before the Minister makes regulations under the Act he must submit the regulations in draft form to the *Industrial Injuries Advisory Council*. This Council consists of a chairman and of an equal number of persons representing employers and employees. All of them are appointed by the Minister. The Council's task is to advise the Minister on draft regulations and on all other matters concerning the administration of the Act.

o

CONTRIBUTIONS

A contribution is payable in respect of an insurable person if he has been employed during any part of a contribution week. A contribution week lasts from midnight on Sunday to midnight of the following Sunday. Contributions are payable also in respect of a week during which the employee was on paid holiday, but not for weeks in which the insured person was sick, injured, or unemployed.

The insurance card of an employee is kept by his employer, but it is the duty of the insured person to obtain it in the first place. The insured person may demand to see his card to make sure that it is properly stamped, but he may not do so more often than once a month.

Contributions are payable at the beginning of each contribution week—that is to say, before the employee's remuneration falls due. The employer may then deduct the insured persons' share in the contribution—but no more than his share—from his wages. If the employer attempted to deduct his own share also he would be liable to a fine. The deduction must be made always in the same week to which the contribution refers. If the insured person is employed by a number of employers in the course of the same week the one employing him first during the week is responsible for the stamping of the card. Arrangements may be made, however, between the various employers for the sharing of the cost.

Apart from his responsibility for the stamping of the insurance card, the employer also must investigate every accident that is reported to him, and must on request furnish information about the accident to the insurance officer. Where the employer is the occupier of a factory, mine, or quarry, or where he employs more than ten persons, he must also keep an accident book.

THE LAW REFORM (PERSONAL INJURIES) ACT, 1948

This Act deals with the problem of 'alternative remedies'—that is to say, with the situation which arises where an insured person has a right of claiming damages from his employer (whether for breach of common law duty or of statutory duty) and also has the right to claim benefit under one of the two national insurance schemes. Since damages are assessed by the court so as to compensate the plaintiff fully for the loss which he has suffered, he would in fact make a profit if he could in addition also claim insurance benefit. On the other hand, however, the benefits are insurance benefits, and the plaintiff will have himself contributed towards the benefit. The dilemma is resolved by the provisions of the Act where it is stated that in awarding damages the court will have to take into account against any loss of earnings or profits which the injured person has suffered because of his injury one-half of the value of any rights which will probably accrue to him in respect of injury benefit, disablement benefit, or sickness benefit for a period of five years. An increase in a disablement pension in respect of need for constant attendance will be disregarded. Similarly, no deductions will be made from damages awarded under the Fatal Accidents Acts in respect of a right to death benefit. The reason why the Act provides for taking into account *one-half* of the value of the insurance rights is that the employee has paid only about one-half of the total contribution for which he will be entitled to a corresponding proportion of the insurance benefits in addition to the damages awarded to him.

Where the damages recoverable in the court action are subject to reduction because of the contributory negligence of the plaintiff the further deduction of the value of half of his insurance rights must be made from the total damages before anything has been deducted for contributory negligence. This may sound a little confusing, and is best explained by means of an illustration.

Assume that the court has assessed the plaintiff's loss at £2500, and has found that he was to blame himself for it to the extent of 20 per cent. Half the value of his insurance rights arising out of the injury for five years comes to £100. The calculation of the amount actually payable to him by the defendant will be as follows:

General damages	£2,500
Value of insur. rights	100
	£2,400
less 20% contr. negl.	480
	£1,920

If the deduction of 20 per cent. for contributory negligence had been made from the general damages before the value of insurance rights had been taken away the plaintiff would have received £20 less. The calculation to be made according to the Act is, then, the one which assures the plaintiff of the larger amount of net damages.

Finally, it should be mentioned that the deduction of probable insurance benefits comes from the damages awarded to the plaintiff for loss of earnings or profits. These damages are known as 'special damages' because it is possible in the action to claim the exact amount of the loss. The damages which the plaintiff may claim for such things as loss of expectation of life, pain and suffering, loss of amenities of life, are known as 'general damages,' and it will be up to the court to decide how much, if anything, he should recover under this heading. From the wording of the Act it appears that the deduction may be made from special damages only, and that no deduction would be possible if the plaintiff claimed no special damages, but only general damages.

CHAPTER FOURTEEN

THE NATIONAL INSURANCE ACT, 1946

THE PRINCIPLES OF THE ACT

THE National Insurance Act, 1946, provides for insurance against the following contingencies: unemployment, sickness, old age, maternity, widowhood, orphanhood, death. It will be impossible in a work of this kind to deal with the many detailed regulations which govern the administration of the scheme, and emphasis will be placed on those matters which are of legal importance. In the same way as in the preceding chapter, no reference will be made to the amounts payable by way of the various benefits. Information may be obtained from the local office of the Ministry of Pensions and National Insurance.

The National Insurance Act differs in one important respect from the Industrial Injuries Act. Under the latter Act a person may claim benefit even if his injury had taken place within an hour or so of his having started on his employment. The National Insurance Act does not allow for claims unless the insured person is able to show that he has satisfied the *contribution conditions* applicable to the benefit which he is claiming. These conditions differ from benefit to benefit, but in each case the insured person must have paid a certain number of insurance contributions before he becomes entitled to full benefit, and, in some cases, he must also show a minimum annual average of contributions paid since his entry into insurance. For the purpose of calculating whether a person has satisfied the relevant contribution conditions, it is important to distinguish between the contribution year and the benefit year. A contribution year is the year covered by a person's insurance card. For administrative reasons insured persons have been divided into four groups, represented by the letters A-D. The cards of the persons falling into the four groups start from different dates in the year. Thus, the contribution year of persons falling under the letter A starts in March, that of persons falling under B in June, and so on. The benefit year for any one insured person starts five months after the expiration of the corresponding contribution year. Any claim submitted during the benefit year will then be judged as far as the contribution conditions are concerned, on the completed contribution years. A contribution week, as under the Industrial Injuries scheme, starts at midnight from Sunday to Monday.

INSURED PERSONS

The purpose of the national insurance scheme is to provide insurance cover for the entire population, subject only to certain exceptions. Some persons are covered by their own contributions, others are covered by the contributions paid by the head of their family. Insured persons are in principle all persons, of either sex, who are resident in Great Britain and who are over school-leaving age (15 at present) and are under retirement age (65 for men, 60 for women). The insured persons are divided into three classes:

(1) employed persons—*i.e.*, those who are gainfully employed under a contract of service;

(2) self-employed persons—*i.e.*, those who are gainfully employed otherwise than under a contract of service;

(3) non-employed persons—*i.e.*, all other persons.

The meaning of being 'gainfully employed' has given rise to some doubts.

Vandyk v. *Minister of Pensions and National Insurance.* V., a victim of poliomyelitis, and suffering from a paralysis of the lower limbs and of the left arm, had been advised by his doctors to follow some purposeful occupation. Accordingly he accepted a research appointment for which he was fully qualified. His pay did not cover the extra expenses (special transport, etc.) which he incurred in connexion with his job. He contended that he was a non-employed person, as his employment was not 'gainful.' *Held,* that gainful employment meant employment for which payment was sought, irrespective of whether the payment actually received covered the costs of doing the work.

The benefits receivable by the three classes of insured persons are not the same. A non-employed person is not entitled to unemployment, sickness, and maternity benefits, while a self-employed person is not entitled to unemployment benefit. The rates of contribution also differ as between the three classes.

As far as married women are concerned, we have to distinguish between those who are solely employed in household duties and those who are employed or self-employed persons. The former will not be insurable (there are exceptions, but these may be disregarded for our purposes), and they will be relying on their husband's insurance for benefits. The latter class have the option as to whether they wish to be fully insured and pay contributions as single women or whether they wish to be exempt from contributions and rely on their husbands' insurance. It should be noted, however, that even where a married woman in employment has decided not to pay contributions under the national insurance scheme, she will still have to pay contributions under the industrial injuries scheme, from which it is impossible to contract out, and her employer will have to pay his full share of the contribution in respect of her. This is intended to prevent employers from giving preferential treatment in employment to married women. The employer saves nothing if a married woman decides not to pay contributions.

The Minister has by regulations provided that certain other classes of persons are exempt from liability to pay contributions. The most important among them are persons undergoing full-time education or full-time unpaid apprenticeship and persons with an income of less than £104 a year. Although the former are not paying contributions, they will be credited with them so that their insurance record will not be spoilt. Persons who are sick or unemployed are similarly exempt from the payment of contributions, and are credited with them.

DISQUALIFICATION FOR UNEMPLOYMENT BENEFIT

A person who is unemployed will not be entitled to unemployment benefit in the following circumstances:

1. Where a person's unemployment is the result of a trade dispute at his place of employment he will be disqualified from receiving unemployment benefit for the duration of the stoppage of work, except where he has in the meantime obtained bona-fide employment elsewhere.

A trade dispute is defined as "any dispute between employers and workmen or between workmen and workmen which is connected with the employment or non-employment of any person, or the terms of employment of any person, or the conditions of labour of any person." The reason for the disqualification of persons from unemployment benefit where their loss of employment was due to a stoppage of work caused by a trade dispute is that the State does not wish to take sides in such a dispute, as it would do if financial assistance were granted to one of the parties.

An employed contributor who appears to be *prima facie* disqualified on the above ground may still claim unemployment benefit if he is able to show:

(1) that he is not himself participating in or financing or directly interested in the trade dispute through which the stoppage of work took place, and

(2) that no other employee, belonging to the same grade or class of workers as he does, and who was employed at the place of employment immediately before the stoppage of work, is participating in, financing, or directly interested in the trade dispute.

It is therefore quite conceivable that a man who did not wish to join a strike, and lost his employment only because his employers were unable to keep the place open in the absence of the bulk of their employees, will be disqualified from benefit.

2. An employed contributor is disqualified from unemployment benefit for a period not exceeding six weeks in the following cases. The actual length of the disqualification will be determined by the insurance officer, who, if it is shown that the case comes under one of the five headings, *must* disqualify the contributor for some period.

(*a*) Where the claimant has lost his employment through his own misconduct or left the employment voluntarily without just cause. Misconduct means here the same as for the purposes of justifying summary dismissal by the employer. Whether or not the claimant had a 'just cause' for leaving his employment will be determined by the insurance officer on the facts of the case.

(*b*) Where the claimant has without good cause refused or failed to apply for suitable employment or refused to accept suitable employment notified to him as vacant or about to become vacant by an employment exchange or by or on behalf of an employer.

(*c*) Where he has neglected to avail himself of a reasonable opportunity of suitable employment.

(*d*) Where he has without good cause refused or failed to carry out any written recommendations given to him by an officer of an employment exchange with a view to assisting him to find suitable employment. The recommendations must, however, be reasonable having regard to the circumstances of the employed contributor and to the means of obtaining that kind of employment usually adopted in the district in which he resides.

(*e*) Where he has without good cause refused or failed to avail himself of a reasonable opportunity of receiving training approved by the Minister of Labour and National Service in his case for the purpose of becoming or keeping fit for entry into or return to regular employment.

The essential words in the above grounds for disqualification are '*suitable employment.*' In view of the subjective nature of this concept, the Act wisely does not attempt to define the term, but merely lays down that employment will *not* be deemed to be suitable in the following circumstances:

(*a*) Where a situation has become vacant in consequence of a stoppage of work due to a trade dispute.

(*b*) Where the employment is one in the claimant's usual occupation, and in the district where he was last ordinarily employed, but at a lower rate of remuneration or on less favourable conditions than those which he might reasonably have expected to obtain if he had not become unemployed.

(c) Where the employment is one in the claimant's usual occupation in any other district, but it is at a lower rate of remuneration or on less favourable conditions than those which are generally observed in that district by agreements between associations of employers and employees or, in the absence of such agreements, than those generally recognized in the district by good employers.

An unemployed person can thus not be compelled by the threat of disqualification for unemployment benefit to act as a strike-breaker or to accept employment at sub-standard wages. This does not settle, of course, the positive issue as to when employment is suitable. Suitability depends largely on the former employment of the claimant. If the employment offered to him is similar to that which he has been engaged in previously he could not suddenly claim that it was unsuitable because he wanted something better. For instance, where a person has been employed part-time in the past, he would be entitled to refuse full-time employment as not being suitable. Where the position offered to the claimant is in a different place it would depend on the claimant's family circumstances as to whether it would be looked upon as 'suitable' employment. The Act provides, however, specifically that after a reasonable time has lapsed, employment will not be unsuitable merely because it is employment of a different kind, provided that the wages and conditions of employment offered are equal to those which are generally observed for employment of that kind. Naturally, here again the claimant could prove that the employment offered to him was unsuitable for other reasons, such as his state of health.

DISQUALIFICATION FOR SICKNESS BENEFIT

A claimant will be disqualified for sickness benefit for a period of up to six weeks if:

(1) he has become incapable of work through his own misconduct, or

(2) he fails without good cause to attend for or submit himself to such medical or other examination or treatment as may be required, or to observe any prescribed rules of behaviour.

A person would have good cause for refusing to undergo some form of treatment if he had either objections on religious grounds to the treatment or if there was contradictory advice on the value of the treatment. If, for instance, one expert recommends an operation and another expert suggests non-surgical treatment the claimant would have good cause for refusing to submit to the operation.

GENERAL PROVISIONS AS TO SICKNESS AND UNEMPLOYMENT BENEFITS

A person is entitled to unemployment benefit in respect of any day of unemployment which forms part of a *period of interruption of employment* and to sickness benefit in respect of any day of incapacity which also forms part of such a period. He is not entitled, however, to benefit for the first three days of any period of interruption of employment, unless within a period of thirteen weeks beginning with the first day of sickness or unemployment he has a further nine days of interruption of employment forming part of the same period of interruption of employment. For this purpose any two days of interruption of employment, whether consecutive or not, within a period of six consecutive days, are treated as a period of interruption of employment. Thus, in order to draw benefit for the first three days of sickness or unemployment, the claimant must have been sick or unemployed for twelve days altogether. These twelve days must have fallen within a period of thirteen weeks, and no day is counted unless it is one of two days falling within a consecutive period of six days. Sundays are disregarded for this purpose.

A claimant for sickness benefit must show that he has been *incapable of work* on every day for which benefit is claimed. A man is incapable for work for this purpose only if there is no type of work which he could be reasonably expected to do, having regard to his age, education, experience, and state of health. Work means remunerated work, so that a woman may be incapable for work, while still able to perform some of her domestic duties.

For unemployment benefit the claimant has to prove that he is unemployed, but capable of work and available for work. It should be noted that where the claimant is paid a guaranteed wage in respect of any week in which work is done the recipient cannot be unemployed during any part of that week, but where the guarantee relates to employment for a minimum of so many days he may be treated as unemployed on the remaining days of the week.

THE ADMINISTRATION OF THE ACT

Responsibility for the administration of the Act rests again with the Minister of Pensions and National Insurance, and is effected by him through the local and regional offices of the Ministry. The rights of an insurance officer in respect of claims for benefit and the constitution and powers of the local appeal tribunals have been discussed already in connexion with industrial injuries.

The highest court of appeal is the National Insurance Commissioner and his deputies, who are appointed in the same way as their counterparts under the industrial injuries scheme. The Minister is responsible for the making of decisions regarding the following matters:

(1) whether a claimant has satisfied the contribution conditions regarding any particular benefits;
(2) where an increase in a benefit is payable (*e.g.*, in respect of dependent children) which of two persons should be entitled to receive it;
(3) which class of insured persons a person should come under;
(4) family allowance matters.

A person who is dissatisfied with the Minister's decision may appeal from it on a point of law to a judge of the High Court.

There is no appeal from a decision of the Commissioner, but any decision, whether made by an insurance officer, local tribunal, or by the Commissioner, may be reviewed by the insurance officer where:

(1) fresh evidence has come to light which was unknown when the decision was given originally,
(2) the decision was given in ignorance of some material fact;
(3) there has been a material change in circumstances since the decision was first given, or
(4) where the decision was based on a Ministerial decision regarding a matter which has to be decided by the Minister, and the Minister has reviewed his own decision.

The Minister is advised in the performance of his duties under the Act by the National Insurance Advisory Committee. This Committee has to consider in draft form any regulations which the Minister proposes to make, and its report on the regulations must be submitted to Parliament with the draft regulations, where the latter require Parliamentary approval before they can come into operation. The Committee consists of a chairman and of four to eight other members appointed by the Minister. The membership of the Committee must contain representatives of employers, trade unions, and friendly societies, but there may also be other persons, such as representatives of the academic world.

CONTRIBUTIONS

Contributions are payable in the same way as those under the industrial injuries scheme. The employer pays the contribution, and deducts then the employee's share from his wages. The rates of contribution which were fixed by the 1946 Act have been altered on a number of occasions now by amending Acts. No advantage has been taken so far of a provision in Section 3 of the Act which permits the Treasury, by order, to vary the contribution rates for a period fixed by the order if in their opinion this is necessary in order to maintain stability of employment. The idea is that during a period of threatening unemployment contribution rates might be reduced, thus leaving both employers as well as employees with more money to spend.

Where the employer should fail to pay the contributions to the national insurance scheme, and the employee has because of that lost any unemployment, sickness, or maternity benefit to which he otherwise would have been entitled, the employee may recover the amount lost from the employer as a civil debt. These proceedings would take place before the local magistrates.

Where contributions have been paid in error at a higher rate than that which was appropriate the employer or the insured person may make a claim for the repayment of the sum over-paid.

CHAPTER FIFTEEN

TRADE UNION LAW

DEFINITION

A trade union in the legal sense of the term is any combination, whether temporary or permanent, the principal objects of which are under its constitution 'statutory objects.' Statutory objects are the regulation of the relations between workmen and masters, or between workmen and workmen, or between masters and masters, or the imposing of restrictive conditions on the conduct of any trade or business, and also the provision of benefits to members. The first point to note in this definition is that a trade union might be a combination of workers or it might be a combination of employers. A trade union by its rules may have any number of objects, but if it is to be a trade union in the legal sense its principal objects must be one or both of the statutory objects. The definition refers also to the provision of benefits to members, but this is merely an ancillary object, and an association formed solely for this purpose would not be a trade union.

At common law, before the passing of the Trade Union Act, 1871, a trade union was looked upon as an unincorporated association, not different in principle from an ordinary members' club set up for cultural or social purposes. It differed, however, from other unincorporated associations in that it was treated as an illegal association if its purposes were deemed to be in restraint of trade. This illegality would affect not only union contracts, which would be unenforceable, but also the relationship between the union and its own officials. A union whose objects were in unreasonable restraint of trade was unable to claim union funds from an official who had misappropriated them.

The status of trade unions was fundamentally altered by the passing of the Trade Union Act, 1871. This Act provides (Section 3) that the purposes of a trade union shall not, by reason merely that they are in restraint of trade, be unlawful so as to render void any agreement or trust. If this section were standing alone the effect might have been that the courts would have been called upon to enforce agreements in restraint of trade entered into by trade unions. A trade union might have been able to bring an action for damages against a member who had refused to come out on strike when called upon to do so by his union. In order to avoid placing the courts into such an invidious position, Section 4 of the Act states that, notwithstanding the provisions of the preceding section, a court should not entertain proceedings instituted with the object of directly enforcing or recovering damages for the breach of any of the following agreements:

1. Any agreement between members of a trade union as such, concerning the conditions on which any members shall or shall not sell their goods, transact business, employ, or be employed.

2. Any agreement for the payment by any person of any subscription or penalty to a trade union.

3. Any agreement for the application of the funds of a trade union

(a) to provide benefits to members;

(b) to furnish contributions to any employer or workman not a member of such trade union, in consideration of his acting in conformity with the rules or resolutions of the trade union, or

(c) to discharge any fine imposed upon a person by sentence of a court of law.

4. Any agreement made between one trade union and another.

5. Any bond to secure the performance of any of the above-mentioned agreements.

Section 4 applies, however, to those trade unions only whose legality rests on Section 3—*i.e.*, those which would have been illegal at common law. It does not apply to trade unions which would have been legal at common law. Their contracts are not affected, and could therefore be enforced by court action. It must be fairly obvious, however, that there cannot be many trade unions to-day whose objects would have been legal at common law.

REGISTRATION OF TRADE UNIONS

The Trade Union Act, 1871, introduced also a system of voluntary registration for trade unions. Registration takes place with the registrar of friendly societies, who acts also as registrar of trade unions. The purpose of introducing registration was to ensure a measure of public supervision over the affairs of trade unions, particularly their constitutions and accounts, in return for which they were given certain privileges not possessed by unregistered trade unions.

The rules of a registered trade union must include the following:

1. The name of the union and its meeting-place.

2. All the objects of the trade union, including particularly the purposes on which union funds may be spent. The circumstances in which a member becomes entitled to any of the benefits granted by the union must be described, and details must be given of the fines which may be imposed on the members.

3. How the rules of the union may be altered or amended.

4. How the officers of the union are appointed and removed.

5. In which way the funds of the union are to be invested, who administers them, and how the union accounts are to be audited.

6. How the union books and records of membership may be inspected.

The registrar would refuse to register a trade union if in his opinion its objects were unlawful or if its principal objects were not statutory objects or if the name of the union was either identical with that of an existing union or so similar that is would be likely to deceive members of the public.

When the registrar is satisfied that a union asking for registration has fulfilled all legal requirements he will issue a certificate of registration.

Of the various privileges which a registered trade union enjoys only the following need be mentioned here:

1. A registered trade union is entitled to exemption from income tax under schedules C and D as far as income in the form of interest or dividends is concerned which is applied by the union solely for the purpose of paying provident benefits. These benefits may not exceed, however, £104 a year per person.

2. As a trade union is an unincorporated association, it is not a legal person, and cannot hold property in its own name. Property has to be held on behalf of the union by trustees. When there is a change in the persons of the trustees the property has to be revested in the new trustees, but where the union is a registered one the property vests automatically in the new trustees without any need for a formal vesting. This saves a good deal of trouble and expense.

3. A registered trade union, though not a legal person, may sue and be sued in its registered name.

4. Where the officials of a registered trade union have kept union property they may be compelled by the court to render an account and to hand over any union property to the trustees of the union. Where they have wrongfully allowed union property to get into unauthorized hands summary proceedings may be taken by the union to recover the property from the persons holding it.

The advantages of registration are procedural rather than material, but even so the large majority of trade unions of workers has registered, as have also many trade unions of employers.

The Rights of Membership

The rules of a trade union, like the rules of any other unincorporated association, represent a contract between the members of the union. Any person joining an existing union does so on the under-standing that he subscribes to the rules. Where a trade union does anything in breach of its own rules any member of the union may appeal to the court for a declaration that the action or resolution of the union is void, being in breach of its rules. Such a declaration will be granted, as it is not looked upon as an attempt of 'directly enforcing' the union rules, which, of course, would be opposed to Section 4 of the Trade Union Act, 1871.

As long as the rules are not directly illegal, the court will not examine their reasonableness. The union rules may therefore give fairly far-reaching powers to the union officials, especially in rela-tion to the expulsion of members of the union. It is only in recent years, when the spread of the closed-shop movement has made expulsion from a union a very serious matter for the person expelled, that the courts have exercised a larger measure of control over union decisions of that kind. The reason for this changed attitude has been clearly explained by Lord Denning. He said: "When a man joins a trade union he is bound by the rules. The rules are said to be a contract between the men themselves and between them and the union to be imposed on all members of the union. A man must accept them or go without employment. They are nothing more nor less than a legislative code laid down by some members of the union to be imposed on all members of the union." Even so, however, in view of the principle of freedom of contract, the court can interfere only if some illegality has taken place in the expulsion of a member. This could happen in any of the following instances:

1. A member may be expelled only if the union rules contain the right of expulsion. Such a right cannot be implied in the rules if it has not been expressly embodied in them.

Spring v. *National Amalgamated Stevedores and Dockers Society.* The defendant union had for some time been admitting to member-ship the members of another union, the Transport and General Workers Union. The latter union complained to the disputes com-mittee of the T.U.C. that this action by the defendants was in breach of the so-called Bridlington resolution, which instructed trade unions not to admit to membership persons belonging to other unions unless they first had been released by their existing union. The disputes committee ordered the defendants to 'return' the members they were alleged to have poached. The defendants then informed the members, the plaintiff among them, that they were no longer members of the defendant union. The plaintiff asked for a declaration that he was still a member of the defendant union, and that they could not expel him. *Held,* that he was entitled to the declaration, since the rules of the union did not provide for expulsion, and such a right, even if exercised in pursuance of T.U.C. directions, could not be implied into the rules.

2. Where a union possesses the power of expulsion the power must be exercised in strict compliance with the provisions of the rules.

Bonsor v. *Musicians' Union.* B. had fallen into arrears with his union dues, and the secretary of his local union branch informed him that his name had been removed from the list of members. The union possessed the power of expulsion for non-payment of dues, but this power should have been exercised by the branch committee and not by the branch secretary. *Held,* that the expulsion was unlawful, and therefore void.

3. Unless the rules clearly state that a member may be expelled at the complete discretion of the committee or other union disciplinary body, this body will be deemed to be acting in a quasi-judicial capacity (*i.e.,* like a court), and it will be expected, therefore, to observe the 'principles of natural justice' in dealing with the case. These principles are generally stated under three main headings:

(*a*) Where a person is accused of some offence against the union he must be informed of the nature of the offence with which he is charged. He must be given sufficient notice to allow him to prepare his answer to the case against him.

(*b*) The member must be given an opportunity of presenting his defence to the body having the power of expelling him. Thus, the case against him may not be heard in his absence unless he has been given a reasonable opportunity of attending and he has failed to take advantage of it.

(*c*) The body conducting the hearing must proceed in an unbiased manner. No person interested in the outcome may be a member of the body, and no issue unconnected with the charge may be taken into account.

Abbott v. *Sullivan.* The plaintiff, a cornporter at London Docks, was a member of the cornporters' committee, formed to protect the interests of its members. No one was allowed to work as a cornporter who was not a member of the committee. The plaintiff had been charged with some minor disciplinary offence and the committee had fined him. After the hearing the plaintiff assaulted on the street a trade union official who was a member of the committee. The official at once recalled the committee, and the plaintiff was expelled from membership. *Held,* that the resolution of the committee was invalid, since the committee had no right to use its disciplinary powers in a matter solely affecting one of its members, and not concerning the interests of cornporters as a whole.

It must not be overlooked, however, that compliance with the principles of natural justice could be excluded by the rules of the union. The rules could provide, for instance, that a member against whom a complaint had been preferred could be expelled by the union without a hearing. The rules could also state that a member could be expelled from the union for any reason which in the opinion of the union's committee warranted this action being taken

4. The member who has been expelled by the union from membership may apply to the court for a declaration that his expulsion was wrongful only where he had exhausted the union's own appeal procedure.

White v. *Kuzych*. A member who had been expelled, in his opinion wrongfully, from a union appealed to the court to have the expulsion set aside. He could have appealed to the union's national executive. He did not do so because in his opinion the appeal stood no chance of success. *Held*, that if the union rules provide for appeals, then the member must first exhaust the appeal procedure before coming to the court.

5. A union member expelled from the union may appeal to the court not only where his expulsion has been procedurally wrong, but also where the expelling committee has misinterpreted some legal term in the rules in deciding on the expulsion.

Lee v. *Showmen's Guild*. The guild is a registered trade union protecting the interests of travelling showmen, and the plaintiff was a member of the guild. A quarrel had developed between the plaintiff and another member as to who should occupy a certain site at the Bradford Summer Fair. The plaintiff being in possession of the site, the other member appealed to the guild, who found the plaintiff guilty of 'unfair competition,' and fined him as they were entitled to do under the rules. The plaintiff refused to pay the fine, and the guild, again in accordance with the rules, expelled him. *Held*, that where an expulsion depends on the interpretation of a term with a legal connotation, such as 'unfair competition' in the present case, the court had jurisdiction to consider whether the domestic tribunal had properly interpreted the term. It was found that they had not done so in this case, and the plaintiff's expulsion was declared to have been irregular.

Where a member has been wrongfully expelled from a union he has a right not only to a declaration that his expulsion was void, and that he should be reinstated as a member, but also to damages for breach of contract. This is a fairly recent development. Until a few years ago it was believed that an action for damages would not lie because the union was an unincorporated association. An action against an unincorporated association is really an action against all its members, and the expelled member is deemed to have given authority to the union officials to act on his behalf. Having done so he could not now withdraw his consent.

P

Bonsor v. *Musicians' Union*. The facts of the case have been discussed already (page 224). There was little doubt that B. was entitled to a declaration that his expulsion was wrongful, and that he should be reinstated, but he had also claimed damages from the union having been unable to find employment in his trade as a band conductor because of the closed shop practised by the union. *Held,* that he was entitled to damages. Although the union's officials acted as agents of the members, it could not be implied that a member had authorized, the officials of the union, even impliedly, to expel him in breach of the union rules.

THE LIABILITY OF A TRADE UNION FOR TORTS

At common law a trade union (as any other unincorporated association) was fully liable for torts (civil wrongs) committed on its behalf. The most important of these wrongs is that of conspiracy, which has been discussed already on page 155.

Taff Vale Railway Company v. *Amalgamated Society of Railway Servants*. The officials of the union had persuaded some of the company's servants to leave their employment in breach of their contracts of service. The company sued the union and the officials for damages. *Held,* that they were entitled to succeed, as the union, though not a legal person, was responsible for the wrongs committed on its behalf.

Trade union pressure led to the passing of the Trade Disputes Act, 1906, which in effect reversed the decision for the future. Section 4 (1) of the Act provides: "An action against a trade union, whether of workmen or masters, or against any members or officials thereof on behalf of themselves and all other members of the trade union in respect of any tortious act alleged to have been committed by or on behalf of the trade union, shall not be entertained by any court."

Any member who has committed a tort may still be sued in his personal capacity, but he could not be sued because he is a member or official of a trade union which has caused the commission of the tort. Section 4 (2) allows, however, an action to be brought against the trustees of union property in connexion with torts committed by the union as the owner of property—*e.g.,* nuisance.

It has been shown already that the general immunity from tort liability extended to trade unions by Section 4 of the Trade Disputes Act, 1906, does not apply to individual members. These members are, however, protected also in certain cases by the provisions of Section 3 of the Act. This section provides: " An act done by a person in contemplation or furtherance of a trade dispute shall not be actionable on the ground only that it induces some other person to break a contract of employment or that it is an interference with trade, business or employment of some other persons, or with the right of some other person to dispose of his capital or his labour as he wills."

Trade dispute is defined by Section 5 (3) of the Act as any dispute between employers and workmen, or between workmen and workmen, which is connected with the employment or non-employment, or the terms of the employment, or with the conditions of labour of any person, and the expression 'workmen' means all persons employed in trade or industry, whether or not in the employment of the employer with whom a trade dispute arises. This definition is important because it is the one which is adopted for the purpose of all the trade unions acts, and it must therefore be carefully interpreted. The following points should be noted:

1. There must exist a real dispute between the two sides; that means to say that some definite demand by one side must be at stake.

2. Disputes between employers are not included in the definition.

3. The dispute must have some industrial connexion because of the definition given to the term 'workmen.' There can be no dispute unless 'workmen' are involved in it.

4. The 'workmen' whose wages, etc., are at stake need not be the employees of the employer with whom the dispute exists. Thus, a sympathetic strike, where workmen come out on strike in sympathy with some of their colleagues employed elsewhere, although they have no dispute with their own employer, is nevertheless a 'trade dispute.'

5. In order for the act to be protected by Section 3, it must have been done 'in contemplation or furtherance' of a trade dispute. This means that the dispute must be either in existence or imminent.

Huntley v. *Thornton and others.* H., a member of the Amalgamated Engineering Union, refused to join a one-day strike called by the union, contending that the strike was unconstitutional. After the strike was over he was called before the local committee of the union to account for his action. After a lengthy argument H. walked out from the meeting and the committee recommended to the national executive of the union that he should be expelled. The national executive refused to sanction the expulsion. T., the secretary of the local branch, then contacted officials of the union in the neighbourhood and suggested to them that they should ensure that H. should not find employment. In fact, pressure by shop stewards led to his losing a number of jobs which he obtained. He sued T. and the other committee members for damages for conspiracy. *Held,* that he was entitled to succeed, as the action of T. was not protected by Section 3 of the 1906 Act. At the time when T. acted there was no trade dispute in existence and he was motivated by personal spite only.

PICKETING

Picketing—*i.e.*, the posting of persons round a place—was wrongful at common law in that it constituted a nuisance. A nuisance may be of two kinds. It may be a private nuisance, where a person interferes with some other person's enjoyment of property, or it may be a public nuisance, where the interference is one with the rights of the general public to pass freely along a highway. A private nuisance is a tort, and is actionable at the suit of the person whose property rights have been interfered with, while a public nuisance is a criminal offence, for which the offender could be prosecuted. At common law, then, pickets could be sued by the occupier of the factory if they barred the entrance to people wishing to go in or out, and they could also be prosecuted if they interferred with the rights of the general public.

The position of pickets has been clarified by Section 2 of the Trade Disputes Act, 1906, which states: "It shall be lawful for one or more persons acting on their own behalf or on behalf of a trade union or of an individual employer or firm in contemplation or furtherance of a trade dispute, to attend at or near a place where a person resides or works or carries on business or happens to be, if they so attend merely for the purpose of peacefully obtaining or communicating information or of peacefully persuading any person to work or to abstain from working."

Picketing is then lawful only if it is:

(1) peaceful;

(2) used solely for the purpose of either obtaining or communicating information or of persuading people to work or not to work;

(3) done in contemplation or furtherance of a trade dispute.

Any show of violence would make picketing unlawful, as would also an attempt to persuade people to break a contract other than a contract of employment—*e.g.*, a contract for the sale of goods. If pickets were to enter private property without the permission of the occupier they would be trespassers. As long as the pickets are merely present for the permitted purposes they would not be guilty of a private nuisance, but they might become so if they engaged in other activities interfering with the reasonable enjoyment of the picketed premises, such as shouting or making noise. They would also be guilty of the criminal offence of public nuisance if they obstructed the highway in an unreasonable manner, such as by lying down in the road to stop traffic to the picketed premises.

STRIKES

A strike may or may not involve a breach of contract. This depends on the way in which the strike has been called. If the strikers give a strike notice, equal to the length of notice applicable to their contracts of service, stating that they will leave work unless their demands are met, they will not be liable either criminally or civilly for breach of contract.

Where no strike notice is given the fact that the strikers cease to work constitutes a breach of contract and gives their employers a right to sue them in damages. The persons who have induced them to break their contracts of service would be liable for conspiracy, were it not for the provisions of the Trade Disputes Act, 1906, though of course where the Act does not apply the liability would still exist. No criminal offence is committed by anyone. The war-time provisions which made the calling of a strike a criminal offence unless certain attempts at arbitration had been made first have been repealed, and there is little doubt that even a nation-wide strike which would cripple the country's economy does not constitute a criminal offence on the part of those who have organized it.

There are, however, certain exceptional cases where a breach of contract (whether or not in pursuance of a strike) would constitute criminal offence. These cases are enumerated in the Conspiracy and Protection of Property Act, 1875.

Section 4 of this Act provides that it is a criminal offence, punishable by a fine of up to £20 or by imprisonment of up to three months, for a person employed in connexion with the supply of gas or water wilfully and maliciously to break his contract of service, knowing or having reasonable cause to believe that the probable consequence of his act, whether done alone or in combination with others, will be to deprive the inhabitants wholly or to a large extent of their supply of gas or water. The Electricity (Supply) Act, 1919, has extended the provisions of this section also to persons employed in the supply of electricity.

Section 5 of the Act provides for the same penalties for a person who wilfully and maliciously breaks a contract of service, knowing or having reasonable cause to believe that the probable consequence of his act, whether done alone or in combination with others, will be to endanger human life, or to cause serious bodily injury, or to expose valuable property to destruction or injury. This provision is likely to apply to persons employed in the hospital service, firemen, and others.

THE POLITICAL ACTIVITIES OF TRADE UNIONS

Trade unions to-day spend large sums of money in giving financial assistance to candidates for Parliament or other public offices as well as directly to political organizations. The attitude of the earlier law to political activities by trade unions was illustrated by a famous decision of the House of Lords in 1910.

Osborne v. *Amalgamated Society of Railway Servants.* O., a member of the Liberal Party, objected to a rule of the union which allowed the use of its funds for the purpose of financing the candidatures for Parliament of some union members. *Held*, that the rule was void since the purposes of a union were limited to those enumerated in the trade union acts.

The decision in *Osborne's case* seriously disturbed trade unions, and they were able to secure the passage of the Trade Union Act, 1913, which altered the position regarding union expenditure on political purposes. The position as it exists to-day is then as follows:

1. A trade union may not spend any of its funds on political objects unless the members of the union have passed by ballot a resolution by a majority of those voting by which the furtherance of political objects has been accepted as one of the objects of the union.

2. Where such a resolution has been passed the union must submit to the registrar of trade unions for his approval rules which must provide for the following:

(*a*) All payments for political purposes must come out of a special fund, known as the 'political fund,' and not out of the general fund of the union.

(*b*) Any member of the union who does not wish to contribute to the political fund may inform the secretary by notice in writing that he does not wish to be a contributor. Unless the notice is given when the member joined the union, it will become effective as from January 1 next.

(*c*) A member who has decided to 'contract out' from the political contribution must not because of this be excluded from any benefits of the union or be disqualified from holding any position within the union, except for a position in connexion with the administration of the political fund.

(*d*) Contribution to the political fund may not be made a condition for admission to the union.

3. A member who is aggrieved by an alleged breach of the rules may appeal to the registrar, who may make such order as he thinks fit in the circumstances. There is no appeal from this order or from a refusal of the registrar to make an order. Where, however, the

rules themselves are not in accordance with the Act any member of
the union may appeal to the court to have the rules declared void.

> *Birch* v. *National Union of Railwaymen.* B., a member of the union
> and a non-contributor to its political fund, had been elected to the
> office of branch chairman. According to the rules of the union, a
> non-contributor was entitled to hold any office except those involving
> administration of the political fund. The political fund was in fact,
> according to another rule, administered by the branch officials. The
> general secretary of the union declared that B. was ineligible for the
> office to which he had been elected. The rules of the union had been
> approved by the registrar, and B.'s complaint to the registrar that the
> rules had been broken was rejected. B. then appealed to the court.
> *Held,* that the court had jurisdiction where the question was not one
> of compliance with the rules but one of whether the rules were legal.
> The rules as drafted excluded a non-contributor from holding a
> general office in the union, and they were therefore void.

4. The political objects for the furtherance of which the political
fund of a union may be applied are enumerated in Section 3 of the
1913 Act:

(*a*) The payment of the expenses incurred by a candidate or
prospective candidate for election to Parliament or any other
public office.

(*b*) The holding of meetings and the distribution of literature
in support of such candidates or prospective candidates.

(*c*) The maintenance of a person who is a member of Parliament or holds any other public office.

(*d*) The registration of electors or the selection of a candidate
for Parliament or any other public office.

(*e*) The holding of political meetings of any kind or the general
distribution of political literature, unless the main purpose of the
meetings or of the literature is the furtherance of the statutory
objects of the trade union.

CHAPTER SIXTEEN

INDUSTRIAL DISPUTES AND THEIR SETTLEMENT

COLLECTIVE AGREEMENTS

A collective agreement is an agreement entered into by a trade union acting on behalf of its members. The agreement may be made either with an employers' association or with an individual employer.

Where the collective agreement is one between a trade union and an employers' association it is in fact "an agreement made between one trade union and another," and such agreements will not be enforced by a court of law in view of Section 4 of the Trade Union Act, 1871 (page 221). We have pointed out already that Section 4 applies only to the agreements of trade unions which would be illegal at common law, so that an agreement made by a trade union which would have been legal at common law—if such a body exists —would appear to be enforceable by court action. Similarly, an agreement made by a trade union with a single employer would also be enforceable.

There is, however, a serious objection to the enforceability of any collective agreement, whosoever the parties may have been. Professor O. Kahn-Freund, one of our leading authorities on industrial law, has suggested that collective agreements could not be enforced at all by court action because they are not 'contracts' in the legal sense of that term, lacking the essential ingredient of a contract—namely the intention of the parties to enter into legal commitments. Professor Kahn-Freund suggests that a collective agreement is a kind of industrial code which is intended to be binding in honour only. There are no real case precedents which would help us in determining whether or not this view is correct, since in practice neither unions nor employers' associations have ever attempted to put this issue to the test of an actual court case.

This brings us to the next question, which is whether a collective agreement between a union and an employers' association does create rights or liabilities for the members of either of the two participating bodies. In the chapter dealing with the law of contract we have noted that a contract between A and B does not create either rights or liabilities for C, except where either A or B acted as C's agent. A trade union when bargaining with employers does not purport to act as agent for their members, and neither does an employers' association. Thus the mere fact that a collective agreement has been made does not entitle a worker to claim from his employer in a court of law the rate of pay which has been agreed upon collectively, even if the employer is a member of the employers' association.

A collective agreement deals generally with two types of issues. There are those which are of concern only to the associations which have made the agreement, such as recognition of a trade union for bargaining purposes, the rights and duties of shop stewards, etc. The other type of issue which may be contained in a collective agreement is of direct concern to the individual member of the trade union in that it deals with rates of pay, methods of remuneration, holidays, and similar matters. As has been shown already, the individual member of the trade union cannot enforce these terms merely because they are embodied in a collective agreement which is supposed to cover also his employment. He may do so only if the terms have become embodied in his own contract of service. This will happen in the following cases:

1. Where an employee has been engaged on the terms of a particular collective agreement, or when it has been agreed that he should be paid 'union rates of pay.'

National Coal Board v. *Galley.* G., a deputy at a coal-mine, was employed by the plaintiffs under a written contract which provided that his wages and working conditions should be regulated by such national agreements as might be in force for the time being. An agreement signed some time later between the plaintiffs and G.'s union provided that 'deputies should work such days or part days in each week as may reasonably be required.' Some years later G., in common with other deputies, refused to work Saturday shifts, and the Board sued him for damages for breach of contract. G. contended that as he had not been a party to the national agreement it could not be binding on him. *Held,* that the agreement had become embodied by reference in his contract of service and that he had broken a term of the contract by refusing Saturday work.

2. If without an express agreement the employer applies the terms of a collective agreement to his employees, and continues to apply them, the terms will have become incorporated in their contracts of service by usage.

3. In employments to which the Fair Wages Resolution of the House of Commons (page 167) applies the employer must pay wages and offer such other terms of employment which are not less favourable than those agreed by collective agreement for the industry. This obligation is, however, one which the employer (contractor) has *vis-à-vis* the Government department from whom

he has received the contract, and his employees do not acquire any right of action against him if he should fail to pay them the appropriate rate of wages. The remedies of the Government department in such a situation have been discussed already.

4. Professor Kahn-Freund, whose views have been discussed already, has suggested that the main effect of a collective agreement is that a kind of 'industrial code of conditions of employment' comes into existence which represents the standard or 'correct' terms on which employees should be employed in the industry. It will be shown below, when dealing with the Terms and Conditions of Employment Act, 1959, that even employers who do not belong to the association which has negotiated the 'code' may be compelled to adhere to the 'code.'

JOINT INDUSTRIAL COUNCILS

In most industries collective bargaining takes place on an *ad hoc* basis. This means that a meeting is arranged between representatives of the two sides of industry if occasion has arisen to examine some demand made by one side on the other.

There are, however, some industries in which there exist permanent bodies, consisting of representatives of the employers and workmen in the industry, meeting at regular intervals for the purpose of discussing any outstanding issues. These bodies are known as joint industrial councils. In the Civil Service and local government service they are also known as Whitley Councils, because the setting up of them was one of the recommendations made by the Committee on relations between employers and employed which sat under the chairmanship of the Right Hon. J. H. Whitley, M.P., between 1916 and 1917.

As the two sides are equally represented on the council, and the chairman, who is usually an independent person, has no voting rights, the sole purpose of the council is to help the two sides to reach agreement. A majority decision is out of the question, and if the parties fail to agree the settlement of the outstanding problems between them will have to be left to some form of arbitration or conciliation.

None of the basic industries in this country have a joint industrial council, but such councils are found in local and central government service as well as in certain minor industries, such as boot and shoe manufacture, pottery, and others.

THE POWERS OF THE MINISTER OF LABOUR AND NATIONAL SERVICE

When a dispute has arisen between employers and workmen, and they have failed to settle the dispute by collective bargaining, a deadlock may arise which would lead to a stoppage of work through either a strike or a lockout. Every stoppage of work will not only affect the interests of the parties immediately concerned, but it must have also serious effects on the national economy as a whole, and it is understandable that the Government will wish to intervene with a view to promoting a settlement. Under war-time conditions it is customary to introduce compulsory arbitration. This means that when a dispute cannot be settled by the parties themselves they must submit it to the decision of an independent arbitrator, appointed in accordance with certain rules, and must accept the decision of the arbitrator. Strike or lockout action aimed at bypassing the arbitration procedure is then declared unlawful.

Under peace-time conditions compulsory arbitration is not generally acceptable to the trade unions of this country, because they conceive of the right to strike as of one of the basic civic liberties of the citizens of this country. The only way, then, in which industrial disputes may be settled is by conciliation or by voluntary arbitration. Conciliation means that a third party tries to help the disputants to reach a settlement, by suggesting to them possible solutions. The parties are not compelled to accept these suggestions, and the dispute will be settled only if they themselves agree. With voluntary arbitration the parties agree to submit their dispute to arbitration, and they also agree to accept the award of the arbitrator, but, of course, they are not forced to agree to go to arbitration in the first place.

We have now to discuss the powers given by Act of Parliament to the Minister of Labour and National Service so that he could promote industrial peace.

THE CONCILIATION ACT, 1896

This Act provided for the formation of conciliation boards—*i.e.,* permanent bodies authorized in writing by the employers and the unions in a particular industry to deal with disputes that might arise between them. The Minister of Labour and National Service (who took over this function from the Board of Trade) has to keep a register of conciliation boards. If he feels that in a trade or district there does not exist sufficient arrangements to have disputes submitted to a conciliation board he can, at his own initiative, appoint a person or persons to inquire into the situation and to consult all parties concerned, including local authorities, as to whether it would be expedient to set up such a board. The above provisions, though still on the statute book, are now in practice obsolete.

Where a dispute exists between employers and workmen the Minister may exercise any of the following powers:

1. He may inquire into the causes and circumstances of the dispute.

2. He may take steps to enable the parties to meet under the chairmanship of a person nominated by him unless the parties have agreed on the name of the chairman.

3. At the request of *one* of the parties, and taking into account the existence and adequacy of the means of conciliation that exist in the trade and district, he may appoint a person or persons to act as conciliators.

4. At the request of *both* parties he may appoint an arbitrator.

The award of the arbitrator would not be legally binding, but since he would be appointed only if both parties asked for it, it must be assumed that they would also be prepared to accept the award. The Arbitration Act, 1950, does not apply to industrial arbitration proceedings, but the principles on which the Act is based would be followed by the arbitrator.

When a settlement of the dispute has been reached, whether by conciliation or by arbitration, a memorandum has to be drawn up and a copy sent to the Minister.

THE INDUSTRIAL COURTS ACT, 1919

This Act consists of two parts. Part I set up the Industrial Court, while Part II made provision for the setting up of courts of inquiry.

The Industrial Court is not a court of law but a permanent arbitration tribunal. The court consists of a number of independent members and of further members who are chosen to represent employers and employees in industry and trade. One of the independent members acts as the President of the Industrial Court, having the status of a High Court judge. All members are appointed by the Minister, who also determines the length of their appointment. The Industrial Court deals with disputes in divisions, consisting generally of three members, an independent member, who acts as chairman, and one member from the employers' and one from the employees' side. The composition of each division is decided by the President of the Court.

Where a trade dispute is in existence or is apprehended, either or both parties may report the dispute to the Minister. The Minister may then take such steps as he considers expedient in order to promote a settlement of the dispute. A trade dispute is defined in the same way as under the Trade Union Acts (page 227). The Minister may do any of the following things, but only if he thinks it advisable and if *both* parties agree:

1. He may refer the dispute for settlement to the Industrial Court.

2. He may refer the dispute for settlement to one or more arbitrators appointed *ad hoc*.

3. He may refer the dispute to a board of arbitration on which, apart from an independent chairman, there are also representatives, in equal numbers, of the parties to the dispute.

The Minister will not use any of the powers shown where there exist in the industry in which the dispute has originated voluntary arrangements for the settlement of disputes unless there has been a failure to obtain a settlement through these arrangements.

It should be noted, then, that arbitration by the Industrial Court is entirely voluntary; unless both parties agree the Minister will never refer the matter to the Court for arbitration. Even if the parties agree, however, it still depends on whether the Minister deems it advisable to use the Court for this purpose.

The awards of the Industrial Court are not legally binding on the parties, but, since they are not compelled to go to the Industrial Court, awards are nearly always accepted by them. The agreement of the parties to a reference to the Court may either come about when the dispute is already in existence, or it may be contained in a collective agreement made by the parties. In such a case the parties have in effect agreed in advance that any dispute arising out of an interpretation of the agreement should be submitted to the Industrial Court for settlement.

No reasons are given for the award. The awards are given in writing and are published by H.M. Stationery Office, but in view of the absence of reasons it is impossible for any Industrial Court case law to come into existence. Where an award is acted upon by the parties, such as where employers apply a wage increase that has been awarded to their employees, the terms of the award will become incorporated in the contracts of service of the employees in question.

Certain statutes make use of the facilities of the Industrial Court. Thus the Road Haulage Wages Act, 1938, provides that employees of persons holding 'C' (private carriers) licences may apply to the Minister of Labour complaining that their wages are 'unfair.' If the Minister feels that the applicants have made out a *prima facie* case, then, in the absence of voluntary arbitration procedure, he must refer the matter to the Industrial Court for an award. Similar powers exist also in respect of the employees of private airlines under the Civil Aviation Act, 1946.

Part II of the Industrial Courts Act, 1919, deals with the appointment of courts of inquiry. The Minister may appoint such a court to inquire into the causes and circumstances of a trade dispute, and to ask it for an investigation and report. The Minister possesses these powers whether or not the dispute has been reported to him by one or both parties to it. The court of inquiry consists of members appointed by the Minister. There are usually three members, of whom the chairman is an independent person—*i.e.*, neither an employer nor an employee (frequently the President of the Industrial Court, or perhaps a university professor), while the other two members are representative figures from industry representing employers and workers, though they must not be directly concerned with the dispute. The court may require persons to give evidence on oath. The report of the court is submitted by the Minister to Parliament. Although the report is not an award, and does not purport to settle the dispute, it frequently suggests the lines on which the dispute ought to be settled, and it is difficult for the parties to disregard the suggestions of such an independent body.

TERMS AND CONDITIONS OF EMPLOYMENT ACT, 1959

When discussing earlier collective agreements we observed that these agreements, in so far as they are binding at all, only concern the members of the organizations which entered into the agreement. If, then, the outsider—*e.g.*, the firm not belonging to an employers' federation—were able to disregard the terms of a collective agreement and possibly pay lower wages than those agreed upon by the parties to the collective agreement, the latter would be seriously handicapped in competing with the non-member firm. For this reason the various orders made between 1940 and 1951 dealing with compulsory arbitration of industrial disputes also included provisions which could be used to compel non-participants in collective agreements to apply in effect the terms of the agreements. With the abolition of the Industrial Disputes Tribunal in 1958 compulsory arbitration has now disappeared from our industrial law, but it was considered desirable to retain the procedure whereby employers could be compelled to apply to their own workers generally agreed terms and conditions of employment. In order to do this, the Terms and Conditions of Employment Act, 1959, contains in section 8 the substance of those articles of the earlier orders dealing with this type of problem.

The provisions of the section may be summarized as follows :

1. Where there exist in a trade or industry or section of it, terms and conditions of employment which have been settled either by an agreement or by an arbitration award, and the parties to the agreement or award are organizations of employers and of workers

representing respectively a substantial proportion of these two sides, either of the organizations mentioned may submit a written "claim" to the Minister of Labour that a particular employer in the trade or industry concerned is not observing the terms and conditions in respect of any worker or workers to whom they apply.

2. The Minister will not examine the claim on its merits, but will only consider whether it contains sufficient detail, and if it does not he may return it to the claiming party for clarification. Once he is satisfied that the claim has been properly reported, he may take such steps as seem to him to be expedient to settle the claim, but if the claim is not otherwise settled the Minister must refer it to the Industrial Court for settlement.

3. The Industrial Court will consider whether in fact there exist in the trade or industry generally accepted terms and conditions of employment. If these are found to exist the Court will examine whether the employer complained about is observing in relation to his workers terms and conditions which are not less favourable than the recognized ones. If the Court finds that he is not observing these terms and conditions it will make an award ordering the employer to observe them. This award is treated as an implied term of the contracts of employment of the workers to whom it refers, operating from a date fixed by the Court. This date may not be earlier than the date on which the employer involved was first informed of the claim. The award ceases to have effect when an agreement or award is made altering the agreement or award on which the claim was based.

A SELECT LIST OF QUESTIONS AND PROBLEMS

The following list of questions and problems is given in the hope that it may be of help to the reader, particularly in revising the contents of the book. For permission to use the questions the author wishes to express his thanks to the Institute of Cost and Works Accountants and to the British Institute of Management. The questions and problems are arranged by chapters: naturally, there are more of them for the longer than for the shorter chapters. Some of the questions concerning Factory Law refer to the Factories Act, 1937. Similar questions set to-day would, of course, refer to the corresponding sections of the 1961 Act.

Chapter Two. The Law of Contract

1. Jones and Smith agreed for the sale and purchase of a house "subject to contract." The form of contract was subsequently agreed between their respective solicitors and counterparts prepared for their signatures. Smith duly signed his part and posted it to Jones, but Jones did not sign or post his part and refused to proceed with the sale. Discuss the legal position. (C.W.A., June 1959)

2. On December 1, Black wrote to White offering to sell his (Black's) car for £350, and White posted a letter on December 2 accepting Black's offer. On December 3 White telegraphed to Black asking him to treat the letter of acceptance as cancelled. In fact White's letter of acceptance never reached Black. State, with reasons, whether you consider that there was a concluded contract. (C.W.A., December 1959)

3. Explain how the rules of offer and acceptance would apply to each of the following:
   (a) a price-ticket is placed on goods in a shop window;
   (b) a bid is made at an auction sale;
   (c) an advertisement offers a reward for the return of a lost watch;
   (d) a letter offers to buy goods for £15 and ends: "If I hear no more from you I shall assume the goods are mine." (B.I.M., January 1960)

4. Under what circumstances will a court
   (a) order the specific performance of a contract, and
   (b) restrain a breach of contract by ordering an injunction ? (B.I.M., June 1960)

5. Explain briefly the main rules relating to consideration. C asks D to collect rents for him while C is abroad, but nothing is said about remuneration. D collects the rents for C, and when C returns he says to D, "I will give you £50 for your work." Can D sue on this promise? (B.I.M., June 1959)

6. Smith sold a cargo of iron to Green. The cargo was to be shipped on a ship named in the contract. If the ship was accidentally stranded, and so damaged that the cargo could not be loaded within the contract period, will Smith be liable to Green?

7. Spendthrift, an infant, has ordered a suit from Thimble, a tailor.

If the infant refuses to take delivery of the suit when it is ready can Thimble sue him for the price? Would it make any difference if Spendthrift had given Thimble a cheque for the price of the suit and then had countermanded payment?

8. A offers to buy a picture, owned by B, believing it to be a Gainsborough. B, sensing that A is under this impression, does not tell him that the picture is merely a good copy, and accepts the offer. Advise A.

9. Jones has bought Brown's house, and it has been agreed that he should get vacant possession on January 1. If Brown does not vacate the building until January 15 will Jones be able to claim any of the following by way of damages for breach of contract?

    (a) the cost of hotel accommodation for himself, his wife and children, and his parents-in-law who had come to visit him;

    (b) the cost of storing his furniture for the fortnight;

    (c) extra travelling expenses, caused by the fact that since buying the new house Jones has found a job near it, while the hotel is near his old home?

10. Is it ever, and if so when, open to a person who signs a document to repudiate his liability thereunder on the ground that he did not know what the contents of the document were? (B.I.M., January 1957)

11. What are the present rules of law governing contracts which have become impossible of performance or otherwise frustrated? (B.I.M., January 1957)

Chapter Three. The Law of Agency
1. What is a breach of warranty of authority?

Dick is authorized by Tom to sell the latter's machinery for £5000. After Tom's death, but without knowing that Tom is dead, Dick agrees to sell the machinery to Harry for £5000. Tom's personal representatives repudiate the sale. Advise Dick as to his legal position in the matter. (C.W.A., December 1958)

2. Outline the duties of an agent to his principal.

A enters into contracts on behalf of a principal, P, without stating the fact that he is acting as agent for P. Explain briefly the position of B and C in the following circumstances:

    (a) A makes a contract in writing with B, without clearly showing that he is signing as an agent for P and not as principal;

    (b) A has entered into a contract with C, stating that he was acting as an agent, but without giving the name of his principal. P subsequently refuses to perform the contract. (B.I.M., January 1960)

3. Smith sold goods on credit to Burke and Hare, who were engaged in promoting a company and who expressly contracted as "agents for and on behalf of the Seamless Clothes Company about to be registered." The company after incorporation used the goods in its business, but subsequently became insolvent and went into liquidation before the goods were paid for. Advise Smith as to his rights of action (if any) against:

    (a) the company through its liquidator;

    (b) Burke and Hare personally. (C.W.A., December 1956)

4. Mrs Bountiful, the wife of a wealthy barrister, who is receiving a generous allowance from her husband, buys large quantities of lingerie from a shop. When Mrs Bountiful fails to pay the bills the shopkeeper wishes to sue her husband. Can he do so with any hope of success?

Q

5. John Bulldog, pretending to be Rudolph Doberman, the well-known violinist, who is a personal friend of his, buys a valuable violin on credit from String, a dealer. When String asks Doberman for payment the violinist discovers his friend's conduct and, feeling sorry for him, decides to ratify the purchase. Will String be able to sue Doberman on this ratification? If not, why not?

6. Tallboy, an antique dealer, accepts for repair a set of antique chairs. Although he has no instructions to sell, he disposes of the chairs at a high price to Gluepot, a collector. Will the owner be able to claim the chairs from Gluepot?

Chapter Four. The Sale of Goods

1. (a) What are the implied conditions of sale in a contract for the sale of goods where no conditions have been stated by the parties?

   (b) D agrees to buy some goods from E. Before the goods come into the possession of E they are destroyed by fire. State, giving reasons, who bears the loss in the following circumstances:

      (i) D has stipulated that the goods shall be held for him until he gives instructions for delivery at his home;

      (ii) E has undertaken to carry out certain modifications before delivery. (B.I.M., January 1960)

2. State the rules governing the passing of property under contracts for the sale of goods in cases where the parties have not indicated an intention that it should pass at any particular time. (C.W.A., December 1952)

3. (a) Tom delivers to Dick a motor-car under an hire-purchase agreement. Before the instalments are fully paid Dick sells and delivers the car to Harry, who pays the price to Dick in good faith. Can Tom claim from Harry the car or damages for its value?

   (b) Would your answer be the same if the transaction between Tom and Dick had been a credit sale? (C.W.A., December 1952)

4. Explain the rights of an unpaid seller against the goods which are the subject-matter of the sale. (C.W.A., December 1953 and June 1957)

5. A firm contracted to deliver a quantity of shirtings according to a sample. After the shirtings had been delivered it was discovered that a certain quantity of china clay had been introduced into the fabric. This defect could be discovered only by a scientific examination of the material. Advise the buyer.

6. Brown agreed to sell to Jones ten crates of oranges. When the crates are delivered Jones discovers that two crates contain tangerines. Advise him.

7. Mrs Green buys a pound of sausage-meat from Bone, a pork butcher. The pork in the sausage-meat has come from a pig infected with trichinosis. If the meat had been cooked it would have been safe for human consumption, but Mrs Green decided to spread it on a piece of bread and eat it that way. She falls ill, and now claims damages from the butcher. Will she be able to succeed?

8. Draper buys a quantity of cloth from Manufacturer for resale. The manufacturer delays delivery, and Draper is thus unable to supply

his customer in time. The customer cancels the order. Can Draper claim damages from Manufacturer for the loss of profit which he has sustained?

9. Explain and illustrate the difference between a condition and a warranty in relation to a contract for the sale of goods. What determines whether a term in such a contract is a condition or a warranty? In what cases, if at all, may a condition be treated as a warranty? (B.I.M., June 1957)

10. Jones, whose house is overrun by rats, buys a tin of rat poison from Crafty, a chemist. He spreads the rat poison in his cellar, but the rats thrive on it, and increase in numbers. Has Jones any remedy against Crafty? Would it make any difference if he had bought "Killall," a branded rat poison?

Chapter Five. The Law of Negotiable Instruments
1. Explain and illustrate the meaning of the expressions 'holder' and 'holder for value' and 'holder in due course' of a bill of exchange. (C.W.A., June 1952) (B.I.M., January 1958)

2. Explain concisely, with reference to bills of exchange, the meaning of: (*a*) accommodation party; (*b*) bills in asset; (*c*) fictitious payee; (*d*) holder for value; (*e*) notice of dishonour *supra protest*. (C.W.A., December 1958)

3. (*a*) Define bill of exchange.
    (*b*) State with reasons whether or not the following are bills of
       exchange:
       (i) a postal order;
       (ii) a cheque drawn in the usual way but bearing the imprint:
          "This cheque must be presented within three months."
       (C.W.A., June 1954)

4. Explain the legal effect of crossing a cheque "A/c payee only." How does the effect of such a crossing differ from that of a crossing "Not Negotiable"? (C.W.A., December 1954)

5. What is meant by 'acceptance' of a bill of exchange? When must a bill be accepted? If acceptance is refused what steps should the holder take? (C.W.A., June 1955)

6. (*a*) Explain the legal nature of the relationship between banker
       and customer.
    (*b*) How is the banker's authority to pay cheques drawn by the
       customer revoked? (C.W.A., December 1959)

7. A crossed cheque payable to John Jones and Company, Ltd., has been endorsed to John Jones, the sole director of the company, and paid by him into his private account. In the winding-up of the company this transaction is discovered and the liquidator who claims that Jones was not entitled to the money wants to claim damages from Jones' bank for collecting the cheque for him. Discuss.

8. Simple, a businessman, draws a cheque for £2 payable to his secretary, Miss Fraud, for minor office expenses. The cheque is carelessly drawn, and Miss Fraud is able to add a nought to the amount and to collect £20 from the bank. Will the bank be able to debit the customer's account with £20?

Chapter Six. The Law of Partnership

1. East and West have for several years carried on business in partnership. It has now been agreed that East shall retire and receive £10,000 in satisfaction of his share, while West shall take over all the assets and liabilities and carry on the business in the old firm name.

Advise East as to the steps which should be taken in order that he may be adequately protected, giving your reasons. (C.W.A., June 1959)

2. (a) Explain the meaning of goodwill.
   (b) Upon the sale of a business, to what extent (if at all) is the vendor, in the absence of an agreement, entitled to carry on a similar business after the sale? (C.W.A., December 1953)

3. Explain the effect of the Limited Partnerships Act, 1907. Why have comparatively few partnerships been registered under the Act? (C.W.A., June 1954)

4. On what grounds can a partnership be dissolved when the articles of partnership are silent upon the matter? (C.W.A., December 1955)

5. Tom Brown and Charles Green are in partnership as Army tailors. Tom Brown joins the Communist Party and addresses on their behalf many public meetings. Some of the customers of the firm indicate their displeasure with Brown's political views, and threaten to transfer their custom elsewhere. Advise Green.

6. Which, if any, of the following partnership firms will require registration under the Registration of Business Names Act, 1916?
   (a) "Long and Short," proprietors Tom Long and Robert Short.
   (b) "Paris Fashions," proprietors Elsie Green and Mimi Blue.
   (c) "Beef and Pork," proprietors Robert Beef and Drusilla Mutton, née Pork.

Where registration is required, what would be the effects of non-registration?

Chapter Seven. Joint Stock Companies

1. What is an 'exempt private company,' and what privileges does such a company enjoy as compared with a public company? (C.W.A., June 1952) (B.I.M., January 1957)

2. To what extent and by what means can (a) the Memorandum, (b) the Articles of Association, of a registered company be altered? (C.W.A., June 1955)

3. Timbermerchants, Ltd., are a registered company. Their objects, according to the objects clause in their Memorandum, include the import and sale of timber. The directors of the company would now like to extend their activities, and also to become undertakers. Will this be possible, and, if so, what have they got to do?

4. Explain briefly the purpose of (a) the Memorandum of Association and (b) the Articles of Association of a limited company. How far, if at all, can these documents be altered? (B.I.M., June 1956)

5. Explain any five advantages which may result from the conversion of the business of a sole trader or partnership into a limited company under the Companies Act, 1948. (C.W.A., June 1960)

Chapter Eight. Commercial Arbitration

1. Discuss the principal differences between an arbitration and an action at law. (C.W.A., June 1952 and B.I.M. June 1959)

2. Discuss the meaning of misconduct on the part of an arbitrator. What courses of action are open to the parties if an arbitrator is guilty of misconduct? (C.W.A., June 1954)

3. In what respects do you consider that arbitration is more advantageous to the parties to a dispute than an action at law? (C.W.A., December 1955)

4. "An arbitration clause in a business document shuts the door to litigation." Discuss this statement with reference to the Arbitration Act, 1950. (B.I.M., June 1957)

Chapter Nine. The Law of Master and Servant

1. Discuss the liability of an employer to pay salary or wages to an employee during the latter's illness. (C.W.A., June 1952)

2. (a) What length of notice should be given by an employer to terminate an employee's contract of service?
   (b) In what circumstances has an employer the right to dismiss an employee without notice? (C.W.A., June 1954)

3. State the obligations of an employer in regard to:
   (a) giving a reference in respect of an employee or ex-employee;
   (b) the contents of such reference. (C.W.A., December 1954)

4. It is an established principle of common law that an employer is under an obligation towards his employees to use reasonable care to institute and maintain a proper and safe system of working. Explain, with examples, the nature and extent of this obligation. (C.W.A., December 1955)

5. (a) What test would you apply in order to determine whether the relationship of master and servant exists in any particular case? Illustrate your answer by examples.
   (b) In what circumstances (if any) is an employee entitled to be paid wages or salary during illness? (C.W.A., June 1956 and December 1959)

6. In what circumstances, if any, has an employer the right to the benefit of an invention made by his employee? (C.W.A., December 1956)

7. Clever, when entering the services of Sly, a solicitor in X, agrees that in the event of his leaving Sly's employment he would not practise as a solicitor or be employed by a solicitor or by a chartered accountant for the rest of his life. The restraint is limited to an area of 50 miles round X. Can the restraint be enforced against Clever?

8. Jones, a detective in the employment of a department store, accuses a woman shopper of having stolen some nylon stockings from a counter. He does so in the presence of other shoppers, and in breach of the instructions of the management, which are that any suspected shoplifter should be followed and stopped only when trying to leave the shop. Has the woman, who denies the charge, a right of action for slander against the proprietors of the store?

9. Beefcake is a branch manager employed by Messrs Butterfingers, wholesale grocers. He commits adultery with Mrs Cheesecake, the wife of one of the assistants employed in the office of which he is manager. The employers summarily dismiss Beefcake. Is this dismissal justified?

10. Green is employed by Brown, and, when seeking a change of employment, requests Brown to provide him with a reference. What are Green's rights, if any, in the following circumstances:

    (i)   Brown refuses to provide a reference of any kind;
    (ii) Brown merely states that Green is competent but lacks initiative;
    (iii) Brown gives a reference which includes defamatory statements relating to Green? (B.I.M., June 1960)

Chapter Ten. Statutory Control of Wages

1. Discuss the conditions to be fulfilled and the procedure to be followed for the establishment of a wages council. (C.W.A., June 1952)

2. Cook proposes to employ Pratt as a packer in his warehouse on the terms that Pratt shall receive £4 weekly and food for dinner and tea in the warehouse canteen to the amount of £1 weekly. Advise Cook as to how the agreement should be made in order to ensure its validity. (C.W.A., December 1953)

3. What deductions can lawfully be made from the wages of a workman? Would the following deductions be lawful:

    (a) a deduction of 6d. per week from the wages of all the workers in a factory in favour of the Works Sports Club, made in pursuance of a resolution passed at a meeting attended by the majority of the workers;

    (b) a deduction of £1 a week from the wages of a factory worker on account of the rent of a company house occupied by him? Give reasons for your answer. (B.I.M., January 1958)

4. Noodle, Ltd., have introduced a bonus scheme for their employees, under which an employee who has not been late for work in the course of a calendar month qualifies for the payment of a bonus of £1. Toadstool, a labourer employed by the company, does not receive the bonus because he has been late on one occasion. Is the company entitled to withhold the bonus from him?

5. Greensleeves is a checkweighman at a pit of the National Coal Board. One day he leaves his place of work, goes down the mine, and engages in an argument with Bottom, a miner, who owes some money to him. Other miners have to prevent them from coming to blows, and work in the mine is seriously interrupted. What can the National Coal Board do?

6. Explain the incidence and effects of "fair wages clauses." (C.W.A., June 1960)

Chapter Eleven. Factory Law.

1. What are the obligations of an employer in regard to providing seating facilities for employees in a factory? (C.W.A., June 1952)

2. Summarize the statutory provisions with regard to precautions against fire. (C.W.A., December 1952 and June 1960)

3. (a) What is the general definition of a factory as given by the Factories Act, 1937, Section 151 (1)?

    (b) A restaurant within the curtilage of a factory is used by executive and administrative employees but not by the workmen, though one of the dining-rooms is occasionally used for conferences between the management and shop stewards. State your opinion (with reasons) as to whether the restaurant would be deemed to form part of the factory for the purposes of the Factories Act. (C.W.A., December 1953)

4. Within what limits is it permissible for women and young persons to be employed overtime in factories? (C.W.A., June 1954)

5. Summarize the provisions of the Factories Acts relating to the notification of industrial diseases. (C.W.A., December 1958)

6. Summarize the provisions of the Factories Act with respect to the safeguarding of machinery. (C.W.A., June 1955)

7. Summarize the general provisions as to welfare contained in the Factories Act, 1937, Part III. (C.W.A., June 1959)

8. State, giving reasons, whether you consider the following to be factories within the general definition given in Section 151 (1) of the Factories Act, 1937:
   (a) a technical institute teaching engineering students how to use dangerous machinery;
   (b) a canteen used for feeding and entertaining the employees in a factory. (C.W.A., December 1956)

9. (a) State the requirements of the Factories Act, 1937, Section 14 (1) as to dangerous parts of machinery.
   (b) A workman was injured by a flying particle of a broken blade in a woodworking resaw which was not fenced. Discuss the employer's liability. (C.W.A., June 1957)

10. Bobtail, an apprentice fitter employed by Messrs Weasel and Company, is seriously injured by a piece of flying metal which has come from a machine used by a fellow-worker. The accident could have been prevented if the machine had been equipped with a different type of guard. Are the employers guilty of an offence under the Factories Acts?

Chapter Twelve. The Law relating to Injuries to Workmen

1. Discuss, with reference to reported legal decisions, the extent to which, if at all, the doctrine of *volenti non fit injuria* applies as between master and servant. (C.W.A., December 1954)

2. How has post-war legislation affected the common law liability of an employer to be sued by an employee for damages for personal injuries? (C.W.A., June 1956)

3. Miss Clumsy, employed by X. Y. Company, Ltd., is scalped when her hair gets caught in a machine. The firm has been providing special protective hair-nets, but Miss Clumsy has refused to use one. Can she claim damages from her employers?

4. Brick, a builder, is told by his foreman to get on a wall which is to be demolished. He objects because of the unsafe nature of the wall, but is persuaded to go there. The wall collapses, and Brick is injured. Will the employers have any defence in an action brought by him?

5. Jones, who is employed by Smith, is injured at work in circumstances where Smith must accept responsibility for the accident. After an illness lasting for six months, Jones dies. What remedies, if any, has his widow against Smith?

6. What is meant by breach of statutory duty? How far does such a breach differ from a breach of the employer's common law duty of providing for the safety of his servants? (B.I.M., January 1958)

*Chapter Thirteen. The National Insurance (Industrial Injuries)
Act, 1946*

1. (*a*)   What principle would you apply in order to determine whether
an employee who sustains an injury during a temporary
interruption of his employment is entitled to benefit under
the National Insurance (Industrial Injuries) Act, 1946?
   (*b*)   Discuss the following cases:
      (i) A night watchman is severely scalded while making tea;
      (ii) A workman on night shift, leaving his work-place with his
employer's permission in order to get supper, is run over
while crossing the street. (C.W.A., December 1952)

2. What 'special questions' may arise upon a claim for benefit under
the National Insurance (Industrial Injuries) Act, 1946? How are such
questions determined, and to what extent may a decision be appealed
from? (C.W.A. December 1953 and June 1957)

3. State with reasons your opinion as to whether a person insured
under the National Insurance (Industrial Injuries) Act, 1946, would be
entitled to benefit in the following circumstances:
   (*a*)   being a factory worker, he is injured in an accident while on
his way from his home to his work and before reaching the
precincts of the factory;
   (*b*)   being an apprentice, he is injured by an accident while
attending a technical school during working hours. (C.W.A.,
June 1960)

4. Under what conditions will an accident be deemed to arise out of
and in the course of employment within the meaning of the National
Insurance (Industrial Injuries) Act, 1946, if the accident happens while
the insured person is:
   (*a*)   acting in breach of any statutory or other regulations applying
to his employment;
   (*b*)   meeting an emergency? (C.W.A., December 1959)

5. State, with reasons, whether a person insured under the National
Insurance (Industrial Injuries) Act, 1946, would be entitled to benefit
in the following circumstances:
   (*a*)   being a locomotive driver, he is injured while driving a train
by a pellet from a shotgun fired by a sportsman whose land
adjoins the railway line;
   (*b*)   being a railway porter, whose duty it is to proceed to a certain
station, he walks along the line in breach of regulations, and
is injured by a passing train. (C.W.A., June 1955)

6. What do you understand by the term 'accident' for the purposes
of the National Insurance (Industrial Injuries) Act, 1946? Give
examples. (C.W.A., December 1955)

7. Carruthers has been injured in an accident at work. The court
found that he was himself to blame for the accident to the extent of
25 per cent. The court assesses the loss which Carruthers has suffered
at £1600. Carruthers is also awarded disablement benefit of £1 a week.
How much will he recover in damages from his employers?

Chapter Fourteen. The National Insurance Act, 1946

1. State the various circumstances in which, as provided by the

National Insurance Act, 1946, a person may become temporarily disqualified from receiving unemployment benefit. (C.W.A., June 1952)

2. Define the following expressions as used in the National Insurance Act, 1946: (a) benefit year; (b) contract of service; (c) contribution week; (d) incapable of work. (C.W.A., December 1952)

3. If an unemployed person has lost a benefit under the National Insurance Act, 1946, by reason of default on part of his employer what remedy is available to him? (C.W.A., December 1953)

4. What do you understand by a period of interruption of employment for the purposes of the National Insurance Act, 1946? In what circumstances, if any, are two such periods treated as one period? (C.W.A., June 1954)

5. (a) What do you understand by the term 'employer' for the purposes of the National Insurance Act, 1946?

(b) By what authority, for what purpose, and to what extent can the rates of contributions under the said Act be varied? (C.W.A., December 1954)

6. In what circumstances is a person insured under the National Insurance Act, 1946, disqualified from receiving unemployment benefit when he is unemployed by reason of a stoppage of work due to a trade dispute? (C.W.A., June 1955)

Chapter Fifteen. Trade Union Law

1. Explain and illustrate the limits within which picketing is lawful. (C.W.A., June 1959)

2. Discuss the legal position of a member of a trade union who is unjustifiably expelled from his union. (C.W.A., December 1954)

3. Jones, the secretary of the Blowpipe-makers Union, orders the members of his union working for Amazonian Exploration, Ltd., to leave their work in breach of their contracts of service. What will be the legal position concerning the following:

(a) the company's right of action against its employees for breach of contract;

(b) the company's right of action against the union and Jones?

4. If in the above situation Green, a member of the union, stayed at work during the strike, and the union secretary after the settlement of the strike compelled the management to dismiss him, would Green have a right of action against anyone?

5. In which circumstances and how in the mentioned case would the union be able to expel Green from membership? If Green feels that he has been unjustly expelled what redress has he got?

6. Compare the legal position of a registered trade union with that of an unregistered trade union. (C.W.A., June 1957)

7. Small induces Large:

(a) to leave Broad's service without proper notice;

(b) to leave Broad's service after giving proper notice;

(c) not to enter Broad's service.

Has Broad any right of action in any of the above cases? Will it make any difference:

(i) if Broad can prove that Small acted with malice towards him, or

(ii) Small is an official of the trade union of which Large is a

R

member, and that union objects to the employment of non-union labour by Broad? (B.I.M., January 1958)

8. Explain:
   (a) The liability of a trade union for its torts.
   (b) The application of trade union funds to political purposes. (B.I.M., June 1956)

Chapter Sixteen. Industrial Disputes and their Settlement

1. Explain and illustrate the statutory definition of a 'trade dispute' (C.W.A., June 1952)

2. If a strike is threatened in a certain industry in consequence of a dispute about wages what steps may be taken by the Ministry of Labour and National Service in order to avert a stoppage? (C.W.A., December 1952)

3. The doorknockers-makers' association and the trade union representing the workers employed in the industry have reached an agreement for an increase in the wages of the workers amounting to 7s. 6d. a week. To what extent is this agreement binding on Brown, an employer member of the association, and on Green, who is a non-member of the association? What can the union do if Green refuses to pay the wage increase to his employees?

4. Write a brief account of the law relating to conciliation and arbitration. (B.I.M., January 1960)

5. What is the effect in law of a collective agreement made between a workers' trade union and an employers' federation setting out minimum terms of employment in the industry? (B.I.M., June 1960)

SUGGESTIONS FOR ADDITIONAL READING

Students who are reading this book for examination purposes should find the contents detailed enough for their requirements. It may be, however, that they find certain subject-matters particularly interesting, or they may require more detailed knowledge for business or professional reasons. In that case, they may find the suggestions below of some help.

Introduction to English Law

ARCHER, P.: *The Queen's Courts* (Penguin Books, 1956)
FRANK, W. F. : *The General Principles of English Law* (Harrap, 1961)
JENKS, E.: *The Book of English Law* (fifth edition by D. J. Ll. Davies) (Murray, 1953)

Commercial Law (Chapters 2–8)

CHARLESWORTH, J. : *The Principles of Mercantile Law* (Stevens, 1960)
GOWER, L. C. B.: *The Principles of Modern Company Law* (Stevens, 1958)
LIGHT, H. R. : *The Legal Aspects of Business* (Pitman, 1959)
MONTGOMERIE, J.: *Stevens' Elements of Mercantile Law* (Butterworth, 1960)
SCHMITTHOFF, C. M.: *The Sale of Goods* (Stevens, 1951)

Industrial Law (Chapters 9–16)

CITRINE, N. : *Trade Union Law* (Stevens, 1960)
COOPER, W. MANSFIELD: *Outlines of Industrial Law* (Butterworth, 1958)
FLANDERS, A., and CLEGG, H. A.: *The System of Industrial Relations in Great Britain* (particularly Chapter II) (Basil Blackwell, 1953)
GAYLER, J. L.: *Industrial Law* (English Universities Press, 1955)
MUNKMAN, J.: *Employer's Liability at Common Law* (Butterworth, 1959)
SAMUELS, H.: *Factory Law* (Stevens, 1957) with supplements.

Law Dictionary

OSBORN, P. G.: *Concise Law Dictionary* (Sweet and Maxwell, 1954)

TABLE OF STATUTES

TABLE OF CASES

[The year given after each case is the year of the court's decision. The letters and figures shown after the date of the decision refer to the places in the various series of law reports where the text of the decision may be found. Where the year is shown in square brackets, the year represents an essential part of the reference to the reports, because the series of reports mentioned is one which is not numbered consecutively; while where the year is shown in round brackets, the series of reports is one which is numbered consecutively. Candidates studying law for professional examinations will not be expected, when quoting a case in an examination answer, to refer to more than its name. They are advised, however, to underline the name, as this is common legal practice. The page references given here are, of course, to the present book.]

256 THE LEGAL ASPECTS OF INDUSTRY AND COMMERCE

Crook v. *Derbyshire Stone, Ltd,* [1956] 1 W. L. R. 432, *page* 153
Cundy v. *Lindsay,* (1878) 3 App. Cas. 459, *page* 29
Currie v. *Misa,* (1875) L. R. 10 Exch. 153, *page* 34
Curtis v. *Chemical Cleaning and Dyeing Company, Ltd,* [1951] 1 K. B. 805, *page* 30

Davie v. *New Merton Board Mills, Ltd,* [1959] A. C. 604, *page* 146
Davis Contractors, Ltd, v. *Fareham U.D.C.,* [1956] A. C. 696, *page* 52
Denham v. *Midland Employers Mutual Assurance, Ltd,* [1955] 2 Q. B. 437, *page* 131
Donoghue v. *Stevenson,* [1932] A. C. 562, *page* 74
Doyle v. *White City Stadium,* [1935] 1 K. B. 110, *page* 19
Du Jardin v. *Beadman,* [1952] 1 T. L. R. 1601, *page* 67

Edwards v. *West Herts Hospital Committee,* [1957] 1 W. L. R. 415, *page* 146
English v. *Wilson and Clyde Colliery Company, Ltd,* [1938] A. C. 57, *page* 144
Entores, Ltd, v. *Miles Far East Corporation,* [1955] 2 Q. B. 327, *page* 25

Felthouse v. *Bindley,* (1862) 11 C. B. (N.S.) 869, *page* 26
Finch v. *Telegraph Construction and Maintenance Company,* [1949] 1 All E. R. 452, *page* 143
Fitch v. *Dewes,* [1921] 2 A. C. 158, *page* 138
Foakes v. *Beer,* (1884) 9 App. Cas. 605, *pages* 36–37
Foley v. *Classiques Coaches, Ltd,* [1934] 2 K. B. 1, *page* 27
Foster v. *Mackinnon,* (1869) L. R. 4 C. P. 704, *page* 30
Frost v. *Aylesbury Dairy Company, Ltd,* [1905] 1 K. B. 608, *page* 72

Galloway v. *Galloway,* (1914) 30 T. L. R. 531, *page* 28
Gaon (Albert D.) and Co. v. *Société Interprofessionelle des Oléagineux Fluides Alimentaires,* [1960] 2 Q. B. 318, *page* 52
Garrard v. *Southey and Company,* [1952] 2 Q. B. 174, *page* 131
General Cleaning Contractors, Ltd, v. *Christmas,* [1953] A. C. 180, *page* 143
Godley v. *Perry,* [1960] 1 W. L. R. 9, *page* 71
Greenwood v. *Martins Bank,* [1933] A. C. 51, *page* 61

Hadley v. *Baxendale,* (1854) 9 Exch. 341, *page* 56
Hampstead Guardians v. *Barclays Bank,* (1923) 39 T. L. R. 229, *pages* 96–97
Hawkins v. *Price,* [1947] Ch. 645, *page* 40
Heil v. *Hedges,* [1951] 1 T. L. R. 512, *page* 72
Henthorn v. *Fraser,* [1892] 2 Ch. 27, *page* 25
Hewlett v. *Allen,* [1894] A. C. 383, *page* 160
Hivac, Ltd, v. *Park Royal Scientific Instruments, Ltd,* [1946] Ch. 169, *page* 134
House Property Company v. *London County and Westminster Bank,* (1915) 84 L. J. K. B. 1846, *page* 98
Hudson v. *Ridge Manufacturing Company, Ltd,* [1957] 2 Q. B. 348, *pages* 142–143
Huntley v. *Thornton and others,* [1957] 1 W. L. R. 321, *page* 227

Inland Revenue Commissioners v. *Hambrook,* [1956] 2 W. L. R. 919, *pages* 154–155
Ingram v. *Little,* [1960] 3 W. L. R. 504, *page* 29

Jerome v. *Bentley and Company,* [1952] 2 T. L. R. 58, *page* 77
Johnson v. *Croggan and Company, Ltd,* [1954] 1 W. L. R. 195, *page* 195
Jones v. *Manchester Corporation and others,* [1952] 2 Q. B. 852, *page* 133
Jones Bros. (Hunstanton), Ltd, v. *Stevens,* [1955] 1 Q. B. 275, *page* 157

INDEX

ACCEPTANCE: by post, 25; by telephone or telegram, 25; communication, 25; conditional, 24; mental, 26; time for, 23–24; unconditional, 24
Accord and satisfaction, 46
Account stated, 18
Acts of Parliament: interpretation, 14; titles, 15
Agent: authority, 59, 68; bribes, 65; by estoppel 62; by necessity, 60; by ratification, 61; commission, 65; company directors, 63, 119; definition, 59; del credere, 66; duties, 64; liability, 63; mercantile, 67, 76; secret profits, 65; sub-delegation, 64; warranty of authority, 63
Agreements—see Contracts
Agreements, collective, 221, 232
Agricultural workers, 159, 167
Apprenticeship, 19, 132, 151, 214
Appropriation of payments, 47–48
Arbitration, commercial: agreement, 126; arbitrators, 127; award, 127; misconduct, 128; popularity, 127; procedure, 127; references, 126; statutory, 126; umpire, 127
Arbitration, industrial: by Industrial Court, 168, 236; by Minister of Labour and National Service, 234; compulsory, 238; voluntary, 236
Assignments, 53, 84, 131
Auctioneers, 67, 80

BANKER AND CUSTOMER, 91–92
Banker's drafts, 95
Bills of exchange: acceptance, 87; bearer bills, 86; days of grace, 87; definition, 85; demand, 87; dishonour, 89, domicile, 87; drawer, 85; endorsements, 88; forgeries, 61, 91; holder in due course, 90; maturity, 87; notice of dishonour, 89; noting, 90; order bills, 86; payment, 88; presentment, 88–89; protest, 90; recourse, 89; rights of holder, 90; transfer, 88. See also Negotiable Instruments
Breach of contract—see Contract
Breach of employer's statutory duty, 194
Breach of warranty of authority, 63
Bribes received by agents, 65
Business names, 101–102

Caveat emptor, 72
Champerty, 43
Checkweighing, 163–164
Cheques: as receipts, 98; banker's duties, 91 ff; banker's protection, 93 ff; crossings, 93; definition, 91; irregular endorsements, 94 ff; payment of debt by, 47; payment of wages by, 163
Collective agreements, 221, 232
Commercial arbitration—see Arbitration
Common law, 9
Companies—see Joint Stock Companies
Conciliation, 235
Conditions: in contracts, 23, 30, 33; in offers, 22
See also Sale of Goods
Consideration: adequacy, 35, 137; definition, 34; good, 34; legal, 37; past, 37, 91; real, 35; valuable, 34
Conspiracy, 155, 226–227
Contracts: acceptance of offer, 24; assignments, 53; breach of, 49, 54; capacity to enter into, 17; conditions in, 23, 30, 33; consideration, 33; corporations, 20; damages for breach of, 54; definition, 16; discharge of, 45 ff; drunk persons, 19; duress, 33; for services, 129 ff; form of, 38; fraud, 31; frustration of, 51; gaming, 42; infants, 18; instalments, 50; invitation to make an offer, 21; legality, 42, 50; lunatics, 19; misrepresentation, 30; mistake, 27; novation, 46; of agency, 59 ff; of apprenticeship, 19, 132, 151, 214; of guarantee, 40; of service, 19, 53, 129 ff; of utmost good faith, 32; offer, 21; parol, 38; privity of, 35; requirement for validity, 17; rescission of, 31; simple, 38; specialty—see Deeds; statute-barred, 48; "subject to contract," 26; time, lapse of, 48; to be evidenced by writing, 39; to make contracts, 26; uberrimae fidei, 32; under seal—see Deeds; undue influence, 33; unenforceable, 17, 39, 49; void, 17, 27; voidable, 17, 19, 31, 33
Contractors, independent, 129, 145, 178, 200

JOINT INDUSTRIAL COUNCILS, 234
Joint Stock Companies: agents, 63;
and partnerships, 124; articles of
association, 109; capital, 109, 112;
charges, 117; debentures, 116;
deferred shares, 114; directors, 110,
111, 112, 118, 119, 124; exempt
private companies, 111; formation,
108; founders' shares, 114; limited,
108, 110; liquidation, 121 ff, 150;
meetings, 120; memorandum of
association, 21, 108, 114; minimum
subscription, 115; name, 108;
objects, 109; offer for sale, 115;
office, 108; ordinary shares, 113;
preference shares, 112; private,
111; prospectus, 114; public, 111;
redeemable preference shares, 113;
registration of business name, 101;
resolutions, 120; share capital, 112
ff; share certificates, 115; share
warrants, 84, 116; statement in lieu
of prospectus, 115; Table A, 110;
trading certificate, 112; transfer of
shares, 39, 116; types of, 110;
underwriting, 115; unlimited, 110;
winding-up, 121 ff

LAND, SALE OF, 40
Law, definition of, 9
Legal tender, 47
Lien of unpaid seller, 79
Limitation of action, 48
Limited Companies—see Joint Stock
Companies
Limited Partnerships, 100, 106
Loaned servants, 130
Lockouts, 214, 227
Lunatics, contracts by, 19, 105

MAINTENANCE, CONTRACT OF, 43
Market overt (open market), 76
Married women, 60–62
Master: common law duties, 139,
193; general, 130; liability for injuries of servants, 193 ff; liability
for wrongful acts of servants, 152
ff; rights against third parties,
154 ff; statutory duties, 194; temporary, 130
Memorandum in writing, 40, 81
Mercantile agents, 67, 76
Misrepresentation: definition, 30;
fraudulent, 31; innocent, 31; remedies, 32; silence as, 32
Mistake, in formation of contract:
as to existence of subject-matter,
28; as to identity of other party,
29; as to identity of subject-matter,
28; as to nature of contract, 30; in

quality of subject-matter, 29; of
fact, 27; of law, 27

NATIONAL INSURANCE ACT: administration, 217; appeals, 218; apprentices, 214; benefit year, 212;
contributions, 218; contribution
conditions, 212; contribution week,
212; contribution year, 212; dis-
qualifications, 214–217; "incapable
of work," 217; insured persons,
213; married women, 213; Minister
of Pensions and National Insurance, 218; National Insurance
Advisory Committee, 218; National
Insurance Commissioner, 218;
period of interruption of employment, 217; sickness benefit, 214;
students, 214; trade disputes, 214;
unemployment benefit, 214, 217
National Insurance (Industrial Injuries) Act—see Industrial Injuries
Natural justice, 224
Necessaries: for infants, 18; for
married women, 60
Negotiable instruments: definition,
54, 85; enumeration, 85
See also Bills of Exchange
Novation, 46

Obiter dictum, 13
Occupiers' Liability, 145
Offer: communication, 22; condi-
tions attached to, 22; definition, 21;
invitation to make, 22; option, 24;
revocation, 23; tickets, 22
Offer for sale, 115
Open market, 76
Options, 24

PAROL CONTRACTS, 38
Partnerships: admission of new partners, 103; and joint stock companies, 124–125; contracts made
by, 104; definition, 100; dissolution, 105, 150; duties of partners,
102; firm name, 101–102; formation, 100; liabilities of partners to
third parties, 103; limited, 106;
ostensible, 100; retirement of
partner, 103; torts, 104
Part performance, doctrine of, 41
Patents, right of servants to, 134
Penalties, 54
Picketing, 228
Political activities of trade unions,
230
Post: acceptance of offer by, 25;
payment by, 47
Power of attorney, 59